DEEP UNDERSTANDING FOR DIVISIVE TIMES

ESSAYS MARKING A DECADE OF THE JOURNAL OF INTERRELIGIOUS STUDIES

Edited by
Lucinda Allen Mosher
Axel Marc Oaks Takacs
Or N. Rose
Mary Elizabeth Moore

Interreligious Studies Press
Newton Centre, Massachusetts

Interreligious Studies Press is a subsidiary of the *Journal of Interreligious Studies* (irstudies.org)— an online, peer-reviewed publication of Hebrew College, Boston University School of Theology, and Hartford Seminary dedicated to innovative research on and study of the interactions that take place within and among religious and ethical communities.

Deep Understanding for Divisive Times: Essays Marking A Decade of the Journal of Interreligious Studies

First Edition

Copyright © 2020 by Journal of Interreligious Studies

Published by:
Interreligious Studies Press
c/o Hebrew College
160 Herrick Road
Newton Centre, Massachusetts 02459
irstudies.org

Printed in the United States of America
Cover design by Paraclete Press
Library of Congress Control Number: 2020920826

ISBN 978-0-57878-508-0

CONTENTS

PART II: PRACTICING INTERRELIGIOUSLY

PART III: TEACHING INTERRELIGIOUSLY

PART IV: ACTING INTERRELIGIOUSLY

AFTERWORD

CB&ED   EOR   CB&ED

FOREWORD
INTERRELIGIOUS/INTERFAITH STUDIES AND INTERFAITH AMERICA

Eboo Patel

The field of Interreligious/Interfaith Studies, of which the *Journal of Interreligious Studies* is a bulwark, continues to grow in intellectual sophistication. The articles it publishes are a powerful illustration of this. They consider interfaith engagement from many angles and perspectives, from ecological to anti-racist. There are excellent pieces here from a range of religious traditions, as well as from perspectives that might be termed spiritualist. There are also place-based perspectives and notes on how to improve interfaith pedagogy and programmatic practice.

Indeed, the past decade has been a time of great growth for Interreligious/Interfaith Studies and its related programs and practices, especially in the academy. Hundreds of faculty members (some of them tenured professors) teach courses in Interfaith (or Interreligious) Studies in colleges across the country. The Interreligious and Interfaith Studies Unit of the American Academy of Religion regularly gathers a full room for its sessions. Several academic books with Interfaith (or Interreligious) Studies in the title or the table of contents have been published recently. The term "interfaith leader" is now regularly used to describe someone with the vision, the knowledge base, and the skill set to create positive connections among people who orient around religion differently. As one sign of this growth, the Arthur Vining Davis Foundations renamed its "Theology" program as "Interfaith Leadership and Religious Literacy." It has been making grants to faculty members and college staff for several years and will hopefully continue to do so for many decades. All in all, we can safely say that we have arrived as a field. The book you are holding in your hand (or reading on your screen), which celebrates the *Journal of Interreligious Studies*, is a powerful proof point for this.

And yet, we all know that there is so much more to be done. We may be teaching more and more Interreligious or Interfaith Studies courses on our campuses, but too few students are taking them. We may be writing articles on the various ways that religious traditions offer wisdom for bringing people from different backgrounds together and creating a bridge to a collective and inclusive future, but not enough people are reading those articles.

My organization, Interfaith Youth Core, in partnership with research teams at The Ohio State University and North Carolina State University, has just completed the most ambitious study of religious diversity ever done in higher education. There were some inspiring findings. Ninety-three percent of students say they have friends across lines of religious difference. Seventy percent say they believe it is important to bridge religious divides.

However, there are some dispiriting findings as well. Only twenty-six percent of students say that they have taken a course that deals with religious diversity. Only fourteen percent say that they have participated in an interfaith dialogue while on campus. And, in this era where identity is of utmost concern to so many young people, it turns out that students spend far less time studying issues of religious diversity than any other form of identity (race, nationality and sexuality).[1]

So, what can the growing field Interreligious/Interfaith Studies do about this? I think we need to engage our intellectual and academic movement into a civic force. In the United States, there is actually a powerful historical reference point for this. It is the story of how the National Conference of Christians and Jews helped create a paradigm shift from America as a Protestant country to America as a Judeo-Christian nation. The Judeo-Christian narrative was, of course, incomplete and imperfect, but it was a step forward. It did good work for several decades. It was, for sure, better to be a Jew or a Catholic in America in 1980 than had been the case in 1930. And the way that the phrase came into existence is an excellent illustration of the point I hope to make.

"Judeo-Christian" did not fall from the sky or rise from the ground. It was not written on Plymouth Rock when the Pilgrims arrived on the Eastern Seaboard or discovered in the ground during the California gold rush. The term is not especially historically accurate or particularly theologically precise. Instead, "Judeo-Christian" was a concrete social response to the anti-Catholicism and anti-Semitism of the early twentieth century. It was an invention of one of the most impressive American civic institutions of the twentieth century, the National Conference of Christians and Jews (NCCJ), a group made up largely of clergy, scholars, and theologians.

The NCCJ emerged in the 1920s specifically to combat the anti-Catholic and anti-Semitic propaganda of the Ku Klux Klan. Over the course of the 1930s and 1940s, it set itself a much more ambitious mission: the creation of Judeo-Christian America, both in the public imagination and in the social infrastructure of the nation. The organization accomplished its mission by running a network of programs whose purpose was to instantiate their big idea. They built a board of prominent Catholics, Jews, and Protestants. They published books like *All in the Name of God*, which made the case against Protestant hegemony and for the three faiths as equal communities with much in common.[2] NCCJ "tolerance trios" comprising clergy of the three faiths went to cities across the nation, organizing what they called "tri-faith dialogues." The organization would then help local religious leaders in those cities organize follow-up interfaith seminars called "Institutes of Human Relations." By 1941, over 200 US cities were organizing such seminars on a regular basis, and up to 2000 smaller towns had similar ad hoc programs.

As the United States got involved in World War II, the NCCJ played a central role in creating the narrative that America was a champion of pluralism. Religiously diverse US troops fighting together exemplified the Judeo-Christian ideal of "the brotherhood of man under the fatherhood of God" combating the evil Nazis, who were intent on destroying all diversity. (Yes: this was at the same time that lynchings were common; and no: the NCCJ did not take on racism with the same zeal as they did religious bigotry—a total travesty.) NCCJ tolerance trios visited 778 different US military installations with their message of Judeo-Christian unity. They distributed literally millions of pamphlets and made a film called *The World We Want to Live In*, which interspersed images of ugly religious bigotry among inspiring stories of interfaith cooperation.

The NCCJ was also exceptional at taking advantage of opportunities. NCCJ leaders immediately sensed the potential in the story of the Four Chaplains—two Protestant ministers, a Catholic priest, and a Rabbi who gave their life jackets to frightened seamen and died holding hands, whispering the prayers of their respective faiths, on the sinking USS Dorchester. They helped make it probably the single most potent symbol of the Judeo-Christian ideal in mid-twentieth-century America.

The NCCJ made mistakes—sins of both omission and commission. It ignored virtually all other religious communities; it barely engaged racism and sexism. Yet, it made an important contribution. Our job in the growing fields of Interreligious and Interfaith Studies is to carry the NCCJ's torch while not repeating its errors. There are now almost as many Muslims in America as there are Jews, and more Muslims than there are Episcopalians. It is time for a new chapter in the story of American religious diversity—a chapter titled "Interfaith America."

We will know we have achieved Interfaith America when it is simply commonplace for cities across the country to have Days of Interfaith Service; when the scholarly field called Interfaith Studies certifies tens of thousands of people every year who have the knowledge base and skill set of Interfaith Leadership; when companies, schools, hospitals, and civil society organizations hire Interfaith Leaders because they recognize the significance of proactively engaging the religious diversity within their organizations; when houses of worship regularly have partnerships across faith lines; when people across traditions can readily articulate the theology or ethic of interfaith cooperation of their own community; when teaching the history of religious diversity in the United States is a robust part of every high school American history course.

We have built Interreligious/Interfaith Studies. It is time to build Interfaith America. In their first-ever anthology, *Deep Understanding for Divisive Times*, the staff of the *Journal of Interreligious Studies* have assembled fresh resources for this effort. Read. Reflect. Act!

NOTES

1   For details, see the report on the Interfaith Youth Core website. http://ifyc.org/sites/default/files/navigating-religious-diversity-9-27.pdf

2   *All in the Name of God* was written and published by Everett R. Clinchy, head of the NCCJ, in 1934. See Keith M. Schultz, *Tri-Faith America: How Catholics and Jews Held Post-War America to Its Protestant Promise* (New York: Oxford University Press, 2011), 15–16.

INTRODUCTION

Axel Marc Oaks Takacs
Editor-in-Chief
Journal of Interreligious Studies

Urging all of us to open our minds and hearts so
that we can know beyond the boundaries of what is
acceptable, so that we can think and rethink, so that
we can create new visions, I celebrate teaching that
enables transgressions—a movement against and
beyond boundaries.

—bell hooks, *Teaching to Transgress:
Education as the Practice of Freedom*

The inaugural issue of the *Journal of Interreligious Studies*, né *Journal of Inter-Religious Dialogue*, was published in May 2009. That issue was entitled "Starting the Conversation," and with this edited volume commemorating ten years of uninterrupted publication, it is evident that the conversation not only continues but also flourishes; it is also being reimagined perpetually. A decade into its publication, I can only hope that there are decades' worth of more issues to come. I am honored to function as the current Editor-in-Chief of the *Journal of Interreligious Studies* and humbled to work with such astonishing authors, educators, leaders, and organizers in publishing this volume.

Much has changed since 2009—politically, socially, religiously, and so on—too much to detail in this short introduction. The timeliness of interreligious studies remains precisely because a deep understanding in divisive times is a timeless necessity. Crossing through, dwelling within, and even moving against boundaries, religious or otherwise, facilitates the creative and liberating transformation of individuals, societies, communities, and the globe. The field of interreligious studies, inclusive of interreligious dialogue and theology, intercultural theology, and even aspects of comparative theology, is tensely situated within numerous interstices. I enumerate four, but perhaps more can be added.

First, the field itself is situated between and within various disciplinary boundaries. It is neither only comparative religion nor only theology of religion, neither only interreligious dialogue nor only interreligious or comparative theology, neither only sociology of religion nor only practical theology for interfaith leaders (and more can be adumbrated). Interreligious studies draws from the theories and methods of these other disciplines, but also extends beyond their boundaries in creative ways.

Second, scholars typically must both recognize and challenge the organic production of boundaries established by religious communities as they practice interreligious dialogue, engagement, and theology. The "multidisciplinary analysis," of a second order, "and theoretical framing of the interactions of religiously different people and groups, including the intersections of religion and secularity"[1] initially presume the boundaries not only between the religious and the secular, but also intra- and interreligiously. However, scholarship quickly turns to challenge and critique those very boundaries in creative ways, often moving beyond the study of religion in that it "serves the public good by bringing its analysis to bear on practical approaches to issues in religiously diverse societies."[2] Indeed, interreligious studies brings to the fore what should be commonplace in the study of religion: religion has always been interreligion.

Third, many interreligious studies scholars are themselves practitioners—faith leaders, interfaith organizers, theologians, and more—seeking to draw from the wellspring of their own tradition while also engaging deeply in other traditions, be it through embodied dialogue, interfaith justice organizing, or the study of discursive religious traditions, from the oral and written, to the ritual, sonic, visual, artistic, and architectural. Scholar-practitioners themselves thus recognize the boundaries of their traditions only to transgress and move beyond them, returning frequently with insight from the journey. These critical insights may be spiritually and mentally rejuvenating, practically embodied in liberating movements for justice, or both.

Fourth and perhaps foremost, interreligious studies scholars early on were quick to incorporate the theories, methods, and aims of various contextual and critical theories and theologies. Scholars, practitioners, and scholar-practitioners from theologians to faith leaders and community members remain shaped—variously liberated or restricted—by what womanist theologian M. Shawn Copeland terms embodied "marks" beyond religion: race, gender, sexuality, class, dis/ability, immigration status, and more. These marks interact and intersect with law and socio-cultural hegemony to produce systems and structures of power that may occlude or suppress the impact of religious traditions and identity. Given the "socio-cultural and religious system of domination . . . constituted by intersecting multiplicative structures of oppression" that feminist theologian Elisabeth Schüssler Fiorenza terms *kyriarchy,* it is unsurprising that interreligious studies quickly became intersectional.[5] It is irresponsible—if not impossible—to offer interreligious analyses, write interreligious theology, or perform interreligious dialogue when religious identity is presumed to function on a body or a community unmarked by these other power constructs. These embodied boundaries matter in the present power construction of our social world, but they also function to transgress other boundaries in the potential they have to unite different religious communities into "transcendent movements of liberation," a phrase I employ to describe angel Kyodo williams' radical dharma.[6]

Boundaries thus matter insofar as they both variously unite and transgress, which is why bell hooks opens this short introduction. Muslim and Hindu may transgress religious boundaries in their shared study and practice of liberation from gender or racial oppression or in their analogous rituals of embodied spirituality; Jew and Bahá'í may transgress religious boundaries in their shared study and practice of liberation from sexual and class oppression or in their analogous engagement with divine covenants; Black Christian and White Christian may unite in their shared practice and study of liberation from patriarchy, homophobia, and White supremacy or in their mutual faith in a God who becomes flesh. Religious and non-religious members of society may transgress boundaries in their shared study and/or practice of the good life, of the true realm of freedom, of justice, mercy, democracy, beauty, truth, faith, and so on. In all these cases, movements that unite transgress the boundaries that divide.

Interreligious studies is uniquely situated to analyze and learn from the fraught nature of marked boundaries: they both unite and divide. *Deep Understanding for Divisive Times* urges scholars, practitioners, and scholar-practitioners to cross boundaries and enter deeply into the experience of other religious communities and traditions in a movement "against and beyond boundaries" that nonetheless takes boundaries as critically formative of the self and larger communities. The field's liminality facilitates this careful attention to these embodied liminal spaces themselves. Nothing is more important in these divisive times.

As Eboo Patel makes clear in his foreword, the past decade has been a time of great growth for Interreligious/Interfaith Studies and its related programs and practices—and the *Journal of Interreligious Studies* has had a hand in that progress! *Deep Understanding for Divisive Times* celebrates the importance of interreligious studies scholarship and education as both a theory and practice of freedom. Our volume brings together original essays from thirty-three contributors, most of whom have published in the *Journal of Interreligious Studies* previously. Their offerings are grouped under four headings. The first part, "Framing Interreligious Studies Discourse," features nine essays concerning theoretical principles of the field. These essays variously situate the field either through meta-analyses of interreligious engagement or through particular textual or embodied studies and the lessons they provide.

In the second part, "Practicing Interreligiously," eight essays shift the discussion from *theoria* to *praxis*. The subjects of these essays are particular examples of interreligious engagement that provide methodological insights into the field. Lessons from essays in this part are drawn from particular contexts that nonetheless remain translatable to other contexts.

The third part, "Teaching Interreligiously," contains seven essays dwelling on pedagogies and classroom practices that center interreligious theories and methods. The study of religion and theology; the divinity school, seminary, and rabbinical curriculum; and even secondary educational institutions are all recognizing the humanistic import of teaching interreligiously. These essays interrogate how interreligious studies is shaping, and being shaped by, teaching and learning in the classroom.

In the fourth part, "Taking Action Interreligiously," another seven essays transpose the theoretical and methodological lessons from interreligious studies into a *modus vivendi*: a way of life that truly shapes one's being-in-the-world. The field of interreligious studies is intended to serve the public good; however, it is also positioned to transform our ways of relating to each other. Indeed, it provides strategies "to open our minds and hearts so that we can know beyond the boundaries of what is acceptable," as bell hooks urges us.

Our volume closes with an afterword by Mary Elizabeth Moore, soon to retire as Dean of Boston University School of Theology, who has supported the work of the *Journal of Interreligious Studies* for many years. In thanksgiving for her leadership, the journal has recently named Dean Moore *publisher emerita*.

No moment in history is more or less in need of "deep understanding in divisive times," even if any given context shapes the methods and goals of such deep learning. The collected essays in this volume provide critical insights and strategies for interreligious studies shaped by our present moment in history, true; however, those insights and strategies may be transposed to new contexts so that new visions may be imagined from the interstitial spaces wherein religious traditions and communities meet. I take to heart what my own study of the Islamic traditions have taught me about the power of these liminal, in-between spaces, known as the *barzakh* in Arabic: the *barzakh* is situated between two things "but is not identical to any of those two things, though it possesses the power (*quwwa*) of both"[7] and "it is nothing but the imagination (*al-khayāl*)."[8] Indeed, it is my contention that interreligious studies is a discipline engaging those interstitial spaces, spaces wherein the powers of manifold religions meet, together constituting an imaginative power to create new theories and practices for communal and liberating ways of living, working, playing, relating, and being in the world.

—October 1, 2020

NOTES

1   Kate McCar≠≠≠er)religious Studies: Making a Home in the Secular Academy," in *Interreligious/Interfaith Studies: Defining a New Field*, eds. Eboo Patel, Jennifer Howe Peace, Noah J. Silverman (Boston: Beacon, 2018), 12.

2   Ibid.

3   This is a feature of Copeland's theological anthropology: "For bodies are marked—made individual, particular, different, and vivid—through race, sex and gender, sexuality, and culture. The protean ambiguity of these marks transgresses physical and biological categories, destabilizes gender identities, and disrupts ethical and relational patterns (who is my brother, who is my sister?). These marks delight as much as they unnerve. They impose limitation: some insinuate exclusion, others inclusion, for the body denotes a 'boundary' that matters." M. Shawn Copeland, *Enfleshing Freedom: Body, Race, and Being* (Minneapolis: Fortress Press, 2010), 56.

4   Elisabeth Schüssler Fiorenza, *Wisdom Ways: Introducing Feminist Biblical Interpretation* (Maryknoll, NY: Orbis Books, 2005), 118. Kyriarchy includes sexism, racism, speciesism, homophobia, classism, economic injustice, colonialism, militarism, ethnocentrism, anthropocentrism, and nationalism.

5   See Patricia Hill Collins and Sirma Bilge, *Intersectionality* (Malden, MA: Polity Press, 2016), 12.

6   See Rev. angel Kyodo williams, Sensei, "A New Dharma: Prophetic Wisdom and the Rise of Transcendent Movements," in angel Kyodo williams, Lama Rod Owens, and Jasmine Syedullah, *Radical Dharma: Talking Race, Love, and Liberation* (Berkeley, CA: North Atlantic Books, 2016), 191–204. Sensei williams herself recognizes the liberating potential of this new dharma that "embraces the mash-up of those ancient teachings coming into contact with traditional Western religions, and earth-based spiritualities" from the Abrahamic to the Jain, Baháʼí, and more.

7   Ibn al-ʻArabi, *Al-Futūḥāt Al-Makkīyah*, 4 volumes, Osman Yaḥya, ed. (Bayrūt: Dār Ṣādir, 1968), volume I, 304 (line 20). (Chapter 63 "Concerning the Recognition of the Subsistence of the People in the Barzarkh/Liminal Space Between this World and the Resurrection").

8   Ibid., lines 20–22.

PART I

FRAMING INTERRELIGIOUS STUDIES DISCOURSE

SACRED INCOMPLETENESS
REFLECTIONS ON THE ORIGINS OF THE
JOURNAL OF INTERRELIGIOUS STUDIES

Stephanie Varnon-Hughes and Joshua M. Z. Stanton

In his seminal work *Intertextuality and the Reading of Midrash* Professor Daniel Boyarin deduces that "It is the incompleteness in the Torah's explanation of itself which provides the space within which these antithetical readings [of the same passage] can be created." Much the same can be said for the process of learning Torah, or the Christian Bible, or any other sacred text. As seminary students, we found the process of formation to be holy and wholly incomplete. When we were younger, we imagined that once established scholars and religious leaders, we might find certainty. The longer we have worked in this field, and as the field itself has grown, we have understood that it is perhaps the incomplete nature of the work (and relationships) that marks this field, enlivens it, and encourages us to move ever forward.

The *Journal of Interreligious Studies* was born out of this incompleteness, and it is nurtured by an incompleteness that leading professors felt in their areas of study and that practitioners experienced in their areas of religious leadership. Scholars felt isolated in their silos. Clergy felt isolated in their houses of worship. Even those who were public intellectuals or scholar-practitioners felt that there was more to know and do and create, especially when it came to understanding the differences within and among religious, spiritual, and humanistic traditions. Some of the luminaries in our respective fields projected a confidence and a completeness, while we felt the humanity of our uncertainty, one borne out of our connection to people with profoundly different worldviews and life experiences.

Our early steps required a lot of gumption in amplifying a problem rather than a solution. Josh reached out to Stephanie during the summer of 2008. He was a recent college graduate, beginning his first year of rabbinical school at the Hebrew Union College–Jewish Institute of Religion in Jerusalem. He was an angsty twenty-two-year-old, trying to understand why his studies in Jerusalem would involve so little connection with other Jewish denominations, much less other religious traditions. How could he be in one of the holiest cities for Jewish, Christian, and Islamic traditions without learning to lead alongside Christian and Muslim clergy, not to mention spiritual leaders from countless other traditions? After some thought and research, he e-mailed Stephanie to see if there were ways that they might collaborate, perhaps even on some kind of academic journal.

Stephanie was more experienced and centered as an educator, working toward her second master's degree while serving as student body president at Union Theological Seminary. Yet her pedagogical experience also piqued her interest in pluralism. Her students

3

in public school had come from every possible walk of life. They were curious about one another. Why did Hinda wear a headscarf? Why was DeAnthony fasting? Why could William not watch movies or read stories that had magic? As a first-year teacher, she had been taught, "You can't talk about religion in the classroom." And yet, her students really wanted to deeply know one another. Was it possible to facilitate that kind of learning in public spaces? What did it mean to learn and lead in such a diverse, complicated society? What did it mean to do so, while exploring one's own firmly held beliefs? When she received Josh's e-mail, she responded enthusiastically.

We spent our first conversation some days later reflecting on our discontentment with existing seminary education and hoped that we might somehow, in acknowledging our own lack of expertise, create a space for openly airing uncertainty and exploring multiple, complicated, contradictory approaches to it. We then began the audacious process of e-mailing and cold-calling religious and academic leaders across the spectra of belief and nonbelief who could advise us, or might even want to join us as unpaid staff on a journal that had yet to be founded. We wondered: did faculty publish peer-reviewed research in this field? What was the canon? Who were the arbiters? Were we talking about "religion," "faith," or "belief"? How could mono-religious institutions (particularly in higher education) respond to growing numbers of "nonbelievers" and those with hybrid identities? With "interfaith" becoming a movement on college campuses and communities across the US, we felt it was time to create some structures for research, reflection, and formalized dialogue practices.

A few hundred hours later, we were a staff of nine with thirty-five thought-leaders on our Board of Scholars and Practitioners. It was a time of political change and social uplift, and we sought to a publication and an organization worthy of our idealism. We would be about sharing work and sharing credit, expressing uncertainty, affirming each other's beliefs while openly expressing our own, brave and compassionate conversations, making ideas accessible, and continually creating new seats at the table for leadership and discourse. We would have uncomfortable conversations about gender, about economic and cultural differences, about leadership styles, and about how to manage our team in ways aligned with our values. We learned from our board members, and alongside them. They became our mentors and our co-explorers in this field.

With a significant anonymous donation and fiscal sponsorship from the Interfaith Youth Core, as well as a growing list of donors and the generosity of a website design firm, Resolve Digital, we built an online platform in the fall of 2008 and issued a call for submissions at the same time. Our Executive Editor, Dr. Aimee Upjohn Light, generously called this chaotic, exhausting, exhilarating process creation *ex nihilo*—out of nothing. We found it to be a sleepless time, juggling our full-time studies, committed relationships, and inspiration to build together, even with seven time zones between us. Above all, we were curious: about each other, about religions and belief systems, about bridging academic and digital spaces, and about the commitments that enlivened each other.

Most gratifying was not simply the launch of a new peer-reviewed, interdisciplinary, academic journal, but the chance for us to be students and leaders at the same time. In the course of editing each volume, we learned from some of the foremost leaders in the emergent field of Interreligious Studies. We could ask them our burning questions and also see what it meant to have a nascent area of academic inquiry. We puzzled through issues of intersectionality, wondering (for example) why we got fewer submissions when we tried to do a special issue on women and feminism, and whether we were privileging those educated within a US system. We sought to discover whether this field was more akin to theology, or social science, or education, or philosophy. Should we center activism, or research? We came to discover that teachers and peers alike were asking similar questions, both in the academy and in interfaith activist organizations all over the world. We were humbled and delighted to reach a point where we had received submissions from every continent but Antarctica. Clearly, our own stumbling toward a *more-completeness* was resonant with questions and longings in many fields and contexts.

Perhaps the most salient lesson was that our own sense of being incomplete might never stop. We were naïve to think that once we each graduated and became "professionals" that suddenly we (and the Journal) would have arrived. We also learned that the hunger that initiated this generative process could both inspire us and ensure that the *Journal of Interreligious Studies* would never stop growing and adapting to the new needs of the academic field it was seeding. Every time we started filling in the gaps of knowledge, new questions emerged—only to be addressed (often provisionally!) and give rise to still more. The iterative process of question and answer, search and solution, embodies the human condition at its best, most empowered, and bravest.

We remain indebted to our countless collaborative partners, as well as those who boldly took on the mantle of leadership after we graduated from our respective seminaries. Their work has far surpassed our own, and we could not be more thrilled. The search for truth(s) with inspiring fellow travelers and the incompleteness of knowledge continues apace, answering new needs in unforeseen circumstances and drawing scholarship and practice closer to the promise of pluralism. As we have grown older, and a bit more experienced, we can say with more confidence: to be incomplete is not a failure at all. To be incomplete is an invitation to curiosity and relationship.

RESPONSES TO SAMENESS AND DIFFERENCE IN INTERFAITH RELATIONS

Jennifer Howe Peace

For the last several months I've been realizing, in new ways, lessons that have been woven into my work as an interreligious educator for the past decade. It is not that I did not know about the dangers of dehumanizing language. It's not that I haven't preached, written, and lectured about the pernicious effects of pathological dualism that divides the world into two camps—us (the good and worthy) and them (the bad and worthless). It is just that I have recently found myself sitting at home in the shadow of a global pandemic with worldwide attention on the violence of racism and I am experiencing a different level of knowing. It is a more visceral knowing that comes from hearing, reading, watching, and listening to people every day who have lived and are living realities in their bodies that give them a "knowing" I can only approximate. This has caused me to think more about the relevance of interfaith work and interreligious education for our civic life as we confront deeply entrenched inequalities and their deadly consequences. What follows is a framework I developed for analyzing responses to similarities and differences. It emerged from decades of work as an interreligious educator and activist, designed specifically with these contexts in mind. However, my hope is that it may also provide an analytical framework for understanding reactions to similarities and differences more broadly and thus have some relevance for analyzing reactions in this current period of reckoning around the legacy and persistence of racism in the United States.

A Framework for Analyzing Responses to Sameness and Difference

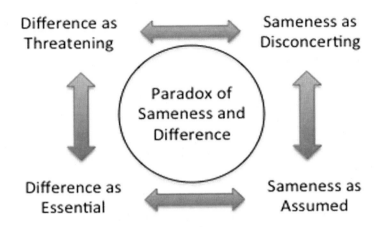

This is a tool for interreligious educators seeking to create transformative learning experiences for their students. More broadly, it is a tool for analyzing and understanding reactions exhibited by individuals and groups when confronted with the reality of difference and sameness. On a more personal level, it can be a useful tool for individuals who want to develop both greater self-awareness and empathy for others as they assess their own reactions to similarities and differences.

I have defined five postures as part of my framework. I refer to these as postures to emphasize that we are all capable of both holding and releasing any of these positions. People may find themselves fixed in one posture when it comes to a particular similarity or differences and in a very different posture in another context. In addition, one can shift postures slowly over time or rapidly—even in the course of a single interaction. An important overarching point is that while people might get "stuck" in particular postures, these postures are not fixed qualities that define a person. They are positions we each can and have likely embodied. While this is not a hierarchical framework, the central posture, which I call the paradox of sameness and difference, is distinct. The other four postures both highlight and obscure particular realities, revealing both strengths and blind spots, while the paradox of sameness and difference is a posture that reconciles seeming opposites and makes visible the irreducibility of our differences alongside the sameness inherent in our shared humanity.

The following overview and examples will flesh out the five postures that comprise my framework for analyzing reactions to sameness and difference.

DIFFERENCE AS THREATENING

In this posture, "we" are seen as superior to "others" and others are seen as a direct threat to us. Any similarities between "us" and "others" are ignored, downplayed, or rejected. There are biological and evolutionary reasons that something new, unfamiliar, or different might be perceived as threatening. Particularly in childhood, our experiences, our socialization, and the reactions of trusted adults around us have a lot to do with when, why, and how often we adopt this posture of difference as threatening. This is the posture underlying extreme nationalism and White supremacy. In religious terms, it is expressed in the idea that my version of my religion is the only true one; all other belief systems are not only false but a threat to me. (Christian supremacy exemplifies this.) Typically, people who adopt this posture have had little or no positive engagement with people outside of their own religious group. This point is important as we consider interventions that can potentially shift this posture.

An example from my classroom: I had a student who grew up in a very homogeneous Christian community. When I asked her to share a story of a significant interreligious encounter, the only example she could come up with was 9/11 when, as she put it, "I became aware for the first time of a strange and foreign religion called Islam." Her early formative experiences provided neither the spaces nor the language to engage with people from religious backgrounds other than her own. So, her only association with Islam was as something threatening. However, she was open to learning. By the end of the class, after reading, reflecting, and meeting both fellow students and guest speakers who were Muslim, her understanding of Islam and her dominant posture towards Muslims shifted significantly.

SAMENESS AS DISCONCERTING

In this posture, religious differences are accepted as inevitable and are generally seen as non-threatening. However, similarities may come as a surprise—and not necessarily a welcome surprise. One example of this posture comes from a story contributed by colleague and friend Homayra Ziad to a collection I co-edited. In it, she describes the disorientation she felt when she saw monks in a monastery in Romania prostrating in prayer. As she writes, "Prostration, resting on palms and knees and placing the forehead on the ground, is the quintessential Islamic act of worship." She continues, "To see my 'own' form of worship performed in an unfamiliar setting unsettled me." This experience of being unsettled by recognizing a similarity between one's own tradition and another is a prime example of a posture of sameness as disconcerting.

As a reflective practitioner and scholar of Islam with a commitment to interfaith relationships, Ziad examines her reactions and moves to a place of new understanding. She writes, "I understood the power of prostration more deeply in that moment than I ever had. Before this experience, prostration was 'mine' and possession had dulled its sharp edge. Now, watching this act as if for the first time, I was struck by the submersion of self that conscious prostration demands of anyone who enacts it."

Ziad uses her experience of sameness as disconcerting as an opportunity for learning. This highlights the broader point that each posture contains the potential for movement, learning, deeper understanding, and transformation. This is realized when, as she models, we recognize and reflect on our reactions to a given encounter and actively shift our posture.

SAMENESS AS ASSUMED

This posture is characterized by the assertion that we are all fundamentally the same, so we should not spend our time arguing about, or fighting over, differences that don't ultimately matter. The assumption here is that sameness is the path to unity. The strength of this posture is the value it places on what connects us. I would say this was the dominant posture of most of the seminary students when they first entered my interfaith studies courses at Andover Newton Theological School.

The challenge, or blind spot, in this posture is that while it can feel like a generous place to the person holding it, it may be experienced by others as a form of assimilation, or even annihilation. The built-in assumption of "we are all one" is that there is only We. There is no room for dissent. Power is a key factor in analyzing this posture. Who is the one asserting "sameness?" What if those listening don't agree with the speaker's characterization? Sometimes, how we are the same ends up meaning how you are the same as me. This posture can in fact involve a kind of unspoken fear of difference, if difference is equated with disruption, division, or dis-unity. Ironically, it can parallel some of the assumptions underlying the posture of difference as threatening.

One example of this posture and how it can shift comes from a class I co-taught with a Jewish colleague on Jewish and Christian relations. We had a Unitarian Universalist student who started the semester resistant to focusing on historical and religious differences between Jews and Christians. It was clearly bothering him that we were spending so much time on theological distinctions as well as the history of anti-Jewish bigotry within Christianity. In his final class reflection, he recognized his own desire to focus on commonalities, writing: "What I had yet to realize was that there is even more need to understand and appreciate each other's differences. Not everything is a commonality, and that is perfectly okay. In fact, it is necessary. In our difference lies our dimensionality, our depth, our richness." His reflection signals a shift from a posture of "sameness as assumed" to "difference as essential."

DIFFERENCE AS ESSENTIAL

In this posture, difference is seen, not as a threat to unity, but rather as what gives community its complexity and texture. Irreducible differences are to be safeguarded. Religious differences are to be celebrated. (There are parallels here to the multicultural movement). I can be Christian and you can be Jewish and you can be Muslim and you can be a secular humanist (and so on) without taking anything away from any of us. In fact, according to this posture, "the more diversity, the better." Using this rubric as a tool for self-reflection, I realized that my tendency was to spend most of my time here. In part, this was because I was often trying to shift students out of the comfort of their "sameness as assumed" postures. Indeed, it was useful for me personally and as an educator to notice my own default posture.

The challenge posed by this posture—its blind spot (as each posture both reveals and obscures something)—is that similarities may be resisted, downplayed, overlooked, or outright rejected. There is a second danger: that of over simplifying and essentializing identities as if there is a single or standard way to be a member of one's particular group (as a Jew, a Muslim, a Christian, a woman, a person of color, and so on).

EMBRACING THE PARADOX OF DIFFERENCE AND SAMENESS

This posture asserts a fundamental kinship that comes from acknowledging our undeniable similarities while simultaneously embracing our irreducible differences. This posture was embodied for me at an interfaith rally in 2018 on Boston Common, organized in response to the tragic shootings at the Tree of Life Synagogue in Pittsburgh. Shaykh Yasir, the Imam of the Islamic Society of Boston Cultural Center (ISBCC), the largest mosque in Boston, spoke at the rally saying: "I want to say something to the Jewish community: As a Muslim, I love you. As a Muslim, my back is your back. As a Muslim my shoulder is your shoulder, as a Muslim my chest is your chest. We have to drown out the propaganda." With each sentence, the downbeat was on the word Muslim. I heard Shaykh Yasir as saying that solidarity doesn't come from a blurring of the differences and asserting that we are all the same; nor does it come from letting our differences stop us from experiencing our shared humanity. Rather, solidarity comes from being our most authentic, diverse selves in all our particularity while granting the same complexity to others and, from that place, saying: I am with you. What hurts you hurts me.

Embracing the paradox of difference and sameness is the posture with the most power and potential to heal. This is the posture I try to expand my capacity for. It is the posture I try to help my students experience or move toward. A rabbi friend of mine said that she believes the closer she moves toward paradox, the closer she moves toward God. This is consistent with my understanding. It is why I see interreligious engagement as a way of being Christian and being Christian as obliging me to engage in interreligious work. The deeper I go into my own faith and practices, the greater my capacity to hold this posture of embracing the paradox of difference and sameness. The opposite is also true. If I neglect my spiritual practice, I can find myself stuck in one of the other postures, leaving me more rigid and less flexible.

One of my underlying assumptions as an interreligious educator is that interfaith work is consciousness-raising work. In order to foster genuine understanding across religious lines (and other lines) we need wisdom that goes beyond intellectual knowledge. As interreligious educators, we have a responsibility to create the conditions for transformative learning in our classrooms. The framework I have developed is one tool for increasing consciousness. It can help identify one's default reactions to sameness and difference while increasing a capacity to live from a place of paradox. Since designing this framework, I have also noticed that it is often in those moments of shifting from one posture to another, and catching oneself in that movement, that transformative learning happens.

NOTES

1   Celene Ibrahim, ed., *One Nation, Indivisible: Seeking Liberty and Justice from the Pulpit to the Streets* (Eugene: Wipf and Stock, 2019), 3–8.

2   The outline of this framework was first developed for a lecture I gave at the Kauffman Institute on November 15, 2018 titled "Responses to Difference and Sameness: A Christian Reflection on Interreligious Engagement," delivered as part of the Triennial Interfaith Dialogue Conference at Grand Valley State University. A recording of the lecture can be found here: https://www.gvsu.edu/interfaith/jewish-christian-muslim-dialogue-29.htm Accessed June 17, 2020.

3   Homayra Ziad, "Oh How You've Spun Me 'Round, Darling" in Jennifer Peace, Or Rose, Gregory Mobley, eds., *My Neighbor's Faith: Stories of Interreligious Encounter, Growth, and Transformation* (New York: Orbis Books, 2012), 117–19, at 118.

DOES INTERRELIGIOUS UNDERSTANDING MATTER IF THE WORLD IS COMING TO AN END?

Rachel S. Mikva

I teach a course that investigates structures of power, privilege, and oppression as they relate to race, class, religion, gender, sexuality, the environment, and the complex web of intersections among them. This is not an abstract study for our community; each of these structures negatively affects some portion of the students directly. I have begun to notice that, even though all the problems seem intractable, it is when we study the climate crisis that most students experience despair. They turn from fiery activists into resigned fatalists, calling into question the value of working on any of the rest of the human equation if the world as we know it might come to an end. Already we are experiencing increasing wildfires, rising seas and collapsing glaciers, increasingly ferocious weather patterns, vanishing forests and species, growing areas of food and water insecurity, and climate refugees. And it will get worse.

Recently, scholars have tried to name this phenomenon: climate depression, ecological grief, solastalgia. The American Psychological Association reported that changes in the climate are surfacing a range of emotions, including fear, anger, exhaustion, and a sense of impotence. A 2018 Yale study learned that 69% of Americans are "very" or "somewhat" concerned about the climate. It should come as no surprise that percentages are higher among young people, with less difference between political progressives and conservatives, because they will be around to feel the growing impact. Young people like the twenty-one plaintiffs in Juliana v. United States, suing the government for denying their rights to life, liberty, and property through its actions that cause climate change. Or the young Swedish climate activist Greta Thunberg, who scolded UN officials (COP24) for not being "mature enough to tell it like it is; even that burden you leave to us children."

Normally, I like to think that there is an expiration date for blaming parents. But these children know that we have mortgaged their future for the comfort of our lifestyle, surrendering to the great Carbon Corporations that make enormous profits from wounding the Earth and then use these profits to purchase elections and fund fake science. These children know that there is no real debate about the fact and urgency of anthropogenic climate change.

This is the Anthropocene era. So does interreligious understanding matter if the world is coming to an end? Of course it does. The question is: How should the crisis shape our work?

The easy part is excavating our traditions to reimagine our relationship with Creation. Every lifestance *can be* interpreted in ways that foster complacency on climate change. Detachment in Buddhism, for example, is sometimes imagined as a lack of concern for the created world—but I learned it as a commitment to do what is right without investment in the outcome. Observance of *halakha* in Jewish tradition can mistakenly be reduced to ritual meticulousness, even though ritual is supposed to be wholly bound up with ethical considerations. Moksha in Jain or Hindu traditions can be seen as concern only for the fate of one's own soul, but there are numerous teachings that connect one's own fate with work to ease the suffering of others and to seek collective liberation. Christians may understand the biblical charge, Fill the earth and master it (Gen 1:28), as license to exploit the earth and dominate its creatures, but it has also spawned a theology of stewardship.

There have always been religious voices that offer alternatives to the politics of fear and greed, colonization and extraction. As illustrated in this tenth-century midrash, we have long known of our interconnectedness: "The whole world of humans, animals, fish, and birds all depend on one another. All drink the earth's water, breathe the earth's air, and find food in what was created on the earth. All share the same destiny—what happens to one, happens to all" (*Tanna d'bei Eliahu*). Humans also intuited that we are composed of the same matter as the rest of creation, well before we had scientific data to prove it. Joseph ibn Kaspi's medieval biblical commentary, for example, asserted that we should be "ever cognizant of the fact that we are of the same stuff as the ass and mule, the cabbage and the pomegranate, and even the lifeless stone" (*ad* Deut 22:6–7). In the Book of Job, one way to read God's response to Job at the end—*Where were you when I laid the earth's foundations . . . have you ever commanded the day to break. . . . Do you give the horse its strength. . . . Does the eagle soar at your command?*—is as a challenge to our anthropocentric view of the universe (Job 38:4, 12; 39:19, 27). These examples come from the Jewish tradition, but there are insights to be gathered from multiple lifestances to counter the domination paradigm. Indigenous traditions, often neglected in interfaith projects, have particular wisdom that should be centered in our efforts.

Our diverse spiritualities also cultivate deep roots for hope. The primary messaging strategy for climate action is to show the urgency of the matter: let's make it better . . . or else. But social scientists have demonstrated that, if you tell people something must be done or we are all going to die, most people opt for Door #2, however strange that seems. Overwhelming fear leads people to disengage. The prophet Isaiah knew this; he called the Israelites to change their ways in order to avert catastrophe, but instead they yielded to the temptations of fatalism: *Eat and drink, for tomorrow we die* (22:13). Succumbing to what Catherine Keller calls "a critically plausible nihilism," and others have named futilitarianism, leads to the same place as reactionary denialism. "I can't do anything about it" or "It's too late" gives in to the culture of consumption and distraction just as readily as "It's not happening."

Hope is not idle optimism that all will turn out for the best, but active faith that the world can be different than it is and that we play a part in shaping it. We must believe it is possible to forestall some of the worst effects of the climate crisis by aggressively pursuing renewable energy resources, developing carbon capture technologies, expanding desalination and other means of sustaining water supplies, changing the human diet and lifestyle, seeking economic equity, acknowledging limits to what can be extracted from the earth and from other human beings, learning to treasure the glorious beauty of the created world, teaching simplicity and solidarity, and modeling compassion. Our spiritual lifestances have other essential ingredients to facilitate adaptation, too. They make meaning, cultivate gratitude, process grief, foster community, teach resilience, acknowledge culpability, practice relinquishment, and so on. Together, they testify to a collective wisdom that can help humanity change course.

The *interreligious* task, one that focuses more directly on building understanding among persons who orient around religion differently, must grapple with the fact that climate change makes our work harder. Disruption and a scarcity of resources can deepen divisions between "us" and "them," and intensify the hunt for scapegoats. Already, we have seen how climate is a major factor in the global refugee crisis that also catalyzed a convulsive wave of White nationalism. Some people viewed nations closing borders, a temporary health measure during the COVID-19 pandemic, as vindication of anti-immigrant discrimination; the crisis also amplified antisemitic voices that painted the disease as a Jewish conspiracy. A recent report speculates that devastation from the 1918 pandemic fueled the rise of right-wing extremists, including the Nazi party in Germany.

To counter these developments, interreligious leaders not only must step up efforts to nurture deep understanding of people who are different than us, but we must also work to reinstill communitarian values and a commitment to the common good. We must resist more robustly and effectively our society's hyper-individualization because communitarian values make us more resilient: capable of adapting to the world we need to fashion in order to prevent catastrophe, capable of thriving in a world that is different from the one we know, capable of planning for and living with uncertainty. As Wen Stephenson titled his most recent book on climate justice, *What We're Fighting for Now Is Each Other*. That is not how everyone thinks about it. In an old Pogo cartoon the mouse warns, "If you are starving with a tiger, the tiger starves last." Some people plan for catastrophe by figuring out how to be the tiger. Experts who study the potential dissolution of the world order, however, argue that we will be dependent on each other in ways we cannot yet imagine.

The most sensitive task for interreligious studies and engagement is to grapple with the role of religion in stifling climate action. In the United States, this work includes challenging the tremendous influence that theologically conservative Christian communities have in shutting down public discourse around climate change. Last summer, I was chatting with an acquaintance who wanted me to understand that his resistance to doing anything about climate change was not that he doubted the science. He just believes that God has a plan.

Either the Second Coming of Christ is upon us, he asserted, or else God will not allow us to destroy ourselves. Since he is a faithful Catholic, I tried citing Pope Francis's encyclical *Laudato si'* and its clear charge to take care of our common home in peril, to acknowledge the human roots of the crisis, and to recognize abuse of creation as ecological sin. It turns out he is not such a "Pope-y" Catholic.

In America, White evangelical Christians and Catholics are most resistant to accepting climate science. One reason is that 58% of White evangelicals believe that Jesus will return by 2050. The worse the world gets, the more it seems to align in their imagination with the Book of Revelation, what David Wallace-Wells called "the inescapable sourcebook for Western anxiety about the end of the world." So, in an unholy alliance with the fossil fuel industries, the Religious Right made the environment a partisan issue. They have taken the Republican Party hostage—the party that created Yellowstone National Park under President Grant, the first national forest preserves under Benjamin Harrison, and the EPA under Richard Nixon (who also signed major environmental legislation such as the Endangered Species Act). Even as recently as the presidency of George H. W. Bush, Republicans pushed to stem acid rain.

To some degree, the religious influence transcends political parties. In a study of Black (mostly Democratic) and White (mostly Republican) evangelicals, researchers found that their theological hierarchy of creation—God, humans, everything else—made individuals suspect of attaching too much importance to environmental concerns. A belief that God is in charge of history also made them less persuadable about anthropogenic climate change and its implications, and less concerned about end-times. Christianity is not alone in eschatological expectation. A large percentage (68–85%) of Muslims in Turkey, Iraq, and Afghanistan, for example, believe the *mahdi*/messiah will come in their lifetime. Multiple lifestances have conjured visions of the end, with their own versions of upheaval and cataclysm that can rationalize inaction.

At the same time, there are evangelical Christians committed to "creation care," like those involved in the Evangelical Environmental Network. African-Americans of various religious stripes helped build the US movement for environmental justice. They have seen how poor people suffer the effects of ecological destruction first and worst; they are not sanguine about apocalypse. Alongside a range of religiously inspired organizations—including GreenFaith, the Indigenous Environmental Network, Hazon, Green Muslims, Faith in Place, the Parliament of the World's Religions Climate Action Task Force, and the Coalition on the Environment and Jewish Life—they demonstrate how people of all faiths are working with courage and creativity to address the climate crisis.

Yet the power of religion is too great merely to hope it is channeled to do good. The First Amendment protects people from government establishment and government interference in the free exercise of religion. It does not require that we smile politely as people deploy their faith to undermine science and doom the planet to destruction. These interpretations cannot take shelter in our commitment to inclusivity. Instead, we must call out the peril and fight harder to establish meanings we see as liberative, even as we recognize the subjectivity of our own perspective.

Interreligious studies and engagement need to develop the capacity to facilitate productive *conflict*, not simply to cultivate common ground and dignify our differences. It may seem logical to manage religious diversity by avoiding argument, but we have important disagreements about how to discuss, enshrine, and embody religious values in our collective public life. Interreligious leaders can help focus civil debates in public theology to advance deeper understanding of texts, beliefs, and praxis. Religious ideas can be subjected to critical scrutiny without succumbing to religious bigotry or reigniting medieval battles between claimants of the "true faith." Pointing out the critical distinction between *condemn* and *contemn*, Cathleen Kaveny urges a public discourse that is not afraid to express strong disapproval without characterizing opponents as despicable. We must develop language to challenge specific ideas rooted in faith when they impact the common good, without negating the faith from which they grow.

NOTES

1   https://climatecommunication.yale.edu/wp-content/uploads/2019/01/Climate-Change -American-Mind-December-2018.pdf.

2   https://www.youtube.com/watch?v=IFIzftwX0Cs.

3   Saffron O'Neill and Sophie Nicholson-Cole, "Fear Won't Do It: Promoting Positive Engagement with Climate Change Through Visual and Iconic Representations," *Science Communication* 30:3 (March 2009): 355–79.

4   Catherine Keller, *A Political Theology of the Earth: Our Planetary Emergency and the Struggle for a New Public* (New York: Columbia University Press, 2018), 2.

5   Kristian Blickle, "Pandemics Change Cities: Municipal Spending and Voter Extremism in Germany 1918–1933," Federal Reserve Bank of New York Staff Reports 921 (May 2020).

6   See https://www.pewresearch.org/fact-tank/2010/07/14/jesus-christs-return-to-earth/

7   David Wallace-Wells, *The Uninhabitable Earth: Life After Warming* (New York: Tim Duggan Books, 2019), 230.

8   Jared Peifer, Elaine Howard Ecklund, and Cara Fullerton, "How Evangelicals from Two Churches in the American Southwest Frame Their Relationship with the Environment," *Review of Religious Research* 56:3 (Sept. 2014): 373–97.

9   https://thebulletin.org/2017/08/ how-religious-and-non-religious-people-view-the-apocalypse/

10 See Rachel Mikva, *Dangerous Religious Ideas: The Deep Roots of Self-Critical Faith in Judaism, Christianity and Islam* (Boston: Beacon Press, 2020), chapters 13–14.

11 Cathleen Kaveny, *Prophecy Without Contempt: Religious Discourse in the Public Square* (Cambridge, MA: Harvard University Press, 2016), ix–x.

INTERSECTIONALITY AND INTERRELIGIOUS ENGAGEMENT
A REFLECTION

Sheryl A. Kujawa-Holbrook

Interreligious engagement during this time in history where all living systems are in decline is an immense challenge. Current national tragedies have awakened many anew to the complex interaction of religion, race, culture, and by extension, other forms of oppression. Indeed, throughout American history, religion itself is as much a tool of oppression as it is a source of human solidarity. Thus, religious oppression, racism, heterosexism, classism, sexism, gender oppression, ableism, and oppression related to immigration status and language are now promulgated as a form of religious, predominately Christian, discourse. On a practical level, it is unrealistic to talk about any religious group in isolation from the complex social identities which characterize adherents, and the others which surround them, either in this country or abroad. Though efforts in interreligious engagement typically focus on relationships between communities, we at times fail to address the intersectional realities inherent in our encounters, and we ignore the social inequities present on a structural level.

Intersectionality is an analytical theory that considers multiple social identities that shape individual and collective experiences of oppression and privilege within hierarchical systems of power. As a framework, intersectionality provides a lens that reveals a deeper understanding of how social power fluctuates between multiple identities and locations, shaping individuals and whole communities. The term became prominent thirty years ago through the work of legal scholar Kimberlé Crenshaw as she explained the overlapping identities of Black women (race and gender) within institutions. Crenshaw, who coined the term, did not claim to originate the concept, but rather traced the occurrence of overlapping identities within earlier Black feminist thought in writers such as Anna Julia Heyward Cooper (1858–1964) and Ida B. Wells (1862–1931). In contrast to interreligious engagement from a single-axis view, an intersectional perspective recognizes differences in social power between diverse constituencies. Methodologically, within the context of interreligious engagement, intersectionality presumes that each person experiences (consciously or unconsciously) social power differently based on their race, gender, social class, sexual identity, ability, nationality, age, language, immigration status, and other forms of social difference. The interplay among the intersections of these social identities within interlocking systems of oppressions are complex. Intersectionality recognizes that people experience both systems of dominance and subordination concurrently. As the late poet and scholar Audre Lorde

(1934–1992) famously wrote, "There is no hierarchy of oppression. I cannot afford the luxury of fighting one form of oppression only. I cannot afford to believe that freedom from intolerance is the right of only one particular group." An intersectional lens disrupts forms of interreligious engagement that favor the dominant culture and the universalizing of religious experience, instead making asymmetries visible and raising up voices from the margins.

"For example, when I participate in an interreligious dialogue, I am never *only* participating as a Baha'i, but as a *Black, male, Baha'i living in the United States*," writes Phillippe Copeland, a professor in the Boston University School of Social Work. "Understanding my faith requires understanding how it is embodied in my experience of being a Black man in America." Similarly, Kristin Garrity Sekerci, a senior research fellow of the Bridge Institute at Georgetown University, writes about gendered perspectives of wearing the hijab within the context of Islamophobia: "Once I started to wear the *hijab,* strangers began to ask me the same question over and over. Suddenly, strangers become uncannily curious about 'where I am from.' . . . When I began to wear the *hijab*, my Western European-American biological hereditary was not only neutralized but supplanted by an entirely separate biological hereditary." Sharing her experiences after a string of antisemitic attacks in New York and New Jersey, Shekhiynah Larks embraces her identity as a Jewish Black woman: "My Judaism is a reflection of self-love and an affirmation of my whole self, Blackness and all. I am walking in a Black body with you every day. . . . For me, being unapologetically Black and Jewish is a revolutionary act. My two peoples are resilient."

Intersectionality within interreligious encounters makes systemic inequalities visible. "Real interfaith work assumes that we have something to teach each other, something to learn from one another. . . . And yet it remains absolutely and indispensably the case that the ground upon which we stand is extraordinarily differentiated," writes Omid Sami, professor of Asian and Middle Eastern Studies at Duke University. "We share radically different levels of access to power, wealth, and privilege that are based on our gender, socio-economic class, sexual orientation, nationalist, and other markers. And there are fundamental structural inequities that shape the parameters in which this conversation take place."

Our intersectional identities are inextricably linked to our religious identities. Identity formation is a spiritual issue, and when positive identity formation is neglected, a common response is to view religious differences (or other social identities) as a threat, with the resultant identities formed in opposition or "over against" the other. We are living now in the midst of the consequences of negative identity formation: fragmentation, nationalism, militant fundamentalism, global confrontations, or what some call the "clash of barbarisms." Agency, empowerment, and resilience, are some of the results of positive identity formation, as well as integral outcomes of interreligious engagement. While there is ample room for philosophical dialogue, interreligious engagement that encompasses daily living, community advocacy, or shared spiritual experiences is based in embodied practice that recognizes the validity of embodied social identities. In contrast to dualistic religious practice that aims to "transcend" the body, or privileges White (male) bodies as the norm, intersectionality embraces whole persons in their communities.

"Life stories are the teacher—the intersecting life stories that evoke emotion and invite people into honest reflections on themselves, their cultures, and social systems, alongside the complex economic, political, and religious forces that shape their lives," writes Mary Elizabeth Moore. Intersectionality is focused on real people's lives and is concerned about creating space for new perspectives and experiences. It cannot be separated from the lives of people who suffer, who hope, and who search for meaning. We are interconnected. Our fates are inseparable. The cultivation of this type of interreligious engagement prioritizes integration over fragmentation and acknowledges the intersectional realities present. Interreligious engagement from an intersectional perspective is always concerned with praxis, that is, with addressing systemic inequities and working for transformative change.

An awareness of the impact of intergenerational trauma on those who have long withstood systemic injustice is key to interreligious engagement that integrates intersectional awareness. In his work on racialized trauma, trauma specialist and healer Resmaa Menakem argues that anyone raised in the United States has experienced the "soul wound" of trauma, though the process is different for people of color than it is for White people. He posits that the ongoing destruction in our communities will not stop until we work through the trauma within our bodies, not just our brains. "Only in this way will we at last mend our bodies, our families, and the collective body of our nation." Restorative relationships through interreligious engagement can become pathways toward healing long-held traumas. Though Menakem's work is focused on the impact of racialized trauma, intersectional theory suggests it is applicable to trauma based in other social identities as well. "Once there's been widespread healing and growing up, fingers of love and trust can begin to reach out from one group to another—and then, slowly, start to intertwine."

As a privileged White, Christian, middle-class, heterosexual, cisgender woman involved in interreligious encounters for many years, I recall conversations about the need to create "safe spaces." Now, though I understand the political, psycho-social, and spiritual dimensions of that need, an intersectional lens informs my awareness that most of my friends and colleagues are never safe, and that to have that expectation is a sign of my White Christian privilege. It may be more realistic for us to cultivate "courageous spaces" where we can listen non-defensively and speak honestly and strive together to engage the work of solidarity.

Interreligious engagement that integrates intersectional awareness will not always be a *comfortable* place, but it has the potential to become a *sacred* space, and a rare opportunity to create communities that welcome differences, push boundaries, and re-examine systemic inequality. For interreligious communities to disrupt systemic oppression more effectively, it is necessary for leaders to become aware of our own biases, prejudices, and complicity. Unchecked, internalized superiority on the part of interreligious leaders (often framed as racism, sexism, and/or heterosexism,) impedes the mutual understanding and deep solidarity that interreligious engagement hopes to achieve. In this regard, the purpose of interreligious engagement is not to stress what we have in common or agree upon. Rather, it is to recognize and accept the realities of our differences because they are the markers of the embodied experiences that constitute our histories and the communities defining and inspiring us. Public anthropologists Adam B. Seligman, Rahel Wasserfall, and David M. Montgomery phrase it eloquently: "Can we learn to live with less-than-perfect knowledge of others and, despite being excluded from their histories, languages, and memories, still have enough trust to allow the construction of a shared world of reference on which to draw when events divide our different communities?"

Many religious traditions teach that seeds of hope are found in the transformation of suffering. The answer to how we access this hope lies in the stories of struggle that our traditions preserve. These stories shape our futures as well as our pasts. One of the heroes of my generation was poet Adrienne Rich. She writes: "So much has been destroyed I cast my lot with those who, age after age, perversely, with no extraordinary power, reconstitute the world." In fact, millions of people are indeed willing to confront despair and the abuse of power in order to restore some justice and beauty to the world. Therein lies our hope.

NOTES

1   Kimberlé Crenshaw, "Demarginalizing the Intersection of Race and Sex: A Black Feminist Critique of Antidiscrimination Doctrine, Feminist Theory and Antiracist Politics," *University of Chicago Legal Forum*, 1 (1989): 139–67.

2   Audre Lorde, "There Is No Hierarchy of Oppressions," in *I Am Your Sister: Collected and Unpublished Writing of Audre Lorde,* eds. Johnetta B. Cole and Beverly Guy-Sheftall (New York: Oxford University Press, 2009), 219–20.

3   Kimberlé Crenshaw, "Demarginalizing the Intersection of Race and Sex: a Black Feminist Critique of Antidiscrimination Doctrine, Feminist Theory and Antiracist Politics," *University of Chicago Legal Forum*, 1 (1989): 139–67; "Why Intersectionality can't wait," www .washingtonpost.com, September 24, 2015. Accessed May 23, 2020; Grace Ji-Sun Kim and Susan Shaw, *Intersectional Theology. An Introductory Guide* (Minneapolis: Fortress Press, 2018), 1–17.

4   Phillipe Copeland, "Faith and Race: A Dialogue Worth Having," *State of Formation*, May 9, 2012, https://www.stateofformation.org/2012/05/faith-and-race-a-dialogue-worth-having/.

5   Kristin Garrity Sekerci, "Sites of Racialization: Headscarves, Turbans and 'Brown Bodies' (@ theTable: Intersecting Islamophobia," www.fsrinc.org, May 25, 2016. Accessed June 7, 2016.

6   Shekhiynah Larks, "As a black Jew, I'm being forced to walk a tightrope after the Monsey attack," www.jweekly.com, January 8, 2020. Accessed June 1, 2020.

7   Omid Safi, "The Asymmetry of Interfaith Dialogue," www.onbeing.org, October 29, 2015. Accessed June 7, 2016.

8   Samuel Huntington, *The Clash of Civilizations and the Remaking World Order* (New York: Simon and Schuster, 1996), 101; Tariq Ali, *The Clash of Fundamentalisms: Crusades, Jihads and Modernity* (London: Verso, 2002), 113.

9   For the traditional categories of interreligious encounter, see Sheryl A. Kujawa-Holbrook, *God Beyond Borders. Interreligious Learning Among Faith Communities* (Eugene: Pickwick, 2014), 37–40.

10   Adeana McNicholl, "Buddhism and Race," in Katheryn Gin Kum and Paul Harvey, eds., *The Oxford Handbook of Religion and Race in American History* (Oxford: Oxford University Press, 2018), 233–35.

11   Mary Elizabeth Moore, "Disrupting White Privilege: Diving beneath Shame and Guilt," *Religious Education*, 114, 3 (May-June 2019), 259. Moore served as dean of the Boston University School of Theology 2009–2020.

12   Vivian M. May, *Pursuing Intersectionality, Unsettling Dominant Imaginaries* (New York: Routledge, 2015), 28–29.

13   Resmaa Menakem, *My Grandmother's Hands. Racialized Trauma and the Pathway to Mending our Hearts and Bodies* (Las Vegas: Central Recovery Press, 2017), 21–22.

14   Menakem, *My Grandmother's Hands*, 310.

15   See Rick Ufford-Chase, *Faithful Resistance: Gospel Visions for the Church in a Time of Empire* (San Bernardino, CA, 2017), 173.

16   Adam B. Seligman, Rahel R. Wasserfall, David W. Montgomery, *Living with Difference. How to Build Community in a Divided World* (Berkeley: University of California Press, 2015), 46–47.

17   Adrienne Rich, *Collected Poems 1950-2012* (New York: WW Norton, 2016), 472.

THE SELFLESSNESS OF INTERFAITH

BUDDHIST "NO SELF" AS A KEY TO DEEP UNDERSTANDING THAT TRANSCENDS RELIGIOUS BOUNDARIES

Russell C.D. Arnold

"As Nagasena I am known . . . nevertheless this word 'Nagasena' is just a denomination, a designation. . . . For no real person can here be apprehended."[1]

It is not really accurate to say that I have been "involved" in "interfaith work," but rather it seems more correct to say that I "am" interfaith. Not that I encompass all of interfaith, but rather to say that interfaith describes the complex process that gave rise to the "person" known as Russ Arnold. And yet, the structures and practices of Interfaith/Interreligious Studies have regularly seemed to marginalize me and my experience. It is my contention that holding to the notion that religions and the boundary lines between traditions are "real" is a cause of great suffering, and it is a significant impediment to deep understanding.

Let me back up a bit to provide a (very little) bit of context. I grew up in a Jewish home, my mom born of Jews from Chicago, my dad, a convert to Judaism who basically remained a Freudian atheist. We did not "belong" to a synagogue, but built a Havurah and made our own Jewish way (it was the 70s and the days of The First Jewish Catalog). In college, I fell in love, "became" an "evangelical" Christian, was confronted with the prospect of war, and consequently was introduced to and became compelled by the Quaker peace testimony. One of my Jewish friends said to me, "we'll miss you." My new Christian friends assumed I must know everything about the Bible and Jesus' context because I was a Jew. When, after college, I "became" a Messianic Jewish leader, those outside saw me either as "neither a Jew nor a Christian, but trying to be both, ending up being neither,"[2] or a (devious) evangelist trying to convert all Jews to Christianity. Some members of the Messianic Jewish movement rejected me as a "pinko commie" working against God because I held progressive views about scripture, society, and justice in Israel/Palestine.

Leaving Messianic Judaism and entering academia nearly twenty years ago, I have experienced consistent efforts by others to fit me into a category based on their notions of the boundaries between religions. For example, I had a student drop my class on Jesus because, when he asked if I was a Christian on day one, I said "no." Some members of the synagogue I belong to distrust me either because of my past involvement with Christianity, or for my regular participation in Friday prayers in local mosques. I was told at the Parliament of the World's Religions that, regardless of what I thought of myself, I was really a Bahá'í. The Religious Studies Department where I used to teach expected me to ignore my or my students' experiences and focus on teaching the "facts" and the official (textbook) understanding of each of the major world religions. The Jesuit, Catholic University where I currently teach encourages engagement with religious experience, but too often still sees me as "the Jew," whom, they suppose, believes and does what the books say Jews believe and do. Even, or perhaps especially, within interfaith activism and the developing field of Interreligious Studies, I have found participation to be built upon the desire for representational diversity, with invited panelists representing the range of discrete religions. Where could I sit on such a panel, except in the seat of the facilitator. Each of these situations, based on the reified categories of religions, create suffering and inhibit sincere efforts at deep understanding and connection.

Given that we live in a world characterized by division and polarization, which is constantly separating us into categories, what resources are available to us that can allow us to alleviate this suffering and move us toward deep understanding? The first step is to acknowledge the suffering, and to recognize its cause(s). Here we can draw on the insights of Sara Ahmed's *Queer Phenomenology*, in which she shows how power and violence is exerted to "straighten" out people's "queer" experiences in order to maintain the lines of "appropriate" orientations.[3] Historically, we can see a similar process being discussed among scholars of late antiquity regarding the emergence of what come to be called Christianity and Judaism. Daniel Boyarin's work, along with numerous others, highlights the efforts to establish "orthodox" Christian identity by creating, defining, and positing an alternate *ekklesia*, which they called "Judaism."[4] The effect of this process of claiming authority was to delegitimize and erase the existence of any who saw themselves as holding together both Jewish and Christian ways of being and doing.[5] While we, today, may not desire to erase the existence of those who do not fit nicely into our categories, our continued reification of these labels has created a category of people we call "nones," whose rich experiences can become invisible, even to themselves.

Is there a cure for this condition? How can we move forward? I have found inspiration in the teaching of the Buddha known as *anatta*, no-self, or selflessness. *Anatta* is one of the three marks of existence, meaning that all things that exist lack an independent, individual, enduring Self. Thich Nhat Hanh carefully describes the complex process that gives rise to what we call a flower. He concludes, "In fact, the flower is made up of entirely non-flower elements; it has no independent, individual existence."[6] He continues by applying this notion of interbeing to Buddhism and Christianity. "Just as a flower is made only of non-flower elements, Buddhism is made only of non-Buddhist elements, including Christian ones, and Christianity is made of non-Christian elements, including Buddhist ones."[7] Like the venerable Nagasena, and King Milinda's chariot, we must recognize that Christianity, Buddhism, Islam, Judaism, Taoism, etc., are "just a denomination, a designation, a conceptual term, a current appellation, a mere name. For no real [religion] can here be apprehended."[8]

Many of us would recognize that the names we give religions are problematic because we recognize that Christianity and Hinduism, for example, are not monolithic or uniform. We may also challenge the notion of religion because of its colonialist origins and Western bias. However, I suspect that most of us still see the traditions that we practice, study, and teach as essentially independent and distinct from one another. The doctrine of no-self challenges us to reject this notion of independence and pay attention to the complex process of interactions that give rise to particular manifestations in the lives of individuals and of communities.

Does this mean that we should do away with all labels and declare all "religions" essentially the same? By no means! In the same way that saying that race is not a biological reality does not mean that each person and culture is essentially the same. We will not diminish the power of religious labels by abstracting them into universal principles or a mystical search for Oneness as Wayne Teasdale would propose.[9] Although Teasdale's "interspirituality" may sound inviting for those individuals engaged in such a mystical quest, this approach can remove a principle or a practice from its context in a way that obscures the roots that tie an individual to the complex, collective, historical process that gave rise to the principle or practice in question. Deep understanding comes not from zooming out until we see only the universal, superficial similarities, but from zooming in toward the particularities to see the relationships, the deep structures of our connections, recognizing the tensions, the differences, and the power dynamics that shape our experiences.

The power of the notion of no-self is that it arises in an effort to gain a deeper understanding of the real nature of existence. So, we understand the thing we call a flower more richly when we understand its arising in connection with soil and seed and air and water and sun and nutrients, etc. Consequently, we understand the soil and seed and air, etc., more deeply when we see them as interdependent with other things. Similarly, we understand our social realities more deeply when we focus on the complex interactions and encounters and seek to understand the interpenetration and interdependence of these experiences. Our deeper understanding of the conditions involved in their interdependent arising allows us to maintain fidelity to their unique experiences while also maintaining the connections between them.

Rima Vesely-Flad provides important guidance for us in this effort based on the experiences of Black Buddhists in her article "Racism and Anatta: Black Buddhists, Embodiment, and Interpretations of Non-Self."[10] She writes, "the experience of non-self must begin with recognition of the social self: the experience of people, tradition, and community and the suffering wrought by living in a degrading social context."[11]

This highlights the importance of being able to bring our whole range of experiences to our interactions with members of our community as well as with encounters with those outside. Acknowledgment of the selflessness of things cannot be used to erase or ignore the particularities of our experience. As Jylani Ma'at says, "if you are asking me to withdraw and be a void of certainness and indelible in my spirit, then you don't really want me to show up. And then you are rendering me invisible almost."[12] No-self does not allow us to pass over the particulars of individual experience, but instead calls us to understand more about those experiences by understanding the deep structures that inform and influence their arising.

When I consider the divisiveness of our world and the social, political, racial, and religious lines that keep us apart and cause our suffering, I approach them as someone who has experienced antisemitism and White privilege, has lived and worked with politically conservative evangelical Christians, and has stood and prostrated in prayer with Muslim friends against Islamophobia. These experiences, and many others, shape me in ways that do not pull me apart (part Jewish, part Quaker, part Evangelical, part Buddhist, part Muslim, etc.), but rather these experiences hold me together, or put another way, these experiences and the people and texts behind them are the conditions that give rise to "me." I did not have these experiences, because I do not have a separate, independent, self or soul. The particular manifestation that is called by others "Russ" is interdependent with all the beings and encounters around me. Every effort to define me using the language of religions or traditions serves as a "straightening device" that does violence to the interpenetration of these experiences, and communicates that you don't really want me to show up. In this, I know that I am not alone. If our goal is deep understanding in these divisive times, we must reject the notion of independent religions, embrace the Selflessness of interfaith, and seek understanding of the rich, complex live encounters that manifest in each one of us.

NOTES

1   Edward Conze, *Buddhist Scriptures* (Harmondsworth, Middlesex: Penguin Books, 1959), 147.

2   See Jerome's description of the "Jewish-Christian" community called the Nazarenes as quoted in Daniel Boyarin, *Judaism: the Genealogy of a Modern Notion* (New Brunswick, NJ: Rutgers University Press, 2019), 122–23.

3   Sara Ahmed, *Queer Phenomenology: Orientations, Objects, Others* (Durham, NC: Duke University Press, 2007).

4   Daniel Boyarin, *Judaism: the Genealogy of a Modern Notion.* See also, Annette Yoshiko Reed, *Jewish-Christianity and the History of Judaism* (Tübingen: Mohr Siebeck, 2018).

5   Daniel Boyarin, *Judaism: the Genealogy of a Modern Notion*, 119–25.

6   Thich Nhat Hanh, *Living Buddha, Living Christ* (New York: Riverhead Books, 2007), 11.

7   Nhat Hanh, *Living Buddha, Living Christ*, 11.

8   Conze, *Buddhist Scriptures*, 147.

9   Wayne Teasdale, *The Mystic Heart: Discovering a Universal Spirituality in the World's Religions* (United States: New World Library, 2010).

10 Rima Vesely-Flad, "Racism and Anatta: Black Buddhists, Embodiment, and Interpretations of Non-Self," in *Buddhism and Whiteness: Critical Reflections* (Lanham: Lexington Books, 2019), 79–97.

11 Vesely-Flad, "Racism and Anatta," 90.

12 Vesely-Flad, "Racism and Anatta," 87.

OUR EMPTINESS IS OUR INSEPARABILITY
A BUDDHIST TEACHING FOR OUR TIME

Wakoh Shannon Hickey

I first encountered the Buddhist doctrine of "emptiness" in a high school humanities class taught by a well-meaning English teacher who, I later learned, had no idea what she was talking about. She presented "emptiness" as void, zero, *nada*, zilch: a common misconception. I wondered why anyone's religious goal would be to achieve *nothing*. Five years later, however, I got a first glimpse into this teaching—a moment that changed my life and set me firmly on the Buddhist path. In the decades since, my understanding has developed, and in my present work as a hospice chaplain who encounters death weekly, if not daily, this teaching comforts and inspires me in the face of my own and others' mortality. It has proven fundamental to my interfaith and anti-racist efforts, as well. Before explaining that last sentence, it seems important to explain some basic Buddhist ideas.

"Emptiness" (*śūnyatā* in Sanskrit) is another way of talking about the Buddhist doctrine of *anātman*, or "not-self." *Anātman* is one of three Buddhist premises about the nature of reality; the others are *anitya* (impermanence) and *pratītya-samutpāda* (dependent origination). *Anitya* means that everything is impermanent; the only constant is that everything changes. Whatever appears solid to us is actually process: transitory confluences of ever-changing events.

The second premise derives from the first: if everything is process, then nothing has any independent, unchanging, eternal existence, essence, or "self": *anātman*. In the Chandogya Upanishad, a Vedic text that predates Buddhism, the *ātman* is said to be one with Brahman, the Ground of Being or Ultimate Reality. An individual *ātman* transmigrates through lifetime after lifetime, in an endless cycle of birth, death, rebirth, and re-death (*samsāra*). One's fate in each lifetime is determined by the cumulative effects of one's actions (*karma*) in previous lifetimes. During the Buddha's life, many people renounced worldly pursuits and became wandering ascetics, devoting themselves to disciplines (yogas) that they hoped would help them realize union with Brahman and thereby achieve moksha, or liberation from samsāra, at death. (Birth isn't so bad, but dying generally isn't much fun.) The Buddha became such a wandering ascetic himself at age 29. When he began teaching six years later, however, he denied that anything has ātman and claimed that attachment to this idea produces *dūḥkha*, or dissatisfaction, even suffering.

An early Buddhist analogy likened the "self" to a chariot that is composed of a frame, wheels, axles, seat, reins, and draught-pole: disassemble these constituents, and there is no essential "cart-ness" to be found in them.[1] Likewise, the human was said to be composed of five *skandhas* ("heaps" or "aggregates"), which are constantly interacting and changing.

1. form   (physical, material, tangible body)

2. feelings   (positive, negative, and neutral reactions to stimuli)

3. perceptions   (inputs from our five sense organs and the mind)

4. mental formations   (thoughts, habits of mind, intellectual constructs)

5. consciousness   (awareness)

Apart from these, the self (our personhood) does not exist. The skandhas collectively are not the "self"; the *skandhas* do not "have" a self and the self does not "have" *skandhas*; nor is the self "in" the *skandhas*; nor are the *skandhas* "in" the self.

The third Buddhist premise about the nature of reality is *pratītya-samutpāda*, which means "dependent origination" or "interdependent co-arising." This doctrine says that all things arise, abide, and pass away according to causes and conditions in a continuous flow. If the causes and conditions producing a particular phenomenon cease, the phenomenon based on them also ceases. The self (and all apparent phenomena) are intersecting, interpenetrating processes, all the way down. This is true moment by moment, as well as lifetime after lifetime.[2]

Some early Indian Buddhist philosophers explained no-self in terms of a constant flow of *dharmas*—the essential building blocks of physical and psychological reality. Dharmas were seen as irreducible, like atoms in Newtonian physics, or like the subatomic and elementary particles discovered since.[3] Different schools of early Indian Buddhism composed their own "periodic tables" of *dharmas*, with differing numbers of elements. Some referred to physical qualities (taste, sound, fragrance, color/shape, tangibility, vitality, decay), but most were mental, psychological, or emotional (volition, perception, memory, determination, faith, shame, diligence, etc.) Phenomena were the result of *dharmas* continually arising, interacting, and disappearing, moment after moment. Each dharma had only one characteristic, and it was "real" in some essential sense, even though its existence was fleeting. The apparent "self" composed of dharmas was not "real," however. It had no essential, irreducible existence; it was just a compilation in a state of change. This is similar to the skandha theory, but dharmas were seen as more fundamental.

Abidharmic speculation got pretty abstract and obscure. The Indian Buddhist philosopher Nāgārjuna (circa 150–250 CE) launched another evolution in Buddhist thought by asserting that all dharmas are also "empty", viz., that they, too, lack any independent, unchanging, eternal essence, however fleeting. To say that phenomena are "empty" is *not* the same as saying they do not exist. It means that phenomena exist *relationally*. Night and day, up and down, faith and doubt, *samsāra* and *nirvāna* only have meaning, and can only be understood or experienced, in relation to their opposites. Their existence is thus *relative*, not absolute.

Nāgārjuna also said there are Two Truths: absolute truth, about which nothing can be accurately said, because it is beyond conception or description; and relative truth, which is our ordinary, day-to-day reality. On the absolute level, there is no essential self and nothing exists separately; on the relative level, we experience continuity as a "self" throughout our lifetime, and we walk around inside separate skins, bumping into things that seem solid. Both are true simultaneously, and awakening entails recognizing both at once. Even though phenomena are "empty" of essence, that does not mean they are "unreal" and that one can do whatever one wishes, as if nothing mattered. Despite the absence of a permanent self on the absolute level, our conduct definitely has consequences on the relative level. Nāgārjuna's Madhyamaka philosophy became extremely influential in Tibetan, Chinese, and Japanese forms of Buddhism.

Nāgārjuna's emptiness teaching was sometimes misunderstood as nihilistic, however. In response, the fourth-century Yogācāra school of Buddhist philosophy developed a theory that multiple layers of consciousness collectively produce an apparent "self," though it, too, is insubstantial on the level of absolute reality. The Hua-yen School of Buddhism developed in China on the basis of teachings in the *Avataṃsaka Sūtra*, which describes no-self in psychedelic or holographic terms. Emptiness is explained there as "interpenetration": the mutual presence of all things simultaneously, everywhere. *Anything* toward which you point contains *everything* else in the universe. For example, a piece of paper is composed not just of wood and chemicals, but of sun and rain and the logger and her chainsaw, and the trucking company and the millworkers and their families, on a planet just the right distance from its sun to sustain organic life, and so on and so on, endlessly. Another simile is a holographic plate that has been shattered, the tiniest fragment of which can be used to project the entire three-dimensional image. Thich Nhat Hanh, a popular modern Zen master from Vietnam, has used the term "Interbeing" to describe this way of looking at things.

Five years after the high school humanities class mentioned above, I began exploring Buddhism again during college. Within a few miles of U.C. Berkeley, a dizzying variety of traditions and lineages are represented, and I visited many of these communities, eventually settling into Sōtō Zen. During the fall semester of 1984, my junior year of college, I lived at Green Gulch Farm/Green Dragon Zen Temple, one of three residential communities run by San Francisco Zen Center. Near the end of my stay, at the end of an all-day meditation retreat, I recalled a riot-geared policeman I had encountered in my job as a reporter for Berkeley's daily newspaper the previous summer, at one of many violent demonstrations against Ronald Reagan's impending re-election to the US Presidency.

Reagan was backed by a coalition of fundamentalist Christians led by Jerry Falwell and Phyllis Schlafly, who dubbed themselves the "Moral Majority." Their self-righteous, exclusivist, homophobic rhetoric seemed profoundly violent to me. So did the rage of protesting groups like the John Brown Anti-Klan Committee, which appeared almost ready to lynch Falwell if they could have gotten their hands on him. And police inflicted brutality on unarmed protesters and volunteer medics. I was devastated by the experience and could not take sides. My timeout at Green Gulch was an opportunity to sift through it all.

I had encountered the police officer I envisioned during that retreat outside a Moral Majority convention, which was scheduled in San Francisco a week before the Democratic National Convention, as a sort of in-your-face to the city's LGBT community. The cop's face behind his face shield was stony, as he shoved unresisting pedestrians onto the sidewalk with his nightstick. He seemed like the antithesis of everything I thought was good, right, and true. And then, for an instant, the boundary between him and me dissolved, and I realized that I was who I was, where I was, doing what I was doing, because (in part) he was who he was, where he was, doing what he was doing. Our lives were utterly intertwined, though we met for only an instant. And I had precisely the same capacity for dogmatism and self-righteousness that I perceived in those I critiqued. In other words, he who seems most "other" than me is inseparable from me; my existence depends on his. The Parable of the Good Samaritan (Luke 10:25–37) conveys a similar teaching. Three years later I formally made vows as a lay student of Sōtō Zen, and sixteen years after that I deepened those vows, receiving ordination as a priest. Since then, I have made my living both as an academic and as a chaplain, serving specifically Buddhist communities as well as hospice patients of any faith or none.

In 2015, I was working as a Buddhist chaplain in Baltimore, which erupted in violent protest after the death of Freddie Gray, who died of spinal cord injuries incurred while in police custody, despite his repeated pleas for medical help. It is part of a long litany of similar tragedies, before and since. At the time, I was leading a group of undergraduates at Johns Hopkins University through a study of the Heart Sūtra, the central scripture of Sōtō Zen. Its key lines are: "Form does not differ from emptiness; emptiness does not differ from form. Form itself is emptiness; emptiness itself is form."[4] Another translation says, "form is not separate from boundlessness; boundlessness is not separate from form. Form is boundlessness; boundlessness is form."[5] How could such a text shed light on the tragedy in our own city, just blocks away from the relatively sheltered university campus?

Answers can be found in our own bodies and minds, and mine had never felt *Whiter* than it did at that time. I had lived in Baltimore for a year and a half, teaching comparative religion at a Catholic university, and visited the neighborhood that burned for the first time on the day before protest exploded into riot. I had gone there to attend a lecture at a predominantly Black American mosque. On the way home, I drove down North Ave., past block after block after block after block of boarded-up, falling-down, blighted buildings, and people obviously suffering poverty, addiction, and despair. I was dumbfounded and aghast. *How had I not seen this before?* I had managed to travel paths through town that ran through the affluent university neighborhoods where I lived and worked, full of tree-lined streets and elegant mansions. I went on to learn the history of Baltimore, where racist policies like redlining and neighborhood covenants excluding Blacks and Jews were pioneered, then spread across the country.[6]

After the city was occupied by the National Guard and curfews imposed to curb violent protest, my neighborhood and the freeway my high-rise apartment building overlooked were silent. But just over the hills, I could see and hear police helicopters circling all night long. Students in my classrooms who lived or worked in occupied neighborhoods spoke of children there who could not imagine living past twenty, much less having careers. The fact that my White privilege depends on this level of disadvantage and suffering for others is a very clear example of interdependent co-arising: because this is, that is. Seeing the interdependence of things, the emptiness *of* forms, can be blissful, but emptiness *is form* means that conventional, relative reality is true too, and our actions, individual and collective, have consequences in this real world. Our individual greed, hate, and ignorance cause suffering, and so does institutionalized greed, prejudice, and the delusion that we are, or could ever be, truly separated.

Emptiness means we are *absolutely inseparable*. In my hospice work, this gives me comfort because I believe that although things change, and people die, love and relationships endure, and nothing is ever truly lost. Because everything is related to everything else, what I do and how I live has consequences far beyond my individual self. When I die, what remains of me and the relationships I've built will still circulate in the world, and hopefully some of it will bring some benefit here and there. My collaborations with religious "others" also arise from a deep conviction that we are all in this hurting world together and can only heal it together.

If we really understood our fundamental indivisibility, might that not change how we walk down the street and encounter people who seem very "other"? What if we said to ourselves, "That person is not *other than* me?" Might this not improve how we organize our economic systems, our political systems, our legal systems? Might it not influence our responses to the most urgent crises besetting humanity today: structural racism, political polarization, income inequality, immigrant and refugee crises, climate change, mass extinction, war? *What if we really, truly fathomed that our own wellbeing, safety, and happiness are intimately connected to the wellbeing, safety, and happiness of not just other people, but all beings everywhere?* The Heart Sūtra says the one who realizes emptiness has no fear. Fearlessness and tenacity in working for change are necessary to create environments in which no one needs to live in fear. In Buddhism, the most basic practice is not meditation but generosity, which is defined as material aid, spiritual aid, and the gift of fearlessness.

The novel coronavirus, the Black Lives Matter movement, and climate change: all are fierce, compassionate Zen Masters whacking us upside the head with a teaching about how we are all connected. If we have ears to hear and eyes to see, they can help us "get over ourselves," our self-preoccupations, and work together with others to make a better world. In doing so, we must never lose sight of the fact that those with whom we passionately disagree are inseparable from us as well, lest we fall into the very evil we oppose. Form is boundaryless; boundarylessness, form. Our emptiness is our inseparability.

NOTES

1   Vajira Sūtra, SN 5:10; Milindapañha, 3.1.1

2   One way to describe the process is the "Twelvefold Chain of Causation."

    1.   Ignorance gives rise to

    2.   Impulses/tendencies/propensities, which give rise to

    3.   Consciousness, which gives rise to

    4.   Name and form (the act of recognizing and identifying objects, and the five *skandhas*), which condition

    5.   The six sense fields (the five sense organs and the mind), which make possible

    6.   Contact (with "the world out there"), which generates

    7.   Feeling, which leads to

    8.   Desire, which leads to

    9.   Clinging, which leads to

    10. Becoming, which leads to

    11. Birth, which leads to

    12. Aging, sickness and death, with their attendant suffering.

    Each link in the chain depends on the previous one; the cycle can be described forward or backward (death depends on birth, which depends on becoming, which depends on clinging, etc.). Through meditation practice, one can become intimately familiar with how such processes occur moment-by-moment within one's own body-mind and create the illusion of selfhood. Seeing through the delusion, one can be freed (at least momentarily) from the cycle. This is one description of what "enlightenment" means.

3   String Theory, which is based on mathematics I do not comprehend, suggests that even these elementary particles can be viewed as one-dimensional "strings" of energy that vibrate in different ways to produce phenomena.

4   Sōtō-shū Scriptures for Chanting and Daily Practice.

5   Trans. Joan Halifax and Kazuaki Tanahashi. Italics mine.

6   Antero Pietila, *Not In My Neighborhood: How Bigotry Shaped a Great American City* (Chicago: Ivan R. Dee: 2010).

PROPHETIC RESISTANCE AS INTERFAITH KEY

Jeannine Hill Fletcher

Critical theory recognizes that the interpretive keys used to study diverse religious traditions derive from the needs of a given era. In the view of Max Horkheimer, the point is not only to study our moment, but to shape it. The key of "prophethood," running through the Jewish, Christian, and Islamic traditions and identifiable as a pattern in socially engaged Buddhism and Hinduism, can be used not only as a tool of analysis and constructive comparison, but also as a resource for interfaith activism today.

THE ORIENTATION OF CRITICAL THEORY

In 1937, the sociologist and philosopher Max Horkheimer made the distinction between traditional theory and critical theory. In traditional theory, the producer of knowledge stands apart from the reality that is studied and plays the role of describer and analyzer of events and dynamics in society. By contrast, the critical theorist was called to recognize how the generation of their ideas would *shape* society. In a compellingly complex essay, Horkheimer urges his audience of fellow scholars to take an active role in the society of which they are a part. The very activity of the critical theorist, Horkheimer wrote, is "the construction of the social present."[1]

As scholars of religion, we too might be challenged to ask whether our research and teaching stands more in line with traditional theory's proposed "objectivity" or whether our work is committed to the construction of our social present. In considering Horkheimer's challenge, we might also listen intently to his concern that past systems of knowledge have brought forth a social reality that is *unjust*. The impact of knowledge production on practice is essential to see; whether one adopts a critically engaged stance or not, the scholar is always producing the social present. If theory has already informed the social reality, and the theorist recognizes that the social reality is *unjust,* they have the responsibility not only to describe it, but also to change it. In this orientation, the responsibility of the critical theorist is not primarily to the audience of students or academic peers, but to those who feel most significantly the impact of injustice. Horkheimer's words gives scholars a new center: "If, however, the theoretician and [their] specific object are seen as forming a dynamic unity with the oppressed class, so that his presentation of societal contradictions is not merely an expression of the concrete historical situation but also a force within it to stimulate change, then his real function emerges."[2] The real function of the critical theorist is to align with those dispossessed by an unjust social reality and to function as a force of knowledge production to create change.

While commitments to objectivity may prevent some scholars from seeing their role in this way, their scholarship also produces the social present. If the theorist is embedded in a social world of injustice yet adopts neutrality, this too is a force at work in constructing the social present. Echoing Horkheimer's concerns, contemporary theorist Barbara Applebaum responds to the charge of a "liberal bias" in the contemporary education system by reminding us that "academic neutrality . . . can support oppression by default."[3] The critical theorist, thus, recognizes that her work is not neutral in its commitment to employ the systems of meaning-making and knowledge production toward liberative ends; the alternative is to do nothing and allow an unjust reality to continue as the status quo.

The theologians among us might have embraced such an ideology rooted within the ethical values espoused by their religious traditions. But, the scholar of religion in the "secular" academy might also identify and articulate an ideological stance from which to build their critical engagement. When we remember that the foundation of so many of our educational institutions—even public institutions—was in service to equipping citizens with practical tools to contribute to the nation, we can recognize the inherent commitments of social engagement within academia. In a brief overview of liberal arts education, philosopher and past president of Bates College Donald Harward articulates the aims of higher education in a threefold way. It is, of course, an academic project (grounded in helping our students acquire knowledge/information/data relevant to our discipline); but it is also civic (designed with the outcome of shaping society); and finally (with any luck) it is also eudemonic, that is, designed for personal growth and happiness.[4] In incorporating the civic dimension, Harward alerts us to the liberal arts commitment that knowledge is not neutral. It is purposeful toward specific ends—whether these ends are articulated theologically as a commitment to human flourishing, ethically as a commitment to moral action, or socially as commitment to the common good. Hence, we do well to recognize that education is *never* neutral.

EVIDENCE OF NON-NEUTRALITY IN THE DISCIPLINES OF THEOLOGY AND RELIGIOUS STUDIES

The studies of Theology and Religion are especially in need of the self-reflective moment of commitment to the common good because of the way the work of our predecessors has functioned to erect sacred systems that have protected injustice. The perceived sanctity of religious forms of meaning-making and academic knowledge production have had devastating effects in our history. Just two recent volumes remind us that we inhabit a dangerous discipline as it has provided the symbolic capital to generate the Western world's most egregious human failures. Under the guise of an anti-Jewish Jesus, scholars in Nazi Germany laid the foundation for genocide, as Susannah Heschel has carefully chronicled in *The Aryan Jesus: Christian Theologians and the Bible in Nazi Germany*.[5] And Craig Wilder has shown the myriad ways universities in the United States incorporated religious principles in the production of knowledge about enslaved peoples and the defense of slavery in *Ebony and Ivy: Race, Nation and the Troubled History of America's Universities*.[6] Our discipline has shaped social realities of death-dealing and destruction under the sacred canopy of elevated knowledge; our discipline has a special responsibility to mobilize our work toward greater humanity.

THE CRITICALLY ENGAGED SCHOLAR-THEOLOGIAN AND THE STATUS QUO OF AN UNJUST WORLD

Setting out to undertake Horkheimer's program in our day, the scholar concerned about our social present might benefit from the sociological analysis of Jaideep Singh in "A New American Apartheid: Racialized, Religious Minorities in the Post-9/11 Era" as he surveys the US landscape of White Christian hegemony that continues to impact the lives and liberties of people of color and/or adherents of non-Christian religious traditions.[7] Khyati Joshi's *White Christian Privilege: The Illusion of Religious Equality in America* provides a current accounting of our present with an eye to the historical and social realities of the moment.[8] With these scholars, we too must read the signs of the times to witness the unjust status quo of White Christian hegemony, where legislation, education, and resource-benefits are skewed to the benefit of those who are White and Christian in our nation's religio-racial project.[9] With this landscape in view, the work of interfaith learning forms a "dynamic unity with the oppressed" and produces knowledge for rebalance, reparation, and resistance.

The field of religious and theological study further provides thematic content for creating the conditions to do our work as socially engaged scholars. When identifying themes for cross-cultural and trans-religious comparison, why not seek in the religious traditions of the world those common threads with a critical edge that might build bridged social capital toward social transformation.[10] One fruitful approach for comparative theology and interfaith learning to develop a project of critically engaged scholarship is through the theme of "prophethood," identifiable in the Jewish, Christian, and Islamic traditions and ripe for comparison with patterns of Buddhist and Hindu thought. Seeing the prophet as one whose "breathless impatience with injustice" compels them to speak, and through whose words "the invisible God becomes audible," the beating heart of a comparative project comes into view.[11] Is there such a reality as "God" that bends the moral arc of the universe toward justice? Does such a reality as "God" care sufficiently about the outcomes of creation to spur involvement in social change? Did such a reality as "God" call forth the Jesus Movement of women and men in the ancient world, who remember a God who has "spoken through the prophets" as the words of their creed confess? Has this God spoken through the prophets to every nation and with finality to Muhammad, the Seal of the Prophets?[12] Do the prophetic activities of engaged Buddhism and Gandhian Hinduism recommend witnessing this God at work beyond the Abrahamic traditions, or does the comparison yield alternative theological conclusions? What complements or complications arise in comparison to the great varieties of indigenous religious traditions and humanistic endeavors when "the prophet" is centered in the discussion? Providing the opportunity to critically engage theological currents, undermining any easy understanding of what a mouthpiece for God might mean, the prophetic lens offers theological richness, an ethical stance and a comparative connection for activists in the faiths, pressing the question of whether there are prophets in our world today. Elevating the theme of prophetic judgment, the selection of comparative themes becomes *purposeful* in creating deep understanding to address the social reality of our times that are divided between those who benefit from an unjust status quo and those who are oppressed by it. For however one adopts a position in relation to the prophet's words, their calls for justice and righteousness, care for the oppressed and exploited, are now on the table for further questioning regarding the justice, righteousness, oppression, and exploitation of our moment.

The practice of the critical theorist of Theology and Religion might find in our discipline rich themes for comparative investigation and collaborative action. But the posture of the critical theorist must also ask where *we* stand in the benefits and dispossessions of an unjust status quo. In the 1930s under the shadow of the rise of Hitler, Abraham Joshua Heschel wrote his dissertation on the prophets of the Hebrew Bible, surely finding this work a resource of response to the injustice rising in his world. In the 1960s with the upsweep of the civil rights movement in the US, Heschel revised his dissertation for an English-speaking audience. As Albert Raboteau reports, in the memory of Heschel's daughter Susannah, "it was revising his dissertation on the prophets for publication in English during the early 1960s that convinced him that he must be involved in human affairs, in human suffering."[13] As with Heschel, our work contributes to our social and political moment, either by default or by design. Interfaith work has a unique positionality to refuse accommodations to White supremacies that have been fostered by Christian exceptionalism, and to produce knowledge to advance the rights and well-being that can dismantles White Christian hegemony. However, we must embrace our place as critical theorists of religion and theology creating coalitions to stand against rise of White Christian nationalisms that continue to deal death by dividing us.

NOTES

1   Max Horkheimer, "Traditional and Critical Theory," (1937) in *Critical Theory: Selected Essays* (New York: Continuum, 2002), 211.

2   Horkheimer, 215.

3   Barbara Applebaum, "Is Teaching for Social Justice a 'Liberal Bias'?" *Teachers College Record* 111 no. 2 (February 2009) 376–408 at 384.

4   Donald Harward, "Engaged Learning and the Core Purposes of Liberal Education: Bringing Theory to Practice," *Liberal Education* 93.1 (2007): 6–15.

5   Susannah Heschel, *The Aryan Jesus: Christian Theologians and the Bible in Nazi Germany* (Princeon University Press, 2008).

6   Craig Steven Wilder, *Ebony and Ivy: Race, Slavery and the Troubled History of America's Universities* (New York, Bloomsbury, 2013).

7   Jaideep Singh, "A New American Apartheid: Racialized, Religious Minorieties in the Post-9/11 Era," *Sikh Formations* Vol. 9 No. 2 (2013): 115–44.

8   Khyati Joshi, *White Christian Privilege: The Illusion of Religious Equality in America* (New York: NYU Press, 2020).

9   Michael Omi and Howard Winant employ the term "racial project" to describe the dynamic configurations of racial categorizations and the distributions of resources along racial lines at any given moment. I include religious categorizations as useful also to have in view in any given moment's racial project. See Omi and Winant, Racial Formation in the United States, 2nd edition (New York: Routledge, 1994), 53–76.

10 Interfaith Youth Core helps to envision the role of interfaith studies in developing appreciative knowledge of other religious traditions that might help to build relationships across religious differences to be mobilized for the common good.

11 Abraham Joshua Heschel, *The Prophets* (New York: Harper and Row, 1962), 4 and 22.

12 Falzur Rahman, *Major Themes of the Qur'an*, 2nd edition (Chicago: University of Chicago Press, 2009), 56.

13 Albert Raboteau, *American Prophets: Seven Religious Radicals and Their Struggle for Social and Political Justice* (Princeton, NJ: Princeton University Press, 2016), 8.

TOWARDS A NEW ECOLOGICAL VISION
AN INTERRELIGIOUS REFLECTION ON
LAUDATO SI'

Thomas Cattoi

In his encyclical letter *Laudato si'*, Pope Francis devotes a brief section to "the gaze of Jesus," where he reminds us that

> The Lord was able to invite others to be attentive to the beauty that
> there is in the world because he himself was in constant touch with
> nature, lending it an attention full of fondness and wonder. As he
> made his way throughout the land, he often stopped to contemplate
> the beauty sown by the Father, and invited his disciples to perceive a
> divine message in things: "Lift up your eyes, and see how the fields
> are already white for harvest" (Jn 4: 35). "The kingdom of God is
> like a grain of mustard seed which a man took and sowed in the
> field; it is the smallest of all seeds, but once it has grown, it is the
> greatest of plants" (Mt 13: 31–32).[1]

This document marked the first instance when a Roman Pontiff devoted a whole encyclical to the question of the environment, thereby following in the footsteps of other religious leaders. For example, Patriarch Bartholomew of Constantinople, known as the "Green Patriarch," has fostered numerous environmental initiatives; the Dalai Lama has issued numerous messages and spoken multiple times about our duty towards the environment.[2] Environmental theology can now be considered a branch of Christian theology in its own right. At the same time, scholars and practitioners working in this field have only rarely stepped out of their confessional and religious context to seek out the wisdom of other religious traditions. In other words, a truly interreligious theology of creation drawing on the resources of different religions has yet to develop. In this brief essay, I would like to sketch the contours of an interreligious response to Pope Francis's invitation to "lift up our eyes" to nature, asking whether a Christian environmental theology can gain any insight from what the Buddhist tradition has to say about the nature and purpose of the natural order.

In the text of his letter, the Pope reminds us that in the Christian understanding of the cosmos, the destiny of the natural order is intrinsically bound to Christ, whose mystery was present from the beginning of time, and who is present in creation through his universal

Lordship. Thus, if the human nature of Christ is the paradigm for a correct relationship to creation, his divine nature is the ontological ground of its ultimate dignity and eschatological transfiguration. Francis devotes a whole chapter to a searing critique of the technocratic paradigm that envisages creation as a mere depository of resources. The underlying theological implication is that humanity lost the Christocentric gaze that was adumbrated at the end of the previous section. Contemporary humanity is no longer able to "see" the world in a way that leaves room for the irruption of transcendence in contingency: even those seeking for transcendence appear to relegate it to a realm that is untouched by their everyday, mundane concerns. What we need to ask ourselves, then, is not only what is the cause of this dichotomy, but also how the wisdom of different religious traditions can help us recover a more holistic way of seeing.

The early Fathers of the church envisaged all natural phenomena as invested with a propaedeutic import. In this perspective, coming to grasp the inner functioning of the natural order also entailed an understanding of its ethical purpose. In a work such as Basil of Caesarea's *Hexaemeron*, for instance, no distinction is drawn between natural sciences on one hand, and ethics on the other. The idea of a "neutral" parsing of natural phenomena, stripped of their ethical relevance, would have been utterly meaningless, since humanity's integrated rationality, guided by the light of revelation, could not explore one and leave aside the other.[3]

This integrated vision started to crumble in the seventeenth century with the epistemological treatises of the English empiricists, but the true moment of crisis for this holistic vision would come with Immanuel Kant's turn to the subject and his conceptualization of distinct forms of rationality. If the panoply of cognitive categories subsumed by the notion of pure reason enables us to explore the natural order, the world of the moral law falls under the purview of something Kant names practical reason, which alone can address issues such as morality or, indeed, the existence of God.[4] The world is thus stripped of the divine touch (*entzaubert*) and its exploration can no longer offer any entrée into the world of morality; science can no longer be assumed to be ethically or spiritually transformative. What we are left with are Lockean substances, inanimate material, a world closed in on itself and from which God has been expunged as an unnecessary nuisance.[5] This is the worldview which the Pope deplores, and which is at the root of the environmental devastation that we all witness: a calculating gaze that is not devoid of insight, but that is unable to look higher than the realization of its own self-aggrandizing goals. This is also a gaze that is fundamentally horizontal, deracinating reason from its transcendent soil, and one that, despite its foolhardy assertion of endless growth and development, is one that denies the very possibility of an eschatological horizon. Some might say that contemporary affluent societies are their own self-realized eschatologies—worlds of inexhaustible material availability, arenas of unlimited shopping, economies of perpetual growth—but eschatologies that leave no room for an external divine intervention, or for an eschatological world which would lack not only a temple, but also a mall.

Pope Francis's *Laudato si'* is not a work of systematic theology, or even of ethics in the strict sense of the term; but it does challenge theologians and, I think, invites them to reflect on the way they can help recover a healthier and more integrated perspective on creation. Is it possible for Christian theology to overcome the reductionist gaze of modernity and retrieve what the Pope calls "Jesus' gaze"? Can other religious traditions offer any resources to Christian theologians seeking to recover a more holistic understanding of the natural order?

In 553, the Second Council of Constantinople condemned a number of propositions taken from the teaching of Origen of Alexandria (185–256).[6] According to Origen and his followers, the goal of spiritual practice was a return to an undifferentiated oneness with God; material creation is just a tool that serves our pursuit of noetic disengagement, but can then be left behind. In addition, and most importantly, the locus of subjectivity was a disembodied *nous*, which used a body to achieve its goals, but was ultimately not tied to it. This vision was colored by an ultimately negative understanding of creation, where the Incarnation had a purely pedagogical function. According to the vision of creation that was developed by the Cappadocian Fathers, and reached its full development in the Christological vision of Chalcedon, spiritual practice is meant to redeem the whole material cosmos in all its plurality and contingency; material creation is part and parcel of the divine plan that becomes fully manifest in the incarnation of Christ. In this perspective, the individual subject is a reality that comprises a soul, as well as a body; the deified individual will be in a relationship with God and with the other members of humanity in her own body, which is not destined to be discarded.[7]

The veneration of icons that is so central to the worship of Eastern churches is a manifestation of the sacramental vision that Francis is calling us to recover. By looking at the icon of the resurrected Christ, we behold God's purpose for creation, as well as God's plan for every member of the human race.[8] A spirituality where the trajectory that brings us to salvation is ultimately inconsequential after the goal is reached seems to foster a kind of spiritual pragmatism, where creation is destined to be erased. Authors like John Damascene and Theodore the Studite, for whom icons are an instance of realized eschatology (that is, the iconographic representation of a universe utterly transformed by God's grace) envisage humanity as continuing in every day and age the task that Christ (the incarnate Logos) had inaugurated in his flesh. The Chalcedonian theology of the hypostatic union undergirds their understanding of sacred images. According to this classical understanding, in the person of Jesus Christ the fullness of humanity and divinity came together without confusion and without separation, thereby making deification possible for every member of the human race. In the icons, we can venerate Christ's own glorified flesh; but we can also witness the testimony of the saints who responded to Christ's invitation and now share in his glory. When commenting on the transfiguration narrative of the Synoptic gospels, both Maximus the Confessor and Gregory Palamas note that the disciples' noetic vision had been purified beforehand, and that alone enabled them to behold the glory of Christ transfigured in front of them.

This notion of "pure vision" that is outlined by these early Christian authors finds significant echoes in the broader tradition of Mahayana Buddhism, which develops what could be termed a "sacramental vision" of reality. From its very inception, Mahayana thought reinterpreted Buddhism's four noble truths in a way that exploded the dichotomy between *samsara* and *nirvāna*.[9] While the earliest Buddhist tradition viewed the reality of suffering and transience as radically distinct from the experience of liberation, Mahayana Buddhism viewed *nirvāna* as already present within *samsara*. As such, the goal of spiritual practice is no longer to move from one state to another, but rather to discover the profoundly nirvanic nature of the whole of conditioned reality. In the Tibetan tradition, characterized by a remarkably high Buddhology, this teaching is compounded by the tendency to conflate the Buddha nature (*tathāgatagarbha*) with *nirvāna*, and ultimately with the whole totality of the natural order.[10]

What are the practical implications of this speculative vision? Reflecting the belief in the all-encompassing character of the Buddha nature, the variety of Buddhas and bodhi-sattvas that people the Buddhist devotional landscape are understood to be conventional manifestations of the nirvanic reality of the *tathāgatagarbha*. Even if *samsara* is *nirvāna*, and *nirvāna* is *samsara*, the greatest majority of sentient beings fails to discern this truth, while the distractions of conventional reality conspire to lower our sights and seek happiness in its transitory material joys. In this perspective, the images of the glorified Buddhas and bodhisattvas turn into pedagogical props, or cues, enabling us to escape this illusion. The iconographic portrayals of these figures in their pure lands, often surrounded by a cloud of disciples and attendants, remind practitioners that it is possible to leave behind this world of attachment and suffering and eventually move towards awakening[11]

How can one move from a samsaric to a nirvanic vision and realize in oneself the all-encompassing nature of the *tathāgatagarbha*? A number of Tibetan schools teach sophisticated visualization practices whereby practitioners gradually purify their perceptions and come to view the world in a nirvanic way. The first step of this practice is the creation in the mind of the practitioner of the image of a tantric deity—a personification of a particular aspect of the Buddha nature such as wisdom or compassion taking the form of a glorified body of the Buddha. The next step is the identification of the practitioner herself with the deity, so that the practitioner comes to see within herself the virtues that the deity represents—in other words, coming to appreciate the inherent nirvanic quality of her own being. Finally, the practitioner dissolves the mental image of the deity into emptiness, thereby confirming the practitioner's intellectual belief in the non-dual character of reality. Through the repeated performance of deity practice, the practitioner acquires a new way of looking at the world where the dialectic of cause and effect, or the separateness of different individual subjectivities, are gradually revealed to be the nirvanic dwelling of the Buddha. The landscape of the pure land is the landscape of the world where we live; it is just that its nirvanic quality is ordinarily hidden from our sight. This kind of intellectual deity practice is a kind of inner transfiguration—a Tabor of the mind, where the natural order is revealed to be the theatre of the Buddha's compassionate activity on behalf of all sentient beings.[12]

Within both the Christian and the Tibetan tradition, sacred images can thus help us overcome the utilitarian and pragmatic approach to the created order that is at the root of the current environmental crisis. Of course, the Christian vision affirms the enduring character of individual subjectivity for all eternity, and humanity's entrance in the embrace of divine relationality; Buddhism rejects the notion of a permanent self, and envisages the whole of the natural order as a transient efflorescence in the undifferentiated stream of emptiness. Despite the tension between their underlying theologies, these two traditions can serve as an antidote to the deceiving, flattened eschatologies of immanence that appear to be the only metanarrative left standing in our globalized world. We can perhaps conclude with a quote from Pope Francis's earlier exhortation *Evangelii Gaudium*:

> Interreligious dialogue is a necessary condition for peace in the world, and so it is a duty for Christians as well as other religious communities. . . . In this way we learn to accept others and their different ways of living, thinking and speaking. We can then join one another in taking up the duty of serving justice and peace, which should become a basic principle of all our exchanges. A dialogue which seeks social peace and justice is in itself, beyond all merely practical considerations, an ethical commitment which brings about a new social situation. Efforts made in dealing with a specific theme can become a process in which, by mutual listening, both parts can be purified and enriched.[13]

NOTES

1 Pope Francis, Encyclical Letter *Laudato Si'* (May 24, 2015) 2:97, at http://www.vatican.va/content/francesco/en/encyclicals/documents/papa-francesco_20150524_enciclica-laudato-si.html (accessed June 5, 2020)

2 See John Chryssavgis, "The Green Patriarch: Ecumenical Patriarch Bartholomew and the Protection of the Environment," at https://www.patriarchate.org/the-green-patriarch (accessed June 5, 2020). For a sample of HH the Dalai Lama's addresses on the environment, see the link from his official site: https://www.dalailama.com/messages/environment (accessed June 5, 2020).

3 Basil of Caesarea, *Hexaemeron: The Six Days of Creation* (Brookline, MA: Paterikon Publications, 2017).

4 See Gary Banham, *Kant's Practical Philosophy: from Critique to Doctrine* (New York: Palgrave Macmillan, 2003), 24–40.

5   See John Locke, *An Essay Concerning Human Understanding*, Book II, Ch. 8 (Indianapolis: Hackett Classics, 1996), 23.

6   See John Meyendorff, *Christ in Eastern Christian Thought* (Crestwood, NY: St. Vladimir's Seminary Press, 1975), Ch. 6.

7   John Meyendorff., Ch. 9.

8   See Thomas Cattoi (trans. and ed.), Introduction to *Theodore the Studite: Writings on Iconoclasm* (Mahwah, NJ: Newman Press, 2014), 7–28.

9   See John Makransky, "Enlightenment's Paradox: Nondual Awareness of Unconditioned Embodied in Dual Activity for Sentient Beings," in *Buddhahood Embodied* (Albany, NY: SUNY Press, 1997), 85–108.

10 Paul Williams, Chapter 5 in *Mahāyāna Buddhism: The Doctrinal Foundations*, second edition (London and New York: Routledge, 2009), 103–28.

11 Paul Williams, Ch. 8, 172–86.

12 For some detailed descriptions of deity practice, see Shechen Gyaltsap IV and Kunkyen Tenpe Nyima, *Vajra Wisdom: Deity Practice in Tibetan Buddhism* (Ithaca, NY: Snow Lion, 2013).

13 Pope Francis, Apostolic Exhortation *Evangelii Gaudium*, at http://www.vatican.va/content/ francesco/en/apost_exhortations/documents/papa-francesco_esortazione-ap_20131124_ evangelii-gaudium.html (accessed June 5, 2020).

THE POWER OF PLACE DURING A PANDEMIC
RELATION, DIFFERENCE, AND ENTANGLEMENT IN MULTIFAITH AND INTERRELIGIOUS ENCOUNTER

Rachel A. Heath

In early June 2020 in Nashville, Tennessee, I found myself surrounded by thousands of people wearing masks, marching from Bicentennial Park and Rosa Parks Boulevard to Lower Broadway, then up to the Legislative Plaza, the Capitol, and back. Six feet of distance was impossible to maintain.[1] A week before, I had left an outdoor gathering on Memorial Day because there were too many people; but on this day, for this march, proximity felt worth the risk to be present-in-place, to protest police brutality, and to express with my body, heart, and mind—next to thousands of others, with those present in body or in spirit—that Black Lives Matter.[2]

The protest was organized and led by four teenaged women calling themselves "Teens-4-Equality,"[3] and as a former multifaith college chaplain who worked with people primarily between the ages of eighteen and twenty-two, I felt invigorated by the energies of the moment. As I walked through the Tennessee streets, an early millennial who had stood on the National Mall when President Obama was inaugurated, I felt as if I was witnessing another potential sea change in generational politics and activism. I was seeing and experiencing the present-future: the possibilities of enfleshing solidarity and imagining the kinds of power needed for a movement to be truly intersectional, place-based, and perhaps even prescient.

These moments and more have given me pause the last several months, as we are collectively experiencing, in increasingly tangible ways, the promises, perils, and potentialities of interconnection and entanglement during a global pandemic. What might it mean, for instance, for us to imagine the pandemic as a *place*—one in which we are living and growing and marching together, yet in too many cases, barely surviving or even dying, both together and apart? We do not have a choice whether or not we are *here*; in some sense, the being-in-the-pandemic is beyond our individual power or control.[4] However, since we are *here*, and here *together*, what kind of wisdom might this pandemic-place hold that is different from the other "normal" places in which we live, occupy, or find ourselves?[5] What is the power that this place might yield?[6]

Place-based epistemology attends to the reality that the concrete matters to our bodies, hearts, and minds.[7] It is a hallmark of the human experience that we can abstract ourselves from place and context in order to imagine what is beyond our present, concrete existence; yet, at the same time, place reminds us that our thinking and be-ing emerge from somewhere, not nowhere.[8] More succinctly: place-based thinking can ground our theories in the concrete matters that characterize both the magical and mundane aspects of the lives that we live, together and apart.

Much of my past work as a multifaith chaplain, as well as my current work as a PhD candidate in religion, has centered on questions of multiplicity, solidarity, and entanglement in a world of interreligious encounter. And what continues to spark wonder in this process are those questions that ask what it means for us to relate to one another between and among our traditions, and often in and through our differences. For some scholars and practitioners, focusing on the similarities or common themes that seem to rise above or beyond these differences is what makes interreligious dialogue or relationships possible. I have heard many versions of this over the years, along the lines of: "at the heart of it all, we are the same" or "at the end of the day, all religions share the same emphasis." Focusing on how we are the same certainly allows us to be in the same room, both proverbially and literally, resting in the knowledge that the intersection of my tradition and yours is one and the same, either now or in a metaphysically ultimate sense. The overarching intention of this language of sameness is to inspire compassion and unity in *places* where there have been imbalances of power, or even trauma and conflict. Yet I cannot help wondering what we ignore, erase, or lose in a relentless underscoring of the sameness in interreligious encounters—or the assumption of similarity—in the effort to be-together across philosophical, religious, and spiritual traditions.

What students from diverse places and traditions have taught me is that assumptions of sameness might bring some of us to the room (or the table, as the popular metaphor goes) some of the time, but sameness will not likely help us stay there. Often it is the crucial act of stopping to pay attention to who is excluded from these rooms, these places of interfaith and multifaith encounter, that might help us identify who has power, who has been marginalized, and what is happening in between. In a similar way, paying attention to who has been included might help us understand what we assume must be the same, or what we require to be "essential," in order to be present with each other or gain access to an interfaith space.[9]

For example, in planning interfaith programs with and for students who identified with more than one religious tradition, I began to notice how interreligious and multifaith dialogues typically require traditional forms of monolithic religious representation of the participants, just to get into the room to be together. What this meant for my students who belonged to more than one tradition is that they often had to choose, in a given moment, who and what they were going to *be* in a given place.

Beyond representation of religious identities, working with LGBTQ+ religious students (as well as embodying that difference myself) I learned how queer folx often have to sever who we are to approach interfaith spaces, simply because visible differences in gender and sexual orientation naturally disrupt spaces and places that are built or held together by assumptions of gender normativity and heteronormativity. As queer theories emphasize, difference can transgress the construction of this "normal," exposing the ways in which normativity relies on sameness to maintain the powers-that-be. Exposure to difference is threatening to safety, to the circumscribable confines that construct normalcy.[10]

This place of assumed-sameness, transgression, and exposure is precisely where place-based epistemology, or the knowledge and wisdom that emerges from our groundedness in place, might be enriching to interfaith-relating in the context of *where* we are together in 2020. Normalcy, or the normal that some of us have been living at the expense of others, is being revealed as unsustainable and detrimental to collective life. At a basic level, experiences of place show us that relying on either sameness or difference to bring unity might miss the point. For example, I can look out my window in Nashville and see trees that are waving their branches in the wind. I know that there are trees in other places, but they are not the same trees I see *here*. You, *wherever* you are reading this, might look out your window and see a different tree, albeit with a similar reaction to the wind. There's something about this sameness and difference that might help us understand something about relating to another across time and space. But, if we both assumed that everyone sees trees when they look out their window, or if we abstracted the concreteness and particularity of the trees we see into some unified tree-truth, then perhaps we would be understanding one point but missing another. And beyond that, what would our experience of these trees mean for those who do not see trees when they look out their window, or when they go outside to experience the different kinds of floral abundance (or lack thereof) in their own contexts?

All of this tree-talk is really just a way of pondering how *being where* I am, in this place called Nashville, helps me relate to you—*wherever* you are—not just because of how we are the same, but because of how and where we are *placed*. Places (and the trees that grow from their ground) cannot be exchanged for one another, and neither can people, nor our religious, spiritual, or philosophical traditions.[11] Nashville is not the same as Cape Town, South Africa; and neither place is the same as Wuhan, China. Christian traditions are not the same as Islamic traditions; and neither can be reduced to Buddhist traditions. These are truths that are full of possibilities, limits, and, maybe even beauty—if we have to courage to risk encountering the spaces and places that we cannot engage with, at a level of deep understanding, before we visit them (or at the very least, before we relate to someone who *lives there* or has *been there*).

This pandemic-as-a-place is a place that we have not encountered or visited before, at least on this global scale and with this kind of collective attention and impact. As I have been writing this piece, cases are surging in the United States again, though the numbers depend on the place in which we live. We are all experiencing this pandemic-place together, and who-we-are in place is revealing starkly some of the power differentials that have been present where-we-are and have-been, all along. Black Lives Matter, for example, is a movement that has been fomenting for the past several years. What about this pandemic-place, though, has helped spark protests and participation in ways that seem somewhat unprecedented? What about this pandemic-place has catalyzed protests, marches, and global uprisings that seem more precise and unapologetic about intersectionality, particularity, and multiplicity?[12]

These questions are in process, and I suspect that answers will continue to surface and change in response to our collective, ongoing experience of this pandemic-place.[13] I do have some intuitions, however, about what being-in-this-place together (and apart) might be revealing, especially to those of us active in interfaith and multifaith work, as writers, activists, scholars, and so on.

One intuition is that the time of emphasizing an interfaith unity that comes from assumptions of sameness is, quite simply, over. Generation Z, those who will be (and should be) leading interfaith work, protests, and global political strategies for the foreseeable future, are unimpressed with single-issue voting or monolithic representation. Too often in the past, movements erased diversity to abstract a generalized-solidarity, which is a strategy that no longer works. Though these truths and realities were being voiced long before the pandemic, there may be something about this pandemic-place that has helped these truths be amplified in new and life-altering ways.

This pandemic-place, with the spread of a virus we cannot yet fully predict or contain, is also revealing the potency of interconnection, a truth we know from physicists, theologians, and theorists who explore the meaning of quantum entanglement. We know that entanglement and porosity characterize our reality on a deep level, all around us; but we are perhaps experiencing it together, for the time being, in a place of discomfort, exposure, and legitimate fear. Interconnection is beautiful but risky—and now we are *here*, together, in this strange and dangerous place that is forcing us to acknowledge the material reality of our entanglement with one another, alongside the importance of safe distances (and yet our inability to be completely separate, absolutely safe), and all the while in the context the disparities of vulnerability and "essential" exposure. Part of what this reality means for my own explorations, as a scholar and practitioner coming from Christian traditions, is a greater awareness of and attention to the ways that power and hegemony flows between my tradition and others, circumscribing and delineating the topography of other places, particularly in moments of interreligious encounter or even solidarity.

Last, for those of us who focus more particularly on religious traditions and practices, maybe part of the wisdom of this pandemic-place is that the solidarity of the sameness *where we are* cannot eclipse the differences in power, access, or survivability that emerge in our diverse experiences of this place. The reality of quantum entanglement does not mean that we are all the same or all one, just because "every particle is vibrating with the same life."[14] Even if matter is vibrating with the "same life" or moving in the streams of an elemental ontology, the wisdom of place may be that we are *still* vibrating differently, experiencing different trees, different streams, different positionalities, especially with regard to privilege and power.[15] Attending to where we are shows us that reducing difference is detrimental to the diverse ecologies that make life happen-in-place.

These intuitions are part of what I understand to be the promises, perils, and potentialities of this pandemic-place: the wisdom that we can be in an interfaith room or space, *to-be-placed*, without having to erase parts of ourselves or our traditions in order to *be* and stay present *here*, together. And that may make all the difference, both for now and for places we are creating together in the time to come.

NOTES

1   Bicentennial Capitol Mall State Park (https://tnstateparks.com/parks/bicentennial-mall) commemorates Tennessee history. But it must be acknowledge that beyond its attention to the topography and other natural wonders of the state, it also commemorates a settler-colonialist history. This place, this land (Nashville, TN) belonged (and still belongs) to indigenous groups, in various capacities, before its current iteration; namely, Yuchi, Muskogee, Shawnee, Chickasaw, Choctaw, and Cherokee tribes and communities. For more information about Tennessee's Native American/American Indian history (and present), consult the Native American Indian Association of Tennessee (http://www.naiatn.org) and/or the Native History Association (http://www.nativehistoryassociation.org/).

2   For more information on this powerful and ongoing BPOC-led movement, consult the Black Lives Matter Foundation (https://blacklivesmatter.com). Please note that, occasionally in this chapter, I hyphenate certain terms, as I did in this sentence with "present-in-place." This practice is influenced in part by theologian-philosopher Mary Daly, as a way to inject movement into terms that seem static; another part of this practice is influenced by poetic practices of my own.

3   For more information on this march: https://www.nashvillescene.com/news/pith-in-the-wind/article/21136294/teens-lead-thousands-in-peaceful-march-through-nashville. To learn more about Teens-4-Equality: https://www.instagram.com/teens.4.equality/?hl=en.

4   What I mean, here, is that despite our efforts to wash hands, social-distance, and wear masks, the realities of global spread are ultimately beyond our individual control. What I do *not* mean is that we should forego these measures just because the potency of the spread is beyond any one place or one person.

5   I am intentional in stylizing *pandemic-place* in this way for poetic, aesthetic, and philosophical reasons.

6   I am indebted to the work of Keith Basso (*Wisdom Sits in Places: Landscape and Language Among the Western Apache* [Albuquerque, NM: University of New Mexico Press, 1996]: see chapter 4) and bell hooks (*Belonging: A Culture of Place* [New York: Routledge, 2009]), among others, for the phrasing and conceptual framing of these questions.

7   As far as I know, this term *place-based epistemology* emerged at the University of Chicago from conversations I had with friends and colleagues Elena Lloyd-Sidle, Rachel Watson, and Hannah Roh.

8   This comes from the work of Edward Casey (*Getting Back Into Place: Toward a Renewed Understanding of the Place-World* [Bloomington, IN: Indiana University Press, 1993], 18ff). Casey also uses Alfred North Whitehead's concepts of simple location and the fallacy of misplaced concreteness as foundations for his own place-based philosophy; Whitehead is crucial to my own thinking and work related to place-based epistemology.

9   I see interplay between philosophical and/or theological discussions of essence/essential, and our current global and societal conversations about what or who is "essential" in this pandemic-place.

10   I have in mind the critical work of Judith Butler, Eve Kosofsky Segdwick, Cathy Cohen, Audre Lorde, Alexis Shotwell, Gloria Anzaldúa, and others.

11   My reference here is to Laurel C. Schneider's discussion of Jean Baudrillard's concept of Impossible Exchange (*Beyond Monotheism: a Theology of Multiplicity* [London: Routledge, 2008]). See chapter 12.

12   I am speaking about my own experience, having been a young adult during the grassroots movements of the mid-2000s; and about how the current moment feels and seems different than before: with more BIPOC-led rallies, marches, and protests (youth and otherwise), along with increased visibility of (White) folks at Black Lives Matter demonstrations to protest police brutality and lift up the names of those killed by police (George Floyd, Breonna Taylor, and countless others), as well as global reaction-participation-response. I am also thinking, here, of the intersectionality of these movements, where LGBTQ+ concerns (and symbols) are also visible at these demonstrations. This presence of multiplicity of concerns and positionalities does not mean everything, but it means something. I am not diminishing movements and participation before the pandemic. I am just trying to identify what feels or seems different about this particular moment and place, as the uprisings and calls to defund the police continue throughout the United States.

13   And who knows, truly, what will have emerged in this pandemic-place by the time this essay is published.

14   Lyrics from the song "One" by Birdtalker (based in Nashville, TN).

15   The elemental ontology of theologian-philosopher Mary Daly—for example, her *Pure Lust: Elemental Feminist Philosophy* (Boston: Beacon Press, 1984) has influenced my thought in this regard, as has the process cosmology and ontology of Alfred North Whitehead. See his *Process and Reality, an Essay in Cosmology* (New York: Macmillan, 1929).

PART II

PRACTICING INTERRELIGIOUSLY

FINDING MYSELF IN THE OTHER
LEARNING FROM THOSE OUTSIDE MY FAITH

Joel N. Lohr

I remember it vividly. It was the first year of my PhD, and I was in the basement of Durham University's massive library. As I would often do, I was browsing religious and theological journals—the physical kind, back when libraries used to purchase these things in great quantities. The journals were lined up on beige, angled metal shelves, the sort you had to swing open in order to access older issues. I recall kneeling down and beginning to skim an article when my supervisor approached. A calm, understated British man, he stood next to me. He had a journal in his hand. And it needs to be said that I was always a bit nervous around him.

"Hello, Joel." A long, awkward pause ensued. These pauses never seemed to be awkward for him. I stood up quickly. "Have you read Joel Kaminsky? He's a scholar who knows who he is." I am sure my stare was completely blank. I distinctly remember thinking to myself: "A scholar . . . who knows who he is." What does that mean? With a slight nod of the head, he handed me a journal and said something like "give it a look," before walking away. In my hand was the latest issue of the *Harvard Theological Review*. Indeed, it contained an article by a Professor Joel S. Kaminsky of Smith College.[1] Although a seemingly small and insignificant event, in the basement of a library of all places, it had a profound effect on me. Every word of that conversation, if it can be called that, is etched in my mind. Its effect was great precisely because (1) I had no idea what "a scholar who knows who s/he is" meant and (2) I came to realize in that moment that I did not really know who I was.

What does it mean to know oneself? What does it mean to know who you are? The ancient maxim "know thyself" has been attributed to numerous Greek philosophers, including Socrates. It is one of three maxims inscribed at the entrance to the Temple of Apollo at Delphi, making it stand out from the other 147 Delphic maxims: γνῶθι σεαυτόν (*gnōthi seauton*, or "know thyself"), μηδὲν ἄγαν (*mēdèn ágan*, or "nothing to excess"), and ἐγγύα πάρα δ'ἄτη (*eggýa pára d'atē*, or "surety brings ruin").[2] All three are worthy of consideration, but for my short reflective essay here I would like to focus on the first, as it relates to what I have learned about interreligious relations and dialogue. For me, to "know thyself" gets at the heart and purpose of dialogue, indeed perhaps what it means to be human—certainly a person of faith. It also relates to the type of dialogue I find most profitable, dialogue that highlights differences and distinctives, rather than commonalities, even while the latter are important to be sure.[3]

THE BEGINNING OF DIALOGUE: BECOMING VULNERABLE

It is not uncommon for me to be asked, typically after people get to know me or have spent time reading my work, why I am religious (or a "person of faith"). This seems to me an entirely fair question; I never resent being asked. This is especially true for me when I think about the many and distinct ways religion has brought conflict and trouble to our world and tends to complicate politics and public discourse—especially in America. My (current) approach is not to defend my faith, or religion, but instead to open up and be as honest as possible—brutally honest—about these things, as well my own shortcomings and foibles. To me, this—the act of becoming vulnerable—needs to be our starting point in religious dialogue with the other, whomever that other might be.

This reminds me of a memorable book review I once read in which the reviewer, Matthew Milliner, begins his review by telling a parable-like story about a debate between an atheist and a Christian. He uses as an analogy for how the book under review achieves its goal by flipping a typical approach to defending religion on its head. He states, talking about a fictional account of an atheist-Christian debate:

> After the predictable sparring over whether or not God exists, the dispute takes its historical turn. The atheist recites the great litany of ecclesial sins—ways that the church has elicited or even sponsored violence. The Christian then comes to faith's defense, relaying as much of William Cavanaugh's *The Myth of Religious Violence* as a pithy sound bite allows. But what if, rather than defending the church, the Christian goes off script, replying instead with a range of accusations against Christians that surpass what the atheist has offered, thereby transforming the debate into an act of public penance? Gone is the fear that Christianity might not be true (one that gives rise to so much nervously animated apologetics). Replacing it is a ... profound sense of disorientation.[4]

Disorientation, I think, is key to fruitful dialogue. It is also a key feature—perhaps *the* key—of why Scripture is powerful, at least the Hebrew Bible if Walter Brueggemann is correct.[5] The phenomenon of disorientation in discussion with others is crucial, I think, to being able to learn from the other, approaching them (singular or plural) as someone who might teach you something, know something you do not, or bless you in some way despite your differences. Losing one's orientation is also key. When we open up to see that we may not have everything right, or that being honest might entail becoming "lower" or "lesser" than our dialogue partner, we become pliable and able to engage in real conversation that is deep and meaningful, much deeper than when we begin with a posture of defensiveness.[6]

And so becoming vulnerable by being brutally honest with ourselves opens up space, I think, for us to engage with others in new and profound ways. It also creates new and real openings for us to know ourselves more fully, and in turn God as creator, from whom we received our form.[7] But a key idea here is that I am not convinced we can truly, or fully, know ourselves without engagement with the other; secondarily, meaningful engagement with the other is dependent upon becoming vulnerable. The former idea could seem counterintuitive in that one might be tempted to think that the best way to know oneself is to examine oneself, preferably in solitude, through long processes of self-reflection. While I do not wish to disparage or discourage self-examination, a worthy exercise,[8] I am not convinced this is the best or only way to come to "know thyself." Knowing oneself, I am convinced, can only fully come by both, but especially through engagement with those who are different than we are, especially in terms of religious perspectives.

FULL DISCLOSURE—SHARING WHO WE ARE

In the interest of full disclosure, let me say a little something about my own religiosity. I have come to realize that my connection to religion is not superficial or a subset of who I am. I was, yes, born into a faith, but I have purposely chosen to continue embracing a Christian religious path, and deeply so. In truth, it defines me, and not by accident. And, to be clear, I would also say that I am not, as many people seem to say they are, "spiritual, but not religious." Increasingly I am starting to think that I may be the opposite—that is, "religious, but not spiritual." But I probably need to unpack this a bit, since it gets to the heart of my first idea about knowing oneself.

I appreciate the religious tradition in which I stand, viz., Christianity, specifically Christianity in the Anglican or Episcopal tradition, because it allows—forces—me to be brutally honest with myself and helps me better understand who I am. Maybe I will rephrase that. *My life as a religious person, through long-standing rituals, traditions, and daily practices, has forced me, regularly—weekly, daily, if not hourly—to examine myself.* Through it, I have come to "know who I am." I have come to see my frailty, my foibles, my ego, my insecurities, my instinct to self-aggrandize, to think of myself as better than others, and my propensity to self-preserve rather than help others. Without it, I would probably buy into the common narrative that, well … I am naturally quite a good person. In fact, I deserve to be pampered and taken seriously because I work hard, or because I am driven, or because I am born into a White family, or what have you. But instead my religious tradition reminds me that I am, in fact, deeply human: frail, broken, prone to mistakes and often self-deluded about those things. And, conversely, it reminds me that I am, even in all my imperfections—along with every other human being, indeed the entire universe, *tov*, which in Hebrew means "pleasing," "beautiful," or "good." I, as well as everyone and everything around me, have inherent dignity and value.

Religion has also helped me interact and reckon with the world, a broken world. It moves me to pray for it, even if I find prayer to be something of an enigma. I am a rational person, and I am not blind to the incredulity of praying to a supernatural supreme being, one previously thought by past generations to dwell in the sky. But prayer for me, as I understand it, is an expression of deeply held hope, and a time for knowing oneself. It has become a daily ritual in which I voice my longings for the world and for those around me—often through set prayers or liturgy—and a ritual in which I confess my shortcoming and wrongs, forcing me to be honest about who I am—to myself, to others, and to the One who is greater than myself. In short, it reminds me of who I am and helps me take seriously the world around me, at a time when it seems increasingly difficult for us as people to do so.

FINDING MYSELF IN THE OTHER: LEARNING FROM THOSE OUTSIDE MY FAITH

Perhaps rather than describe the process of coming to know oneself through the other, I might share a story from earlier in my life that exhibits the process. It goes back to my time as a university chaplain and director of religious and spiritual life, the first year I served in such a role. It also relates to something I call "appreciative curiosity," building upon the important work of Eboo Patel and his idea of "appreciative knowledge."[9]

The event at which this story takes place was part of a series. When I first started in my position at University of the Pacific in Northern California, I was named University Multifaith Chaplain—a title meant to signal that I was there to serve the needs of all students, whatever one's religious or spiritual position (or even lack thereof). In truth, I had little idea of what that really meant, though of course in my interview for the job I tried to act as if I did. I recall speaking at some length of my experience in Jewish-Christian dialogue, something I was familiar with, and claimed, for the purposes of the interview, to be an expert in. I guess that was not a lie in that I had published a few things about it. And—something I was quite proud of—I had just finished co-authoring a book on the Torah with a Jewish scholar, so I felt I could make some kind of case.

At any rate, not only was I supposed to know something about Christianity, my own religion, and perhaps something about Judaism, but now I was expected to be some kind of multifaith expert, someone with a knowledge of the multitude of religions. Sure, I had taken courses in world religions in my undergrad days, so I guess I knew a thing or two. But to say I was "winging it"—doing anything I could to get by—is probably an understatement. To make up for it I decided to live by two pieces of advice. The first was given to me by a much-loved former colleague who once told me that the key to success in this kind of work is *listening*. You need not be a dispenser of information so much as simply listen. That is the sign of a true expert chaplain. The second is the old adage that eighty percent of success is showing up. Both listen and show up I did.

When I started, I decided it would be a good idea to have some kind of weekly or biweekly event, something multifaithy (if that is a word), the sort of thing I thought chaplains like me should organize. I had no idea what to plan, but the previous weekend I had been on the phone with a friend; she was interested to hear how my new job was going. She was a synagogue educator and she recommended that I look up a popular book titled *How to be a Perfect Stranger*, by Stuart Matlins and Arthur Magida.[10] She told me about using it in her own classes at the synagogue. In essence, the book provides brief summaries of major religious traditions and gives tips on how to conduct oneself in foreign religious settings: attending a Bris, going to a Confirmation, or finding oneself at a mosque, gurdwara, or Buddhist temple. The book was a great help—short, concise, and to the point—and so I decided to base a series of events for students on it.

I titled the series something wildly creative like "Perfect Stranger Meetings," and the concept was simple. I would circulate a specific chapter from the book to students in advance (back when I thought students would actually read something outside of their course work) and then ask two or three students from that particular religion to present on it. I asked them to address three things: What can you tell us about your religion? What has your experience been like? and, Why are you a follower/adherent/practitioner? Sessions were set up to include a time for questions and answers, followed by a shared meal. It was usually a lunch or dinner event and lasted about an hour or so, depending on how long people stayed and chatted.

I was proud that the events went so well. There are interesting and amusing stories to tell for each session, but for our purposes I want to share a story from the Muslim presentation that involves *jihad*. Serious jihad. Jihad in earnest. Jihad of the students. The jihad of one student in particular.

The three Muslim students who presented were all female, and two of the three wore hijabs (head coverings or headscarves). Their polished presentation included a rather slick slide-show along with touching stories. And then it was time for questions from the audience. The first question came from a student who asked if it was hard to be a Muslim, and if they had difficulties coming to college or going to high school. The answer was an unambiguous and unanimous yes, and one presenter, one who seemed to have the best grasp of the material being presented, spoke especially eloquently, sharing in a way that let us into her life, and heart.

The student proceeded to talk about her jihad. "My jihad has been great," she explained. I started to raise my hand, to ask her to explain the term, but there was no need. She immediately realized her need to clarify. "Jihad," she said, "is a term in Arabic that simply means struggle." She paused, noticing the faces of a doubtful and troubled audience. "When used in American news programs, the term usually means struggle against the West." "But," she continued, "regular Muslims use it just to speak of personal battles or struggles." She now seemed a touch reluctant, but mustered enough courage to continue, cautiously. "I have many struggles, but my headscarf is my greatest jihad." The other two students, one with a headscarf and one without, nodded along in agreement. It was clear the headscarf, whether wearing one or not, was a struggle for them too.

This is where both appreciative curiosity and vulnerability crept in for me. I couldn't help wanting to know more and ask them to elaborate. I wanted to understand what that really meant, what the heart of the struggle was like. I wanted to be informed. I cared. And I was not afraid to show my ignorance. I think I did not even raise my hand. I think I just blurted out "can you share more?," probably not realizing I was speaking aloud. The main student speaking was again open to explaining. I had no idea what I was about to hear. I had no idea it would turn everything I thought I was about to hear on its head.

"My headscarf is my jihad," she explained, "because I come from a very moderate Muslim family. My mother does not wear one." She went on, "My family is from Los Angeles," and this was a place, she explained, where her father had hoped they, as a family, would "fit in"—assimilate to American life despite being Muslims and foreigners. So, she continued to explain, she never wore a hijab as a child or later as a high school student, a time when many Muslim girls start to wear them. In fact, her father was opposed to them altogether and would have none of it. But the young student was very interested in her faith, started asking questions about it, and ultimately, she explained, wanted to be obedient to God and live out her faith, a faith that she said inspired her to be modest and help the weak in the world. So, she decided—against her father's wishes—that she wanted to start wearing a headscarf; she decided she would start wearing one when she started university. She figured it was a time of transition and meeting new people anyway.

But her father was opposed. He did not want her to wear it and he insisted that she not. He made it clear that he thought she would be perceived as an extremist, a fundamentalist, or worse. He encouraged her (I think she said "pleaded with me") not to wear one. But she felt strongly enough to go against her father's wishes, something she said was very hard for her to do; she wanted to honor her parents' wishes but was compelled by her faith not to. *This* was her struggle; *this* was her jihad.

There she stood, now a few years into college, wearing her headscarf and talking about how it was a struggle because her father did not want her to wear it. And here I thought the struggle would be over *having* to wear one, being *forced* to wear one, or *not wanting* to wear one but feeling compelled to be obedient to the Qur'an, or a dominant father, or tradition, or whatever. Or maybe I thought the struggle would be over how hot it was to wear one, living in the Central Valley of California with its 100-degree heat and 300 days a year of sunshine. What did I know? How wrong I was. How little I really knew Muslims.

I came to know myself—to find myself—a little more that day through the other, through a student. I learned more about myself—my biases, my ignorance, and the fact that even in all our differences as people of faith we share a great deal. We are all on journeys, ones others probably have no idea about. Slowly, I was coming to know who I am.

CONCLUSION

Joel Kaminsky, the author of that article my supervisor handed me to read long ago, has since become a friend and writing partner. Not long after reading that article, I wrote an email to him, asking if he might meet me at a conference to talk about his work. He does not share my faith; he is Jewish, and I am quite certain it will stay that way for the rest of his and my life. As we have penned books and articles together over the years,[11] he has helped me see things about my life and career that I would not have otherwise recognized. It has been one of the most rewarding and meaningful processes of my life. He is indeed "a scholar who knows who he is;" and he, like the Muslim student in that sharing event and so many others, has helped me understand who I am. Interreligious dialogue, and becoming vulnerable with the other, has brought me a gift I never realized imaginable, the gift of learning who I am, of finding myself. For that I am grateful.

NOTES

1   The article was Joel S. Kaminsky, "Did Election Imply the Mistreatment of Non-Israelites?" *Harvard Theological Review* 96, no. 4 (2003): 397–425. It came to be important to my dissertation, later published as *Chosen and Unchosen: Conceptions of Election in the Pentateuch and Jewish-Christian Interpretation*, Siphrut: Literature and Theology of the Hebrew Scriptures 2 (Winona Lake, IN: Eisenbrauns, 2009). More on Kaminsky below.

2   See Eliza Gregory Wilkins, *The Delphic Maxims in Literature* (Chicago: University of Chicago Press, 1929), 1.

3   Especially important to my thinking on fruitful dialogue has been the work of Jon D. Levenson. A helpful entry point is the discussions between him and others around the 2000 statement Dabru Emet. See "Dabru Emet," in *Christianity in Jewish Terms*, ed. Tikva Frymer-Kensky, David Novak, Peter Ochs, David Sandmel, and Michael Signer (Boulder, CO: Westview Press, 2000), xvii–xx; Jon D. Levenson, "How Not to Conduct Jewish-Christian Dialogue," *Commentary* 112.5 (2001): 31–37; David Novak, "Instinctive Repugnance," *First Things* 123 (May 2002): 12–14; and Tikva Frymer-Kensky, David Novak, Peter Ochs, and Michael Signer, "Jewish-Christian Dialogue: Jon D. Levenson & Critics," *Commentary* 113, no. 4 (2002): 8–21.

4   Matthew Milliner, "Lenten Reading: How the Church Has Betrayed Christ," in *Books & Culture* (March/April 2013), a review of Ephraim Radner, *A Brutal Unity: The Spiritual Politics of the Christian Church* (Waco, TX: Baylor University Press, 2012). Available at https://www.booksandculture.com/articles/2013/marapr/lenten-reading.html.

5   Brueggemann makes much of the way Psalms in particular, but also Christian Scripture as a whole, forces the reader through a process of orientation, disorientation, and then reorientation. See, especially, Walter Brueggemann, *Spirituality of the Psalms* (Minneapolis: Fortress, 2002); *The Message of the Psalms: A Theological Commentary* (Philadelphia: Augsburg Fortress, 1984), as well as his *Theology of the Old Testament: Testimony, Dispute, Advocacy* (Minneapolis: Fortress, 1997).

6   See, for example, James W. Tamm and Ronald J. Luyet, *Radical Collaboration: Five Essential Skills to Overcome Defensiveness and Build Successful Relationships* (New York: HarperCollins, 2004), as well as Tamm's Ted Talk on the same topic titled "First Step to Collaboration? Don't Be So Defensive" (available at https://www.ted.com/talks/jim_tamm_first_step_to_collaboration_don_t_be_so_defensive).

7   Jews and Christians alike often point to the reference in Genesis 1:26 to human beings having been made in the image and after the likeness of God, even while the concept is not a strong emphasis of the larger narrative (e.g. Richard S. Briggs, "Humans In the Image of God and Other Things Genesis Does Not Make Clear," *Journal of Theological Interpretation* 4, no. 1 [2010]: 111–126). Regardless, literature on *Imago Dei* within Judaism and Christianity is extensive, too much to list; lesser known is the concept within and connection to Islam. A helpful entry point is Yahya Michot: "The Image of God in Humanity from a Muslim Perspective," in Norman Solomon, Richard Harries, and Tim Winter, eds., *Abraham's Children: Jews, Christians and Muslims in Conversation* (London: T&T Clark, 2006), 163–174. Although a connection might be found within strands of Sufi Islam, Michot shows that according to the Qur'an nothing is in the likeness of God; God is wholly other, yet he is the one who gave humans form. It might be best, he argues, to consider Muhammad as the human with the highest of callings, and in essence Islam would be "*imitatio Muhammadi*" (174).

8   Especially well known and helpful, in my view, is Ignatius's practice of the daily Examen. For more, see Mark E. Thibodeaux, *Reimagining the Ignatian Examen: Fresh Ways to Pray from Your Day* (Chicago: Loyola, 2015).

9   See Eboo Patel, *Interfaith Leadership: A Primer* (Boston: Beacon, 2016), especially 113–119.

10   Stuart M. Matlins and Arthur J. Magida, *How to be a Perfect Stranger: The Essential Religious Etiquette Handbook*, 6th ed. (Woodstock, VT: Skylight, 2015).

11   Joel S. Kaminsky and Joel N. Lohr, "Exclusion," in *New Interpreters Dictionary of the Bible* (Nashville: Abingdon Press, 2007), 2:362–64; Joel S. Kaminsky and Joel N. Lohr, *The Torah: A Beginner's Guide* (Oxford: Oneworld, 2011); Joel S. Kaminsky, Joel N. Lohr, and Mark Reasoner, *The Abingdon Introduction to the Bible: Understanding Jewish and Christian Scriptures* (Nashville: Abingdon, 2014); Joel S. Kaminsky and Joel N. Lohr, *The Hebrew Bible for Beginners: A Jewish and Christian Introduction* (Nashville: Abingdon, 2015); and Joel S. Kaminsky and Joel N. Lohr, "Election in the Bible," in *Oxford Bibliographies in Biblical Studies*, edited by Christopher Matthews (New York: Oxford University Press, 2017).

FINDING BALANCE
ON SUSTAINING HOPE IN OUR DIVISIVE ERA

Jeffery D. Long

Reflecting on my own work as an interreligious scholar and practitioner, I find that one of the greatest challenges I have personally faced over the last twenty years has been sustaining the hope that the work I am doing will actually do some good in a world that seems to be plunging in an increasingly divisive and hopeless direction. I have had many occasions, over the course of my career, to question whether doing scholarship and writing on religious pluralism is a worthwhile activity at all, given that the world appears to be moving in a less pluralistic direction all the time, with large numbers of adherents of practically every tradition gravitating toward more exclusivist ways of thinking and being. I have even joked with friends that since, during the same period in which I have written and published and spoken on religious pluralism, the world seems to have become progressively less pluralistic, it has led me to wonder if my work is actually having the opposite of its intended effect!

I do not seriously believe that the rise of religious exclusivism and extremism is my fault alone. I am not nearly so hubristic as to believe I could have such an impact on global trends. At the same time, though, whenever any of us writes, speaks, or teaches, there is at least an implicit hope that what we are doing is going to lead to *some* good in the world. Even an infinitesimal move in the right direction is a reason to feel encouraged.

The deeper question is whether scholarship, as such, really can facilitate change in society as a whole. It is very easy to feel, cynically, that what we do is for such a small audience, and that it is such an elite and privileged activity, that it is too remote to really be relevant to what is happening "in the streets" in regard to racial and social justice, or climate change, or interreligious understanding. At the same time, this is work to which some of us feel not only passionately committed, but also irresistibly drawn. I find that I would be thinking about the issues that preoccupy my work even if I were not a professional scholar of religion: an "academic," to use the popular term.

How, then, do I resist the despair that sometimes threatens to paralyze my work and sustain the hope that I really am contributing something constructive and meaningful to the contemporary discourse? One response—perhaps almost too personal and confessional for a scholar to be making—is that, as a committed practitioner in a religious tradition, I turn to my spiritual practice for comfort. A particularly dramatic experience that I recall takes me back to the early days of my career. I had just begun teaching full time at Elizabethtown College, in rural Pennsylvania, where I have, as of this writing, now taught for twenty years. In the year 2000, at the University of Chicago I completed my doctoral dissertation, which was entitled *Plurality and Relativity: Whitehead, Jainism, and the Reconstruction of Religious Pluralism.* The title was a deliberate reference to a masterful essay called *Plurality and Ambiguity*, by David Tracy, who was a member of my dissertation committee. In my dissertation, I sought to use a synthesis of Alfred North Whitehead's process metaphysics and the Jain "doctrines of relativity" to argue for the central teaching of the religious tradition that I had been drawn to practice, the Vedānta tradition of Sri Ramakrishna Paramahamsa and Swami Vivekananda, viz., that there are many paths to the Infinite. My aim, as my subtitle indicated, was the "reconstruction" of the religious pluralism articulated by thinkers such as John Hick, Paul F. Knitter, and Raimon Panikkar, after it had been heavily critiqued by such thinkers as my doctoral advisor, Paul J. Griffiths. My belief was that, if I could develop a model of pluralism that could successfully run the gauntlet of Professor Griffiths' criticisms, then I would strengthen the case for this view among scholars of religion and (I hoped) the larger public.

After starting my job at Elizabethtown College later the same year, I also began working on my first book. I had been drawn to a Hindu tradition in large part because of its affirmation of pluralism, a view that I was convinced was essential to getting humanity out of its current conflicts and on the path to a better and more humane world. Yet, I kept encountering the fact that, in the minds of many of my fellow scholars, Hinduism was increasingly a tradition that was associated with an aggressive religious nationalism.[1] And there was, of course, no way I could deny that Hindu nationalism was a real phenomenon. I therefore configured my first book, not so much as a critique of Hindu nationalism, though that is one factor in it, but as an argument for a Hindu alternative to Hindu nationalism. Because I found pluralism to be such a central feature of Hinduism as I understood it, and because I viewed pluralism as so important to human survival, my aim was to "rescue" Hindu pluralism *from* scholars who dismissed it as part of a rhetoric of Hindu superiority; *for* the Hindu community itself, for which it seemed to be an increasingly endangered inheritance; and indeed *for* all humanity, for which I believed Hindu pluralism held an essential key to survival—a belief I still hold today.

My book was published in 2007 as *A Vision for Hinduism: Beyond Hindu Nationalism.* Recently, Elaine Fisher cited it in her own excellent book on this topic. She writes:

> Hindu pluralism, in contrast to the endemic communalism of post-independence India, itself has genuine roots in the subcontinent's precolonial heritage.... [T]he genuine theological work done by Vivekananda and his contemporaries in constructing a viable pluralistic worldview . . . holds meaning for practitioners past and present. Inclusivist pluralism, for many, is a sincerely held theological commitment and can viably be promoted as a genuine emic Hindu pluralism.[2]

I, of course, could not agree more with the view Fisher expresses here. The extent, however, to which scholars have tended to dismiss Hindu pluralism as a cynical rhetoric of Hindu nationalism—as a way for Hindus to pat ourselves on the back for being inclusive even while not always being so in practice—is shown by the fact that Fisher feels the need to make an argument for what would otherwise be seen as a fairly obvious point: that pluralism is a widely held Hindu position.

Allow me to return, however, to my spiritual practice as a source of hope that the work I am doing is actually capable of making a helpful contribution to humanity. When I had just begun writing what would become *A Vision for Hinduism*, just at the beginning of my second year of teaching at Elizabethtown College, there occurred the horrific events of September 11, 2001. Soon thereafter, the United States appeared to be readying itself to launch a massive war in retaliation for the attacks—which, of course, it did. It invaded Afghanistan that same October; and in March 2003, it invaded Iraq, which of course had not been involved in the 9/11 attacks. Some days later, as I recall, I sat in my office, intending to return to work on my manuscript. This was a project fueled by my hope for a world where all human beings would, as Hindus had been doing for centuries, move with ease across religious boundaries, participating in the practices of many traditions, reading their sacred texts, and learning from the insights of their wisest sages. It was propelled by my hope for a world like that of Ramakrishna, who could say, "I have practiced . . . all religions . . . I have found that it is the same God toward whom all are directing their steps, though along different paths."[3] To this day, my work is energized by such a hope.

On *that* day, however, I found that I could not write. I just looked out the window, pondered the news of the last couple of weeks, and thought, "What possible good could this book ever do? What a silly, vain project, to think that anything I could ever say could address all of this pain, anger, hate, and suffering!" Starting to feel desperate, I closed my eyes to meditate. After clearing my thoughts and entering the state of peace to which that practice can take me, even in the worst of times, I heard an interior voice say, "Now, more than ever, you need to write this book." I opened my eyes and went back to my writing. The words now flowed easily. This episode has been repeated a number of times during subsequent years.

The wise contemplative practices that are our collective human inheritance, the practices that are available to us from the world's spiritual traditions, are an essential tool for keeping despair at bay. Are there also other ways to resist despair, and sustain the hope that is essential to doing any kind of constructive work in interreligious studies? Another form of resistance is to remind ourselves that ideas do matter. What may initially appear as the musings of small elite in a society can indeed be seized upon by policymakers, then used to transform our collective experience, for good or for ill. I recently found further support for this understanding in Cole Stangler's review, published in *The Nation*, of economist Thomas Piketty's book *Capital and Ideology*. In that book, Piketty argues that the current, unsustainable situation is not, as both Marxist and neoliberal orthodoxy might have it, the result of inexorable economic forces, but the result of specific historical policy choices that could have been made differently, and that were made on the basis of ideology: because of views and values about property, race, class, and so on. As Stangler points out, "To truly understand inequality, [Piketty] posits, one must think globally. And to think globally, one must also turn to . . . the ideological frameworks that justify social arrangements."[4]

This calls to mind, for me, some words by David Ray Griffin that I am fond of citing on those occasions when I raise the question in my writing, "What good is it to develop a philosophy of religious pluralism?" In Griffin's words:

> The human proclivity to evil . . . can be greatly exacerbated or greatly mitigated by a world order and its worldview. Modernity exacerbates it about as much as imaginable. We can therefore envision, without being naively utopian, a far better world order, with a far less dangerous trajectory, than the one we now have.[5]

And if we can envision such a world order, and if such envisioning can find its way into and shape the larger social consciousness, then we certainly have an obligation to do so.

Finally, one last but also important resource that I have found for sustaining hope is my tradition's injunction, found in the *Bhagavad Gītā*, that we should work "without attachment to the fruits of our actions" (*karma-phala-vairāgya*). It is certainly hubristic to believe we have the power to change the world for the better. Indeed, the temptation to such power is precisely a source of evil and suffering, for it does not come from a place of humility, but of ego. Even the despair that can threaten to overwhelm us is a form of egotism, stemming from the view that we personally have the power to change the world, and that, if the state of the world is not to our liking, it must be because we have not done enough to change it. However, we are neither omnipotent nor omniscient. Whatever understanding or insight we have, we must also realize that there is much that we do not know. This realization leads us not to despair, but to a surrender to the higher power within each of us—however we might conceive of it in our respective traditions: the knowledge that *we* do not do anything, but that it is this higher power within us that works *through* us.

The prayer that then emerges from this understanding is, in the wise words of St. Francis of Assisi, "Lord, make me an instrument of your peace!" And from the Hindu tradition, let us be, like Lord Krishna's musical instrument, his flute, empty—empty of all egotism and all vanity—that through us a beautiful song might be played.

NOTES

1   See the contribution of Anantand Rambachan in this volume, p. 83.

2   Elaine Fisher, *Hindu Pluralism: Religion and the Public Sphere in Early Modern South India* (Oakland: University of California Press, 2017), 191.

3   Swami Nikhilananda, trans. *The Gospel of Sri Ramakrishna* (New York: Ramakrishna-Vivekananda Center, 1942), 35.

4   Cole Stangler, "Tipping Point: Thomas Piketty's New History of Global Inequality," *The Nation* (June 1/8, 2020), a review of Thomas Piketty, *Capital and Ideology* (Cambridge, MA: Belknap Press, 2020). See https://www.thenation.com/article/society/thomas-piketty-capital-and-ideology-inequality-origins/

5   David Ray Griffin, "Introduction to SUNY Series in Constructive Postmodern Thought," in *Primordial Truth and Postmodern Theology* by David Ray Griffin and Huston Smith (Albany, NY: SUNY Press, 1989), xiv.

THE ONENESS OF US ALL IN OUR CURRENT AGE

Michael M. Cohen

The word *pandemic* reminds us that we cannot escape the human world wide web we share. Pandemic literally means "all the people."[1] The COVID-19 virus underscores the countless ways we are connected. That outlook is related to a core principle of many religions: the notion that we all come from One Source and from that interconnectedness we are therefore responsible for each other. This chapter will explore discussions of that foundational underpinning and what insights we can glean today from those deliberations.

We will examine those related theological conversations found in Christian and Jewish sources. However, a clear chronological order of what was said first is not so simple, and with most of these sources there is a lag in time from when something was said and when it was written down. The Letter of Paul to the Galatians was written some twenty years after Jesus died, while the Gospels were written decades after Jesus lived and taught. When it comes to the Jewish sources we have the dynamic of rabbis who lived from the beginning of the second century CE through the end of the fourth century CE in "conversation" across those centuries as recorded much later in the Talmud and Genesis Midrash Rabbah.[2] In addition, as Shaye Cohen points out, "the seven genuine Pauline letters are written by a known author, the gospels by an unknown author (or compiler), and rabbinic texts are large anonymous anthologies (school literature)."[3]

These Christian sources are all earlier than those Jewish sources, which raises the question: how aware were the rabbis of those Christian sources and were they at all responding to them? While we label the two groups as Christian and Jewish, we need to remember that Jesus was born and died a Jew, and he mostly addressed Jewish audiences. The implication is that both Christian and Jewish sources were teaching and interpreting verses from the Torah, the Five Books of Moses, a Jewish source redacted hundreds of years earlier, around 400 BCE.

We tend to think of the Jewish and the Christian traditions as linear; the reality is much more convoluted. There is a view within Judaism that, "there is no early and no late in the Torah."[4] That is to say, chronology is not always of paramount importance. The light of a star we see in the heavens has traveled light years to get to us. The starlight we see may have left the star 100 years ago; yet we perceive it as happening now.[5]

When it comes to our current age, this reminds us that things may not always be what they appear to be. Understanding complexity and nuance are critical to addressing the challenges before us, from COVID-19, to anthropogenic Climate Change, to racism, to identity politics, to name a few. Humility and empathy are critical for those conversations. Empathy itself is a manifestation of an orientation that we share a Common Source and by that affinity we are bidden to take care of each other and repair the world [*tikkun olam*].

In Galatians 5:14, Paul quotes Leviticus 19:18 when he writes, "For the entire law is fulfilled in keeping this one command: 'Love your neighbor as yourself.'" In Matthew 7:12 we read of Jesus teaching, "So in everything, do to others what you would have them do to you, for this sums up the Law and the Prophets." A similar idea is expressed in the Talmud when a gentile asks Hillel to explain the entire Torah with Hillel standing on one foot to which Hillel replies, "That which is hateful to you do not do to another; that is the entire Torah, and the rest is its interpretation. Go study."[6] Trying to sum up the essence of all of the commandments we find in the Jerusalem Talmud, "Charity [*tzedakah*] and acts of kindness [*gemilut hasadim*] are the equivalent of all the commandments [*mitzvot*] of the Torah" [*Jerusalem Talmud, Peah* 1:1]. In all of these passages, empathy for the other is paramount to how we should act.

Later, according to Matthew 22:35–40, Jesus offers a different hierarchy of importance. There we find, "And one of them, a lawyer, asked him a question to test him. 'Teacher, which is the great commandment in the Law?' And he said to him, "You shall love the Lord your God with all your heart and with all your soul and with all your mind [Deut. 6:5]. This is the greatest and first commandment. And a second is like it: You shall love your neighbor as yourself [Lev. 19:18]. On these two commandments depend all the law and the prophets" [Matt. 22:35–40]. This is echoed and elaborated in the Gospel according to Mark:

> One of the teachers of the law came and heard them debating. Noticing that Jesus had given them a good answer, he asked him, "Of all the commandments, which is the most important?" "The most important one," answered Jesus, "is this: 'Hear, O Israel: The Lord our God, the Lord is one. Love the Lord your God with all your heart and with all your soul and with all your mind and with all your strength.' [Deut. 6:4–5][7] The second is this: 'Love your neighbor as yourself.' There is no commandment greater than these." "Well said, teacher," the man replied. "You are right in saying that God is one and there is no other but him. To love him with all your heart, with all your understanding and with all your strength, and to love your neighbor as yourself is more important than all burnt offerings and sacrifices." When Jesus saw that he had answered wisely, he said to him, "You are not far from the kingdom of God." And from then on no one dared ask him any more questions." [Mk. 12:28–34]

We see a vacillation, a tension, in these texts between whether loving your neighbor or loving God is the most important commandment. It appears resolved in the Gospel according to Luke:

> On one occasion an expert in the law stood up to test Jesus. "Teacher," he asked, "what must I do to inherit eternal life?" "What is written in the Law?" he replied. "How do you read it?" He answered, "Love the Lord your God with all your heart and with all your soul and with all your strength and with all your mind" and, "Love your neighbor as yourself." "You have answered correctly," Jesus replied. "Do this and you will live." [Lk. 10:25–28]

Equating the love of God with the love of each other becomes more apparent in a later Jewish source. In *Genesis Midrash Rabbah* we read,

> Ben Azzai said, "This is the book of the descendants of Adam" [Gen. 5:1], is a great principle of the Torah. Rabbi Akiva says: "Love your fellow as yourself" [Lev 19:18], is even a greater principle. Thus one should not say, "You should not say, since I have been put to shame, let my neighbor be put to shame." Rabbi Tanhuma explained: "If you do so, know whom you are dishonoring—'God made him in the likeness of God'" [Gen 1:26–27].

Rabbi Tanhuma finds that Rabbi Akiva's position comes up short since if a person was shamed, they may decide they can also shame the other person, since loving your neighbor as yourself does not mean loving your neighbor more than yourself. To counter that, Rabbi Tanhuma adds the idea that we are all created in the image of God and we should treat one another accordingly.[8] Combined with Ben Azzai's great equalizer position that we are all descended from a single ancestor, the discussion here strongly teaches us that loving our neighbor is a manifestation of the recognition that we are all from one source and that human reality in and of itself commands us to be responsible for each other.

Relatedly, a student asked the Hassidic Rabbi Shmelke of Nikolsburg, "We are commanded to love our neighbor as ourselves. How can I do this if my neighbor has wronged me?" The Rabbi answered,

> You must understand these words correctly. Love your neighbor *like something which you yourself are*. For all souls are one. Each is a spark from the original soul, and this soul is wholly inherent in all souls, just as your soul is in all the parts of your body. It may come to pass that your hand makes a mistake and strikes you. But would you then take a stick and beat your hand, because it lacked understanding,

and so increase your pain? It is the same if your neighbor, who is of one soul with you, wrongs you for lack of understanding. If you hurt him, you can only hurt yourself." The Disciple went on asking, "But if I see a person who is wicked before God, how can I love him?" "Don't you know," Said Rabbi Shmelke, "that the original soul came out of the essence of God and that every human soul is part of God? And will you have no mercy on him, when you see that one of his holy sparks has been lost in a maze, and is almost stifled?"[9]

Rabbi Shmelke teaches that one element that unites our shared human experiences is the pain, fear, hate, and mistrust others have caused us, as well as the profound reality that we are all linked one to the other.

A century after Rabbi Shmelke lived, the Reverend Martin Luther King Jr., elaborating on that same biblical verse to *love your neighbor*, wrote, "Forgiveness does not mean ignoring what has been done or putting a false label on an evil act. It means, rather, that the evil act no longer remains a barrier to the relationship. Forgiveness is a catalyst creating the atmosphere necessary for a fresh start and a new beginning."[10] In addition, we read in *Pirkei Avot* 1:6, "judge everyone favorably," to which the Talmud adds, "One who judges others favorably in the scale of merit is judged favorably by others."[11] That is to say, the interpersonal dynamic can profoundly change when we switch our focus from solely accusing others of wrong and try better to understand them.

In our current times where identity politics has pushed civil discourse to the side, we need to remind ourselves that empathy and compassion are the only way to overcome our differences. We need to see our individual responses as part of a greater collective effort. Discussing COVID-19, Michael Polifka advises us to look at "risk" from both personal and public vantage points:

> Personal risk: if one skydives the risks are pretty much all on the individual person. But if one drives drunk there is the personal risk for driving into a tree but also the risk to another person being hit by the drunk driver. The risk for the latter is mitigated for the rest of us in the public by the rules and social mores we have set up. The more they are followed the less the public risk for all of us.[12]

We know that reduced speed limits, mandatory wearing of seat belts, and installing baby seats have saved thousands of lives. Now most of us avoid car accidents, but we wear seat belts as a communal, societal, and social response, and we are all the safer because of that.

At the end of the *Shabbat* [Jewish Sabbath] there is a short ritual called *Havdalah* [separation] that involves wine, spices, and a braided candle. Its function is to separate *Shabbat* from the other days of the week, and so we say, it *"separates between holy and secular."*[13] Rabbi

Michael Graetz insightfully comments that there is no difference between saying, "*separates between holy and secular*," and "*separates between holy and holy*."[14] Separations, divisions, chronology—as we discussed at the beginning of this paper—are manifestations of human perception. Those categories are necessary and helpful in how we make sense of our lives and the world. We must never forget, however, that they are a means and not an end. At the end of the day, those separations, manifestations of our One Source in common, are actually profound connections if we allow them to be experienced that way.

NOTES

1   It combines the Greek word for "all" (*pan*) with the Greek for "people" (*demos*, from which the word *democracy* is derived.

2   The Talmud was compiled around the year 500 CE; Genesis Midrash Rabbah was compiled in the mid-fifth century CE

3   Correspondence with author, June 24, 2020.

4   *Babylonian Talmud, Pesachim* 6b.

5   The star Alkaid in the handle of the Big Dipper is 101 light years away with light traveling at 186,282 miles a second.

6   *Babylonian Talmud, Shabbat* 31a.

7   Here is the basic affirmation statement of monotheism in Judaism plus the command to love God.

8   *Imago Dei, b'tzelem elohim.*

9   Shai. Cherry, *Torah Through Time: Understanding Bible Commentary from the Rabbinic Period to Modern Times* (Philadelphia: The Jewish Publication Society, 2007), 29.

10 Cat Meurn, "Love and Forgiveness in Governance: Exemplars: Martin Luther King, Jr." *Beyond Intractability.* https://www.beyondintractability.org/lfg/exemplars/mlking.

11 Jerusalem Talmud, Shabbat, 127b.

12 Correspondence with the author, June 15, 2020.

13 *hamavdil beyn kodesh lechol.*

14 *hamavdil beyn kodesh lekodesh*; which is said when *Shabbat* ends and a Jewish holiday begins.

HOW TO BE UNCOMFORTABLE, TOGETHER

Stephanie Varnon-Hughes

> . . . men and women are not only themselves; they
> are also the region in which they were born, the
> city apartment or the farm in which they learned
> to walk, the games they played as children, the old
> wives' tale they overheard, the food they ate, the
> schools they attended, the poems they read, and
> the [gods] they believed in.
>
> —W. Somerset Maugham,
> *The Razor's Edge* (1943)

When I first saw the internet, in 1995, I was seventeen years old. The parents of one of my high school friends were pharmacists, wealthy for our coal mining town. They had a computer with internet in the basement of their pharmacy. On weekends, after "making laps" (driving around town with other teens) and maybe stopping by the Dairy Queen, we would stock up on chips and soda and gather around the computer. I no longer remember what we searched for, or found. Our high school still used typewriters to teach typing. I was about to leave for college at University of Illinois, where I would get my first email address. I do remember feeling a kind of fear and excitement: we were connected to the outside world, somehow. We could talk to people far away, unlike us. Maybe even in different counties or states.

I turned out to be right. Indeed, we could share information, images, and ideas immediately. Instead of sticking my hands into the card catalog and hoping our library had a copy of James Joyce's *Ulysses* (it did not), or even having my parents drive to the nearest college town to find a bookstore with a copy (Southern Illinois University in Carbondale, Illinois, and they did have a copy, but it was an abridged version), I could find hundreds of articles about Joyce, and even (soon) buy a copy online and have it sent to me. All of us of a certain age have had similar journeys, from simple discovery to overload to conflict. Fast-forward another ten years, and I found myself defriending, deleting, blocking, and furiously debating politics on LiveJournal, MySpace, and Facebook. During the election season leading to the election of President Obama, I took a posture of self-righteousness. If I deemed someone to be racist, ignorant, xenophobic, or misinformed, I either blasted them publicly or smugly ended our online relationship. In the 2016 election cycle, I

71

discovered that my posture of certainty had ended or foreclosed many relationships with people I now needed to understand, learn from, and collaborate with.

We are all now, for better or worse, in public together. What does this mean? What are our responsibilities? What are particular challenges, and are there areas gilded with hope and promise? Ought we be moral in the public square? What does a robust interreligious theology have to teach us about how to be interreligious in public?

Encounter with difference can lead to conflict or to deepened learning; sometimes, it leads to both at once. When exposure to diversity takes a negative turn, we see conflict, fear of difference, and reaction without critical or creative thinking. Reaction can appear as an impulse to flee, to resist, to deny, and to avoid difference. Each of us could log in to our preferred social media or online news source this very minute and see examples of this kind of fear-based reaction and conflict. Encounter with difference can also be an opportunity to lean into the dissonance and expect transformation. In this space we interreligious educators lead and facilitate. As I grew as an interfaith leader, especially in digital spaces, I realized I had failed in my online dialogical practice.

Here's how I've failed: in the last US presidential election, I had 125 unanswered friend requests (with 297 friends) on Facebook. I had actively unfriended some two family members, former colleagues, or classmates per month during the election and aftermath. Why do I do this? Because I want to be right, because I fear change, because I want to be liked, because I am stuck in struggle for preeminence. I'm not the only one behaving this way online.

According to a report in the *Proceedings of the National Academy of Sciences* (June 2017), researchers evaluated 563,312 public tweets. They sought to understand how social networks transmit moral attitudes and norms. They remind us, "Our moods, thoughts, and actions are shaped by the entire network of individuals with whom we share direct and indirect relationships. Thus, we often develop similar ideas and intuitions as others because we are socially connected to them."[1]

When we began socializing online, many of us may have thought this transmission of ideas would be similar to real-life conversations and learning. Our thoughts and practices are shaped by everyone with whom we have direct and indirect relationships. We develop similar ideas to theirs as we consume information and share experiences *with* them. Does this work online? These researchers found that when tweets concerned polarized issues, and if they included moral-emotional words, the "diffusion" happened within political in-groups, but did not move to out-groups. As passionately as we feel about "sharing," we are sharing within a space of folks exactly like us. That is, "With respect to politics . . . communications about morality are more likely to resemble echo chambers and may exacerbate ideological polarization."[2] When I saw this research, I realized that our experiences online with debate, discussion, and diatribe may feel important, urgent, and meaningful—but they are not dialogue. Fewer learning, relationship-building, or transformative opportunities are happening than we would like.

If we are invested in authentic, transformative dialogue, we need to turn to what we know about education and spiritual/ethical formation. Shared interpretative activity generates social space. If you gather people around a concern or cause, you create a social space of common intentions and understandings. William Schweiker calls such settings "spaces of reasons," that is, settings in which people speak a common language and understand one another because they share a certain vocabulary and a certain set of perceptions.[3] He notes that in much social media debate, we are operating from a place of certainty and trying to convince others. However, for our interactions to be fruitful, he points out, we must generate meaning and interpret information *together*. We must shift from a posture of certainty to one of inquiry. I must be willing to meet my co-meaning-makers with a willingness to be wrong; I must overcome my desire to convince them. This is hard! We love being right, pointing out the faults of others. If we continue in this modality, though, relationships are weakened and when we really need to collaborate (on issues of immigration, hunger, housing, health care, joblessness), we face serious obstacles.

In *The Gift of Responsibility*, Lewis Mudge reminds us, "Dialogue begins with the sheer fact of meeting and getting to know one another. Partners in discussion want to be sure that their faiths are held in respect by their interlocutors and that participants are *both* valid representatives of their religious communities *and* sufficiently open-minded for the discussion to be fruitful."[4] If we cannot enter into one another's reasoning spaces, we will struggle for dominance and remain stuck in our echo-chambers, never being willing to be changed, and so remaining unchanged. Mudge uses the metaphor of armature for sculpture as a way to invite us to build relationships with those we disagree. He exhorts us, "If you live for a while with a 'thin' agreement, you begin to supplement it with other sorts of relationships. At the very least, the agreement needs to be commonly interpreted, founding a shared legal culture, grounded in a shared moral 'framework.' Confidence raised by forgiving, trust-building, and solidaristic behavior at one point spawns confidence at other points."[5]

That is, we don't have to know exactly what to say, exactly how to convince an opposing side, how to solve a fraught conversation. Those are the wrong questions because, in real relationship, there is no convincing and not much solving. Instead, we must come along together to a space that we cannot imagine alone. We need our interlocutor to help us find and expand that space. With this understanding in mind, two years ago, I began accepting all of those friend requests, and reaching back out to those I had defriended, blocked, and blamed. I began following family members, old friends, and strangers who disagreed with me. I wrote notes of connection and question. I asked what we had in common. I asked them to help me understand their pressing issues. I sought to suspend my certainty as a spiritual practice. I love being right! (After all, I sailed through school winning awards and earning a PhD; I've been acculturated and affirmed to be "right.") However, this was keeping me from finding community and collaborators in dire times. This work of leaning into gray spaces, of setting aside our gold stars of certainty for provisional questions, is a key ingredient for interfaith learning.

In *Conflict Across Cultures: A Unique Experience of Bridging Differences*, Michelle LeBaron and Venashri Pillay call for "conflict fluency" in addition to "cultural fluency." They define cultural fluency as ". . . developmentally advanced work even for adults to 'remain conscious' of the influences 'embedded in our . . . processes.'"[6] In our current systems of politics, civic leadership, religious/ethical leadership, and higher education, it's rare to see humility and curiosity. We raise up and edify leaders who are certain, charismatic, unflappable, and confident. But these traits hinder dialogue and block change. LeBaron suggests that we must, instead, interrupt embedded patterns of thinking. In short, her questions foster disequilibrium and call for pause—time for the individual and the group to reconsider and perhaps begin the work of repatterning. The repatterning (of conversations, of models of engagement, of ways we relate to one another) should be our primary focus, not convincing others of our way of thinking.

When what we know about the world comes into contact with new perspectives, we naturally feel disequilibrium. Many of our community members resist that shaky feeling! They want us to be certain. We are all seeking certainty. But, we cannot allow our stakeholders to either retreat into non-participation (blocking, deleting, ignoring) or avoiding dialogue. These are ripe opportunities for growth, and it is our responsibility as religious, ethical, and inter-religious leaders to shepherd communities through these shaky places into growth and transformation. We know from interfaith engagement that encountering difference has often widened our worldviews and transformed our own spiritual/ethical perspectives and practices. The same will be true for any civic or political encounter. Indeed, if we must live together, we fail to enter this practice at our continued detriment.

Here are the three key ingredients I have found for maintaining the conditions for being uncomfortable: relationship, reflective practice, and resilience. We interfaith practitioners are excellent at cultivating relationship and invitations for developing neighborly encounter. Reflective practice is already a key ingredient of many of our personal religious or ethical traditions; we need also apply it to conversation, civic dialogue, and online debate. Time for pause should be modeled, exemplified, and practiced just as much as having a pithy, memorable retort. No one will give me "likes" for stepping back and reflecting; but, if I try, my relationship with my racist cousin may be deepened enough that we can work together on opioid addiction in our hometown. Finally, resilience. We need to name and frame that this is hard work, and we need to foster and sustain it. Instead of seeing a given conversation or encounter as a chance to share all of the reasons our point of view is correct, we must learn to be more uncomfortable. This is a hard recommendation. I'm saying that there is no final point, no place where we'll know we've accomplished what we set out to do. Relationships that grow and deepen don't have endpoints; they are fluid. All members of a given community change together and individually, over time.

Resilience can be understood to be a willingness to enter unknown or uncomfortable spaces and the skills to practice coping there long enough to maintain new relationships. Resilience as a virtue and practice ought to be co-requisite to dialogue and relationship in enabling communities to withstand dissonance long enough for deep understanding to take root and flourish. For decades, interfaith work has centered on hospitality and what we have in common. This is helpful at the starting places of building relationship and community. Now, at the mid-point of 2020, we find that we need to work with, and get along with, those with whom we have little (or nearly nothing) in common.

It may be easier for many of us to apply these principles to wider contexts—in neighborhoods, in large interfaith organizations, in political work. For me, I struggle with provisional space and resisting self-righteousness in personal conversations with family members and colleagues. The same principles apply. I need to invest time and energy in building relationship, more than I spend in debunking their points of views or criticizing their new sources. As leaders and creators of a field and related canon, we need also center discomfort (and the related skill of resilience) as a primary source of shared interpretive space and potential change. When we are with others who do not think, believe, or vote like us, we must frame it as an opportunity to remain in dissonance for as long as possible—longer than we think is possible. This is a counter-cultural move, and different from what we've been trained to do as pastors, preachers, teachers, and elected officials. But, our current way of being in opposition isn't working. And the possible fruit of exploring unanticipated meaning, together, will be worth the feeling of certainty. In our multifarious and ever-shifting world, it really isn't possible to be certain—as seductive as that sensation may be. Let's champion a shift away from being right, and a movement to knowing that part of being human includes the messiness of provision, missteps, not being sure, and not knowing everything we will need at the end when we begin. The "thin places" feel uneasy to begin, but they will lead to rich places for discovery and solutions, if we can tolerate the discomfort, together.

NOTES

1   William J. Brady, Julian A. Wills, John T. Jost, Joshua A. Tucker, and Jay J. Van Bavel, "Emotion Shapes the Diffusion of Moralized Content in Social Networks," in *Proceedings of the National Academy of Sciences*, 114, no. 28 (2017): 7313–7318, at 7313.

2   Brady, et al., 7317.

3   William Schweiker, "Starry Heavens and Moral Worth: Hope and Responsibility in the Structure of Theological Ethics," in *Paul Ricoeur and Contemporary Thought*, eds. John Wall, William Schweiker, and W. David Hall (New York: Routledge, 2002), 117.

4   Lewis Mudge, *The Gift of Responsibility: The Promise of Dialogue Among Christians, Jews, and Muslims* (New York: Continuum, 2008), 31, emphasis original.

5   Mudge, 246.

6   Michelle LeBaron and Venashri Pillay, *Conflict Across Cultures: A Unique Experience of Bridging Differences* (Boston: Nicholas Brealey, 2006), 58.

TOGETHER ON THE JOURNEY
THE ROLE OF SPIRITUAL CARE
IN INTERRELIGIOUS RESISTANCE WORK

Abigail Clauhs

I came into interreligious work through community organizing, never guessing it would land me at the bedsides of the dying. Yet here I find myself, student activist turned chaplain and minister, offering spiritual care to people at the end of life. Perhaps that trajectory is not all too surprising. The act of spiritual care—of tending to our humanity, our souls, our spirits—should, after all, be entwined with the work of community, the work of change, the work of justice-making.

Indeed, I believe that the skills and work of chaplaincy—the work of spiritual care—is necessary to the "deep understanding for divisive times" that we are all exploring in this collection. I hold that spiritual care and chaplaincy is needed in our interreligious organizing, in our social justice movement spaces, in any and all of our efforts to create change and transformation. This is not the task of chaplains alone, limited solely to those employed professionally as spiritual care providers. Yet chaplains, with our focus and deep training in spiritual care, may have some unique learnings to offer as we collectively seek deep understanding, exploring how to be in interreligious relationship and navigate this divided world together.

Now, I could begin by talking about how chaplains are uniquely positioned, particularly in the current religious landscape of the United States, to make interreligious connections and build those relationships; about how here, in a society where people are increasingly unlikely to hold a religious affiliation or to be connected to a religious institution (the number of religiously unaffiliated US adults had risen to twenty-one percent by 2014, while religious service attendance continues to fall), chaplains are often the trained religious leaders that people—especially the religiously unaffiliated—are coming into contact with.[1]

I could tell you that, according to a recent national survey, nearly a quarter of American adults had contact with a chaplain during the past two years, and that more than half of these encounters occurred in a healthcare setting.[2] I could talk about how this phenomenon has been especially highlighted in the midst of the ongoing COVID-19 pandemic, where articles about chaplains caring for the dying, for families, for staff, have lit up the headlines of the *New York Times, The Atlantic, BBC News*, and other publications, telling the story of the need for spiritual care amidst loss and trauma.[3] I could tell you about the many contexts that chaplains serve in—from ICUs to hospices, universities to prisons, seaports to the military;

about the credentials many chaplains are required to have, from in-depth theological training to the action-reflection-action model of Clinical Pastoral Education; about the spiritual assessments we do; about the debriefings, the grief support, the inclusive rituals. Yet, what I keep returning to is this concept of what chaplaincy has to offer to our larger world. To you, reader. To us. The art of spiritual care itself: the accompanying, the journeying—through trauma and heartbreak, yes, and also through joy and renewal and myriad human experiences. Something that may be best described not in statistics or facts, but rather in an image.

You may be familiar with certain popular images of spiritual care. You need only look as far as the historical terminology used in our field, so often featuring the classic Christian imagery of a shepherd (invariably male) providing "pastoral" care to his flock. Indeed, the shift toward the language "spiritual care" and away from "pastoral care" is a current and ongoing one in the field of professional chaplaincy. However, the image I return to again and again, especially as I reflect on the need for spiritual care in the wider community—the need for a model of collective, liberative spiritual care—is that of the midwives. You know the midwives. They must have a history nearly as long as humanity itself. Of existing in the liminal spaces of transition, of birth and death, or joy and loss. Of attending to transformation, of accompaniment, of journeying with, into moments both beautiful and terrible. Of using their skills and knowledge to empower another person, engaged in a co-creative process to bring forth something new. You know the midwives. They embody what spiritual care, at its most fully realized, can be.

I came across this image of the midwife early in my chaplaincy, around the same time as I was doing my first round of clinical chaplain training, where I served on the perinatal units of a major urban hospital. There, among the incandescent happiness and staggering grief encountered in the units for Labor and Delivery, for Neonatal Intensive Care, for OB/GYN, I drew on the model of the midwives. The metaphor is certainly not mine. I was first introduced to it through hospital chaplain Karen R. Hanson's chapter, "The Midwife," in the foundational chaplaincy text *Images of Pastoral Care*, where she writes that "the intent of both professions is to be with people, to attend people in a process . . . using our skills and our personhood to focus on the unique context and process of the patients and families we are privileged to attend."[4] It is an image that has been used by many feminist and womanist theologians, especially as a way of highlighting the communal care done by women and communities of color. Midwives through the ages have been holders of collective and intergenerational knowledge, ensuring the survival of the community in the face of danger and oppression.

I invite us to reflect on the stories of midwives in our traditions, in our communities' histories. For me, the narrative I always come back to is from the Exodus text of the Hebrew Bible, a source I consider sacred as a Unitarian Universalist minister connected to the early origins of my faith community in Christianity (despite our long history of being labeled heretical by Christian communities along the way). In Exodus 1, which tells us of the oppression of the Israelites and the cruel Egyptian rule over them, we meet the midwives:

> The king of Egypt said to the Hebrew midwives, one of whom was named Shiphrah and the other Puah, "When you act as midwives to the Hebrew women, and see them on the birthstool, if it is a boy, kill him; but if it is a girl, she shall live." But the midwives feared God; they did not do as the king of Egypt commanded them, but they let the boys live. So the king of Egypt summoned the midwives and said to them, "Why have you done this, and allowed the boys to live?" The midwives said to Pharaoh, "Because the Hebrew women are not like the Egyptian women; for they are vigorous and give birth before the midwife comes to them." So God dealt well with the midwives; and the people multiplied and became very strong.[5]

In "Midwives and Holy Subversives: Resisting Oppression in Attending the Birth of Wholeness," a powerful examination of the midwife as a model for spiritual care, Karen B. Montagno writes that these midwives of Exodus—in the face of oppressive and genocidal power—"take 'subversive,' risky, and strategic steps to interrupt and dismantle oppression and to ensure the wholeness and future of their community."[6] Here we find the role of the midwife, the chaplain, the spiritual care practitioner: to care for the community in ways creative and subversive, as an act of resistance which safeguards new life and possibility. The story of the ancient midwives is all too relevant to this question of the role of chaplaincy in our current divided context. Because right now, there is a need for spiritual midwives, for communal spiritual care. We are, together, losing an old world and birthing a new.

Yes, these are deeply divisive times. The polarization is tangible. Many are waking up to the painful realities of injustice that others have always known, the trauma carried from generation to generation. For some, there is deep grief and fear about what a changing world might mean and what it might cause them to lose—feelings that can take root as denial and refusal to acknowledge another's pain. For yet others, there is hope in the possibility of transformation, after so much hurt. It is a liminal time, a risky time, a dangerous time. I find myself thinking often of the words of Sikh activist Valarie Kaur, who asks:

> What if this darkness is not the darkness of the tomb, but the darkness of the womb? What if our America is not dead but a country that is waiting to be born? What if the story of America is one long labor? … What does the midwife tell us to do? Breathe. And then? Push.[7]

This is a time in need of spiritual midwives, in need of spiritual care, in need of voices and hands and hearts encouraging our breathing, strengthening our collective pushing. It goes beyond gender, beyond the biological act of birthing. It is about the necessity for all of us, across our religious traditions and interreligious initiatives and myriad of contexts, to have spiritual care skills for this collective journey of deep understanding and transformation:

1. To be able to listen deeply.

2. To hold silence.

3. To cultivate grounded, compassionate presence.

4. To seek out the feelings beneath the words.

5. To stay curious.

6. To be self-reflective and self-aware.

7. To be trauma-informed, recognizing that trauma is not just an individualized experience but one that can be collective and intergenerational.

8. To honor the universality *and* the particularity in each of our spiritual traditions, knowing where we are different and still offering the care and connection we are able.

9. To be able to do this not just in theory or in academic or professional contexts, but on the streets, in the homes, at the bedside, in a million everyday contexts with the people we meet in our lives.

10. To see ourselves as spiritual care practitioners, as midwives of the human spirit, and to understand that practice to be an integral part of whatever titles we might hold or job that we might do.

Many of the skills I use as a chaplain at the bedside, after all, come out of my beginnings in interreligious community organizing, learning how to have difficult conversations with care. This is heart work, this work of collectively caring for each other, of making the journey of transformation together. And it is necessary work. It is resistance work.

For if there is anything these deeply divisive times have shown us, it is that our religious communities, our interreligious coalitions, must act decisively. We must be the midwives resisting. As great thinker and Holocaust survivor Elie Wiesel, a mentor and inspiration for me during my undergraduate years at Boston University, once said: "We must take sides. Neutrality helps the oppressor, never the victim."[8] The movement for interreligious studies, dialogue, coalition-building—we cannot, must not, be neutral.

Across religious lines, we need each other, in real ways, in this time. As White nationalist movements continue to rise, relying on their foundational narratives of antisemitism and Christofascism, we need each other. As Judaism, Islam, and other traditions continue to be racialized and made "other" by White supremacy, we need each other. As we all do our own intra-faith work of examining how racism, patriarchy, and so many other forms of oppression live within our own religious communities' walls, we need each other. As a pandemic rages and mass movements for racial justice fill the streets (so present in my mind as I write these words), we need each other.

We need each other to form real relationships that will sustain us through the journey still to come. We need each other to care, to listen, to trust. We need each other to grieve, to cry, to sing, to hope. We need each other to share our stories of resistance, our histories of care—not just the Exodus midwives, but the narratives from each and all of our long traditions. We need each other to share the grounding we find in the sacred, especially in a society where the language of faith and spirituality has been so often co-opted by those who would do harm. We need to be committed to an ethos of spiritual care in our interreligious coalitions.

We will certainly not all be chaplains at the bedside (nor do we have to be—this is the beauty of shared movements); but I dream we will all be part of this larger work of midwifing, of becoming. Of being unafraid to touch our tender hearts and feelings, to name our grief and fear. Of creating interreligious relationships of love and care which respect and honor our differences, just as chaplains do with theologically diverse care-seekers. Of deep listening to others, and deep knowing of ourselves. Of noticing what might be underneath the words, hiding below the actions—the truth not readily apparent. Because that type of spiritual care is what we need for the collective journey.

CRCRCR

Just recently, I was at the bedside of one of my patients, suited up in my mask and face shield and gown and gloves that are all too commonplace for me during this pandemic. He was dying, and I was holding his hand. Most of the time, his cloudy eyes were fixed somewhere else, on something I could not see, as his breath rattled in his chest. He'd been in bed for days, unable to get up, but as I sat there, I noticed him shuffling his feet beneath the bedsheets. I considered calling the nurse, wondering if he might be in some discomfort; but as I watched him move one foot, then the other, I realized: "You're going on a journey." For the first time in a long time, still looking far away ahead, he spoke to me. "Yes . . . I am." . . . "It's been a long road." . . . "It's like a river. . . . It keeps on going." And I sat there, as he gripped my hand, taking one step and then another, going nowhere I could see but on a journey nonetheless. Somewhere I was not going with him. But for a little piece of that passage, that long river of becoming, that transition from life to death so often compared to birth itself, there I was present. A reminder:

You are not alone. You are loved. You matter.

Breathe. Push.

It's like a river. It keeps on going.

We need each other, in real ways.

This is how we go on.

NOTES

1   Wendy Cadge and Michael Skaggs, "Chaplaincy? Spiritual Care? Innovation? A Case Statement" (Chaplaincy Innovation Lab, September 15, 2018), https://chaplaincyinnovation .org/wp-content/uploads/2018/12/Cadge-Skaggs-2018.pdf.

2   Wendy Cadge, George Fitchett, Trace Haythorn, Patricia K. Palmer, Shelly Rambo, Casey Clevenger, and Irene Elizabeth Stroud, "Training Healthcare Chaplains: Yesterday, Today and Tomorrow," *Journal of Pastoral Care & Counseling* 73, no. 4 (2019): 211–21, at 212.

3   Emma Goldberg, "Hospital Chaplains Try to Keep the Faith During the Coronavirus Pandemic," *The New York Times* (April 14, 2020), https://www.nytimes.com/2020/04/11/ health/coronavirus-chaplains-hospitals.html; Wendy Cadge, "The Rise of the Chaplains," *The Atlantic* (May 17, 2020), https://www.theatlantic.com/ideas/archive/2020/05/ why-americans-are-turning-chaplains-during-pandemic/611767/; Barbara Plett Usher, "Coronavirus: The Chaplains Toiling on the Frontlines," *BBC News* (July 12, 2020), https:// www.bbc.com/news/world-us-canada-53284610.

4   Karen R Hanson, "The Midwife," in *Images of Pastoral Care: Classic Readings*, ed. Robert C. Dykstra (St. Louis: Chalice Press, 2005), Kindle edition.

5   Exodus 1:15–20 New Revised Standard Version.

6   Karen B. Montagno, "Midwives and Holy Subversives: Resisting Oppression in Attending the Birth of Wholeness," in *Injustice and the Care of Souls: Taking Oppression Seriously in Pastoral Care*, eds. Sheryl A. Kujawa-Holbrook and Karen B. Montagno (Minneapolis: Fortress Press, 2009), 8.

7   Valarie Kaur, "Watch Night Speech: Breathe and Push," *Valarie Kaur* (May 8, 2018), https:// valariekaur.com/2017/01/watch-night-speech-breathe-push/.

8   Elie Wiesel, "Nobel Acceptance Speech" (Oslo, December 10, 1986), *Elie Wiesel Foundation for Humanity*, https://eliewieselfoundation.org/elie-wiesel/nobelprizespeech/.

TENSIONS IN THE HINDU FAMILY
THE CHALLENGES OF
INTRARELIGIOUS DIVISIONS

Anantanand Rambachan

I want to begin my contribution to this volume of essays on a very personal note that high-lights the challenges and divisions in the Hindu community. In May 2020, the city council of Saint Paul, Minnesota, passed a resolution censoring India's ruling party, the Bharatiya Janata's Party, for what the council described as its "Islamophobic ideology." The resolution also made reference to India's National Registry of Citizens and the Citizen Amendment Act. The full text of the resolution is as follows: "Reaffirming Saint Paul as a welcoming city, expressing solidarity with Saint Paul's South Asian community regardless of religion and caste by rejecting the Bharatiya Janata Party's Islamophobic ideology, and opposing India's National Registry of Citizens and Citizenship Amendment Act."[1]

The resolution attracted the attention of various India-American and Hindu organizations in the United States.[2] The India Association of Minnesota (IAM) strongly rejected the decision and accused the Council of portraying India and Indian Americans in a negative light. The Council, argued IAM, failed to speak of persecution in other South Asian nations. The Hindu American Foundation (HAF) also joined in opposing the resolution, writing a formal letter calling attention to human rights atrocities in Afghanistan, Bangladesh, and Pakistan. HAF highlighted a letter by its Advisory Board Member, Vishal Agarwal, arguing that the resolution "creates an unnecessarily hostile environment for Hindus."[3] Others argued along similar lines, claiming that the resolution reflected negatively on Hindu Americans and promoted Hinduphobia.[4] Although the resolution itself did not mention the Hindu community, this equation of the Hindus and the Bharatiya Janata Party is significant; I will return to it later.

I was not involved in either drafting or sponsoring this resolution, and I became aware of it only when the text was debated for the first time on May 6, 2020. The lead sponsor of the resolution, City Council Member Jane Prince, acknowledged working on the resolution with the Minnesota Chapter of the Council on Islamic Relations (CAIR–MN). Soon, however, I was drawn into the controversy on the Facebook page of Vishal Agarwal. It started with a comment from Hindu American Foundation Executive Council Member Ramesh Rao. Here is a snippet from that Facebook exchange:

Ramesh Rao: *Oh, this is yet another Anantanand Rambachan and gang initiative.Idiots, fools, knaves, and finally destructive in their approach to the world.*

Venkat Nagarajan: *Is Rambachan part of this initiative?*

Vishal Agarwal: *No but he is on the board of Sadhana that would support it.*[5]

Venkat Nagarajan: *What a pity. He has masqueraded for years as a so-called supporter of the Hindu-American community and has hoodwinked many people into holding him in high esteem.*[6]

This is not a pleasant social media exchange to cite in this essay, but I do so to illustrate the challenges that I face as a Hindu scholar and activist. All of the participants in this exchange are fellow Hindus; two hold official offices in the Hindu American Foundation, perhaps the most influential Hindu lobby group in the United States.[7] One worships in the same temple as I do.

This is only the most recent example. In 2015, for example, Rajiv Malhotra, Hindu activist and writer, spearheaded a campaign, unprecedented in the history of the Hindu tradition in North America, to prevent me from speaking at a Hindu-Catholic Dialogue event at the Durga Temple in Virginia. Malhotra described those who invited me as "ignorant Hindu leaders." His supporters were encouraged to flood my inbox with letters expressing their opposition to the "Trojan horse" in the Hindu community. Strategies were formulated for protests and the organizers were bombarded with requests to disinvite me. I was warned ominously by one of his supporters "not to come to the Durga Temple in Virginia."[8]

What are the lines of division between us as Hindus? What explains the hostility expressed on social media? At the heart of the matter, I believe, is a difference in our respective understandings of the nature of the Hindu tradition and its relationship with the Indian State. The controversy over the St. Paul City Council resolution is only another recent example that throws these intra-Hindu differences into relief. Although the resolution expressed opposition to policies of the Indian state, these criticisms were received as Hinduphobic attacks on the Hindu community in the United States. The World Hindu Council of America (VHPA), for example, spoke out against the resolution, describing it as both anti-Hindu and anti-India.

> The real purpose of this resolution is to create hatred for Hindus and people of Indian origin residing in Minneapolis—St. Paul area. This resolution, if passed will lead to bullying of the children of Indian origin in schools and colleges and intimidate the hardworking people of Indian origin who work at the gas stations, 7/11s and motels among others.[9]

Many of the respondents to the resolution, both organizations and individuals, did not critically separate nation-state and religion; but rather, assumed their identity. They moved uncritically from one to the other. When these two are not separated, criticism of the nation of India is treated as criticism of the Hindu tradition, and criticism of the tradition as criticism of leadership of the nation of India. Hindus who are critical of state policies are accused, not only of treason, but also of Hindu apostasy. Identification of the tradition with the state means, in effect, its identification with the person of the state leader who assumes a sacrosanct status and immunity from critique. Those who are regarded as enemies of the state are treated as enemies of the religion; those who are friends of the state are regarded as friends of the religion. All of this holds true, in general, for theocratic states. My interrogation of the ideology of Hindu nationalism, in the form advocated by leading members of India's ruling party, makes me, in the eyes of fellow Hindus, an enemy both of India and the Hindu tradition.[10]

What are the roots of this identification of state and religion, spoken of as *Hindutva* [Hinduness]? The earliest systematic exposition of this ideology was by V.D. Savarkar (1883–1966) in his well-known work *Hindutva*.[11] Savarkar's definition of Hindu identity has several important components. The first is geographical. A Hindu is "primarily a citizen, either in himself or through his forefathers of 'Hindusthan.'" The second is common blood or *jāti*. A Hindu is a descendant of Hindu parents and shares with other Hindus a common blood traceable to the Vedic fathers. "We *feel* we are a JATI, a race bound together by the dearest ties of blood and therefore it must be so."[12] The third is the tie of homage to Hindu culture or civilization. Savarkar names this common culture as Sanskriti on the basis of the claim that Sanskrit is the language that expresses and preserves all that is worthy in the history of the Hindus. It includes a shared history, literature, art, law festivals, rites, rituals and heroes. This criterion was the basis for the exclusion, not only of Indian Muslims, but also of Indian Christians. Despite sharing birth and blood, they had, in Savarkar's words, "ceased to own Hindu civilization (Sanskriti) as a whole. They belong or feel that they belong to a cultural unit altogether different from the Hindu one.[13]

> For though Hindusthan to them is Fatherland as to any other Hindu yet it is not to them a Holyland too. Their Holyland is far off in Arabia or Palestine. Their mythology and Godmen, ideas and heroes are not the children of this soil. Consequently, their names and their outlook smack of foreign origin. Their love is divided. Nay, if some of them be really believing what they profess to do, then there can be no choice – they must, to a man, set their Holyland above their fatherland in their love and allegiance. That is but natural. We are not condemning nor are we lamenting. We are simply telling facts as they stand. We have tried to determine the essentials of Hindutva and in doing so we have discovered that the Bohras and such other Mohammedan or Christian communities possess all the essential qualifications of Hindutva but one and that is that they do not look upon India as their Holyland.[14]

A Hindu, according to Savarkar, is someone who looks upon India as fatherland, but also as holy-land.[15] In his view, Indian Muslims and Christians are not as qualified, as Hindus, to be citizens of India. In 2003, the BJP honored Savarkar by installing his portrait, amidst great controversy, in the Central Hall of the Indian Parliament.[16]

There are, as well, groups in India, and increasingly in the Hindu diaspora, which do not distinguish between Hindutva and Hinduism and are enthusiastic defenders and advocates for both. They see no conflicts between the core religious claims of the Hindu tradition and the nationalistic ideology of Hindutva. They advocate vigorously for India to become a Hindu Rashtra or Hindu State. They are unapologetic defenders of the state and its policies and are incapable of developing moral critiques of the state from the values of the Hindu tradition. They brand all criticisms of Hindutva as denunciations of the Hindu tradition.

Although quite cognizant of the complex relationships between religion and state power throughout history, including nations that claim separation between both, I critically distinguish Hindutva and Hinduism. I understand Hindutva to be an ideology of religious nationalism that confers a quasi-divine status to the nation and proposes the highest aim of life to be the service and defense of the nation. Hinduism, on the other hand, affirms the immanence and transcendence of the divine and does not limit this geographically. Although the Hindu tradition does not exclude love and service of one's country, the aim of the Hindu tradition is a liberated life, devoted to the universal common good, and not the deification of a nation.

Hindutva makes and thrives upon a sharp distinction between Hindus and non-Hindus. It is a definition of the meaning of Hindu identity based on exclusion and otherness. It overlooks the universalism of Hinduism as well as its human appeal and narrowly identifies it with nation and clan. Hinduism, contrary to Hindutva, affirms a vision of the world's unity and a commitment to the well-being of all. A parochial identification of Hinduism with nation, clan, and ethnicity makes it impossible for Hinduism to legitimately proclaim itself as a world religion. If the Hindu tradition claims universal validity for its teachings, these must transcend such specificities. Hinduism must detach itself from Hindutva if it wishes to be relevant and to speak to human beings across our rich diversity.

There are various implications in these two positions for interreligious relationships. Hindutva champions a form of majority rule that appears to be intolerant of plural identities; it asserts a definition of nationality and loyalty that excludes large numbers of people for whom India is home. There is, however, an ancient and powerful tradition of hospitality to religious diversity in the Hindu tradition that, for centuries, made possible the accommodation of a wide diversity of religious beliefs and practices; the Hindu community historically offered shelter to persecuted religious groups. It is this genuine hospitality that can once again point the way forward as India agonizes over its identity as a nation.

Hindutva's disposition to the Hindu religious tradition is generally uncritical. There is a tendency among Hindutva's ideologues to blame "outsiders," especially Muslims, for the creation of hierarchical systems such as caste.[17] However, there is good evidence of distinctions in Vedic times between those who regarded themselves as noble (*arya*) and those referred to as *dasyus*. The *dasyus* were considered subhuman, hypocritical, without virtue, observing different customs, and likened to a famine. They were excluded from the community and its sacred rituals.[18] I believe that we can critique Hindutva as well as specific interpretations of the Hindu tradition that do not promote human dignity, equality, and flourishing. Commitment to a tradition must not be measured by unquestioning assent and defense of all that is done in its name. We can lift up and commit ourselves to the profound liberative teachings of the Hindu tradition that affirm the unity of all life, and the values of justice and compassion for all.

The Hindu tradition does not regard Hindus as constituting a perfect community that has been corrupted by outsiders. We are subject to the universal human problem of ignorance (*avidya*), as a consequence of which we develop greed and self-centeredness and exploit others to satisfy our desires. Our liberation from ignorance comes as a consequence of overcoming the ignorance of our separate selfhood and discovering our fundamental unity with all beings; this results in relationships of compassion and generosity.

We are not only subject to the distortions of ignorance. We ought to be humble in our relationships with persons of other traditions. The divine is always more than we can define, describe, or understand with our finite minds; descriptions will, of necessity, be plural. The acknowledgement of the limits of language and the relativity of the human condition preclude any Hindu claim to the ownership of truth in its fullness and finality. Hinduism espouses an epistemological and philosophical humility that is antithetical to the privileging of a single viewpoint, be it religious or political, and recognizes the enrichment that diversity affords. The desire for religious or political hegemony and homogeneity, intrareligious or interreligious, is not in accord with the foundations of the Hindu worldview.

The rise of Hindu nationalism challenges Hindus to think deeply about what it means to affirm a Hindu identity. Is this identity linked inextricably to a specific historical nation or does it transcend allegiance to a nation-state, its leader and policies? Hindutva reduces the role of religion to that of servitude to the state and, in doing so, undermines its moral and ethical power. In addition, it is associated with attitudes of hostility, mistrust, and increasing violence towards those minority communities that do not satisfy a very narrow criterion of national identity that privileges Hindu cultural and religious traditions.

I believe that Hindu Americans have a special obligation to contest Hindutva ideology. Such challenges should not be regarded as hostile to Hinduism or to India and ought to be welcomed in the spirit of respectful debate that is a part of the tradition's history. Hindu Americans know well the fears and the challenges of being a religious minority. We have participated in many legal and lobbying efforts to ensure that federal, state, and city policies are not partial to the interests of the religious majority or a single tradition. We contest monolithic definitions of American identity that would marginalize and exclude us. It is hypocritical of us to fight for such rights here, while condoning their violation elsewhere.

NOTES

1   https://stpaul.legistar.com/LegislationDetail.aspx?ID=4430178&GUID=6413F8CE-8E77
-43CA-9300-8C3F67093180. Accessed June 15, 2020. For a good summary of the history
of this resolution as well as a brief description of the National Registry of Citizens and the
Citizen Amendment Act, see Joey Peters, "St. Paul City Council approves measure declaring
Indian government Islamophobic" in *Sahan Journal* (May 20, 2020) https://sahanjournal.com/
politics/st-paul-city-council-approves-measure-declaring-indian-government-islamophobic/

2   Peters, "St. Paul City Council."

3   "12,000+ letters sent to St Paul, Minnesota City Council opposing anti-India
resolution," HAF press release, May 20, 2020. https://www.hinduamerican.org/
press/12000-letters-sent-saint-paul-city-council-opposing-anti-india-resolution.

4   "How Resolution 20-172 by St. Paul City Council Incites Hindu Phobia," *Newsgram* (May 19,
2020). https://www.newsgram.com/resolution-20-172-st-paul-city-council-incites-hindu-
phobia/ Accessed June 15, 2020.

5   I serve on the Advisory Board of Sadhana, a progressive Hindu organization. See https://
www.sadhana.org/ Sadhana also had nothing to do with this resolution, but Agarwal is critical
of Tensions in the Hindu Family on the basis of his assumption that the organization may
support such a resolution.

6   Vishal Agarwal, May 6, 2020.

7   See https://www.hinduamerican.org/. The Hindu American Foundation was the
organization behind the "Take Back Yoga Initiative" of about a decade ago. See Paul
Vitello, "Hindu Group Stirs a Debate Over Yoga's Soul" in *New York Time*s (November 29,
2010). https://www.nytimes.com/2010/11/28/nyregion/28yoga.html#:~:text=The%20
campaign%2C%20labeled%20%E2%80%9CTake%20Back,to%20the%20faith's%20ancient%20
traditions.

8   See my essay, "The Hindu Terror" in *Open Magazine* (October 7, 2015). https://
openthemagazine.com/voices/the-hindu-terror/.

9   Hindupost Desk, "VHPA urges US City Council to reject Hinduphobic, anti-Bharat
resolution," in *Hindu Post* (May 18, 2020). https://www.hindupost.in/politics/
vhpa-urges-us-city-council-to-reject-hinduphobic-anti-bharat-resolution/.

10 See, for example, my essay, "Hindus Have Choices: Identity, PM Modi and American Hindus,"
at *Patheos* (August 6, 2014). https://www.patheos.com/topics/2014-religious-trends/hindu/
hindus-have-choices-anantanand-rambachan-08061.

11 V.D. Savarkar, *Hindutva* (Delhi: Bharti Sahitya Sadan, 1989).

12 Savarkar, 89–90.

13 Savarkar, 100–01.

14 Savarkar, 113.

15 It is important to take note of the fact that the very idea of the nation-state is a construct of the Western world. For further reading see the works of Anthony D. Smith and especially *The Nation in History: Historiographical Debates about Ethnicity and Nationalism* (Hanover, NH: University Press of New England, 2000). One of the prominent Indian critics of nationalism was the famous writer and poet Rabindranath Tagore (1861–1941). See M. Chatterjee, "The Critique of Nationalism," in Margaret Chatterjee, *Studies in Modern Jewish and Hindu Thought* (London: Palgrave Macmillan, 1997), 123–44.

16 "President unveils Savarkar portrait in Parliament" in *Rediff India Abroad* (February 26, 2003) https://www.rediff.com/news/2003/feb/26prez.htm.

17 "Muslim invasion created Dalits and tribals in India, says RSS" in *India Today* (September 22, 2104). https://www.indiatoday.in/india/story/rss-mohan-bhagwat-hindu-dalits-tribals-muslim-invasion-293816-2014-09-22.

18 See Prabhati Mukherjee, *Beyond the Four Varnas: The Untouchables in India* (Shimla: Indian Institute of Advanced Study, 1988).

REALIZING KINSHIP
SPIRITUAL PRACTICE TOWARD
HEALING OUR DIVIDED WORLD

Ruben L. F. Habito

As advances in information technology facilitate instantaneous communications across continents, and as the impact of globalization is felt on all fronts throughout the populated areas of our planet Earth, on the one hand, we feel a heightened sense of interdependence and interconnectedness throughout our world. Yet, on the other hand, ironically and lamentably, our global society is beleaguered by recurrent incidents of violence and conflict, manifesting deep-seated divisions across different levels of our being as humans navigating our way through this life on Earth.

With racial, ethnic, national, political, social, economic, religious, and other factors in play, we human beings construct identities associated with a need for belonging to specific groups set off from others outside of that group. This is a frame of mind called "tribalism," an "us vs. them" mentality that informs attitudes and behavior, based on adherence and devotion to an in-group that by definition demarcates itself from those outside.[1] An extreme form of this is one that harbors hostility, and desires or even actively works toward the elimination of those considered outside the group. This tribalistic mindset is arguably at the roots of the major problems faced by our global society today.[2]

As of this writing, the global pandemic COVID-19 continues to ravage societies throughout the world, cutting across national, social and other boundaries, exposing us human beings to a common vulnerability as humans to the virus. Thus, on the one hand, the pandemic provides an occasion for the global human community to transcend our tribalistic attitudes and find solidarity in our common plight against this pervasive threat to our human lives, urging us to go beyond our self-imposed boundaries in seeking to care for one another. However, on the other hand, regrettably, the pandemic has in effect, served to heighten the inequities among us and further bolster the demarcations that already set us apart, based on economic, social, racial, and other factors. It puts sectors of our global community at greater odds with one another vis-à-vis strategies to contain the virus, even as it wreaks havoc on the lives and causes the death of multitudes of the more economically disadvantaged sectors of our human community.

Surveying our contemporary world, one cannot help lamenting a highly dysfunctional and violence-prone global society marked by deep-seated divisions and animosities among different sectors, heading toward a disastrous future. An earnest cry wells up from the depths, echoing the words of Rodney King, an African American construction worker whose beating by LAPD police sparked riots in the Los Angeles area in 1992: "Can't we all get along?"

In his analytical look at the human condition, the Buddha describes the fundamental human problematic as *dukkha*, a term often translated as "suffering," but more appropriately rendered as "dis-ease, dissatisfaction, dislocation, dysfunction." The term refers to a wheel that is not correctly centered and consequently is malfunctioning. With this as starting point, the Awakened One presents a therapeutic approach to our human problematic in the well-known Four Noble Truths, based on a fourfold set of principles for healing deriving from the Āyur Vedic tradition. This entails:

1. laying out the symptoms of the disease, that is, bringing to light the manifestations of *dis-ease and dissatisfaction*;

2. determining root causes, thus pinpointing to *craving*, which plays out in the three poisons of greed, ill-will, and delusion;

3. envisioning a healed state of well-being that comes to the fore with the *eradication* of the causes of the disease; and

4. prescribing the *path* toward healing, i.e., the eightfold path beginning with Right View and culminating with the practice of meditative concentration.

David Loy, Buddhist philosopher and Zen teacher, takes these Four Noble Truths and transposes them from the individual, personal level to the societal and institutional levels of our being.[3] Taking cue from this transposition, we can describe our contemporary world situation as one of global *dukkha*. Loy traces the causes of this global dis-ease to the three poisons in institutionalized form, i.e., in the institutionalized greed of a globalized economic system propelled by our consumeristic attitudes and values; the institutionalized ill-will harbored by tribalistic mindsets against the perceived "other" regarded as a threat to their existence, which spawns a lucrative military industrial complex that feeds on the insecurities of the populace; and the collective delusion brought about by the corporate interests that control the mass media, highlighting the titillating and sensational items that capture the headlines, sidetracking our gaze, and shifting our attention from the more urgent issues we face as a global community.

In a another work, Loy reframes the second Noble Truth as a sense of lack we humans feel within ourselves, springing from the delusion of a false, constructed self.[4] This deluded self is propped up by a false sense of security as it finds belonging in a constructed tribal group-identity set up in opposition to those who are outside of that group. The animosity engendered toward "those others" who do not belong to "my group" is what escalates into the violence that we see in so many forms in our world today.

Christianity attributes the woes of humanity to "sin," understood as a state of separation and alienation from our divine source. We human beings are originally created in the image of God (Genesis 1:26–27), but through an act of willful disobedience, came to be exiled from our original home (the Garden of Eden), and thereby also came to be alienated from our neighbor, that is, our fellow human beings, and from the Earth, our natural habitat. This state of separation on three levels is at the roots of the dysfunctional state in which we now see ourselves, adversely affecting the personal, social, and global dimensions of our being.[5] This acute sense of inner dislocation is what drives us to crave for a sense of belonging with some tangible entity larger than ourselves, and thus feeds the tribalistic mentality and its accompanying patterns of destructive behavior.

With their respective diagnoses of the ailing human condition, Buddhist and Christian traditions also offer their respective prescriptions toward healing. The overcoming of our dis-eased and dysfunctional human condition (*dukkha*) begins with the due acknowledgement of this condition, and proceeds to the identification of its root causes. In identifying this delusive, egoic self as the cause of this dysfunction, we are enabled to forge a path toward liberation, which lies in the cessation of this delusion. This liberation is actually an awakening to our "true self that is no-self," understood as the realization of our intimate interconnectedness with each and every thing in this universe. Mindfulness and meditative concentration, in diverse forms as taught in various schools of Buddhism, is the prescribed form of spiritual practice that allows for this overcoming of the delusion of a separate self, that is, awakening to and realizing our intimate interconnectedness with everything and everyone in the world. To awaken to my true self is in fact to recognize and see everything and everyone as *kin* to myself: there is literally nothing, and no one, who is alien, or "other" to me. I behold everyone and everything around me and realize my deep kinship with all: I am *that*.

In Christianity, the overcoming of our state of separation from our divine source, from our fellow humans, and from the world of nature, that is, the overcoming of being in a state of sin, begins with the acknowledgement and confession of that sin. The Good News is a call to reconciliation, which entails a *metanoia*, literally a change of heart and mind. This is no less than a total transformation of our entire way of being, from an alienated, insecure, self-preoccupied life, to one that has now been reconciled with God and has reclaimed its divine image, reconciled with our neighbor, and with the entire Creation. In theological terms, this is "dying to our old self with Christ on the cross and being reborn in the newness of life in the Risen One." This is "putting on the mind of Christ," which effects a transformation from a self-centered, alienated state of being, to a mode of being and way of life that is now reconciled with our divine source, reconciled with our neighbor, and with the entirety of creation.[6] This reconciliation opens our hearts to embrace everyone and everything "in Christ," as members of the same extended, all-inclusive family, together basking in unconditional Divine Love. This reconciliation empowers us to actively work together toward everyone's collective well-being grounded in that love.

In a multi-volume series exploring the spiritual teachings of living religions of the world (under the common subtitle *World Spirituality*), with renowned international scholars contributing essays on Hindu, Buddhist, Jewish, Christian, Islamic, Indigenous, Secular, and other forms of spirituality, the common preface to all the volumes offers a working definition of the key term "spiritual" that is notable. *The spiritual core is the deepest center of the person. It is here that the person is open to the transcendent; it is here that the person experiences ultimate reality.*[7] I venture to suggest that this spiritual core, where the person is open to the transcendent, in whatever way this may be named, is also where a person experiences an intimate connectedness with everyone and everything that exists in the universe, that is, where one realizes a deep kinship with all.

In this regard, Buddhists and Christians need only turn to their own respective spiritual teachings and practices and "walk their talk," thereby becoming agents that will bring about a new world order based on the understanding and realization of this kinship of all. Adherents of other religious traditions are also called to find a way to go beyond their own religious-based tribalistic mindset and reexamine their own core message to humanity. In this light they are called to join hands with all peoples of goodwill to work toward shared goals of a harmonious, equitable, just, and compassionate world order, empowered by their own religious vision. And for those who regard themselves as "spiritual but not religious," taking on a form of spiritual practice that enables them to return to their home in the deepest center of their being, whether it be through Zen, Buddhist insight meditation, Hindu, Jewish, Sufi, Christian contemplation, or some form of "non-religious" mindfulness practice, may open them to an experiential realization of that intimate interconnectedness with all, and bring about a transformation in the way they see themselves and the way they live their lives.

Spiritual practice that puts us in touch with this innermost core of our being, thereby opening our hearts to our intimate connectedness with each and everyone in the universe, enables us to overcome a self-preoccupied, tribalistic mindset, and instead live in the light of the vision of the kinship of us all.[8] The heart and mind of one so awakened is conveyed by a well-known line from the early Buddhist treatise On Lovingkindness (Mettā Sutta): *As a mother would give her life to protect her child, her only child, have this boundless heart in you toward all beings.*

The realization of this all-inclusive and intimate kinship in a truly experiential way will inevitably unfold in the personal, social, political, economic, ecological, and all levels of our being, and bring about a palpable and effective transformation of our global society.

NOTES

1   The Macmillan dictionary (2018) defines this term "tribalism" as "a way of thinking or behaving in which people are loyal to their social group above all else," and can entail a type of "discrimination or animosity based on those group differences" (Merriam-Webster, 2018). The term as used in current intellectual discourse is not intended to be derogatory or demeaning to indigenous communities which are also referred to as "tribes." See Bruce Rozenblit, *Us Against Them: How Tribalism Affects the Way We Think* (Kansas City, MO: Transcendent Publications, 2008).

2   See Robert Wright, *Why Buddhism is True: The Science and Philosophy of Meditation and Enlightenment* (New York: Simon and Schuster, 2017), 18ff. See also Wright's lecture series, *Beyond Tribalism: How Meditation Can Save the World*, available online at https://learn.tricycle.org/courses/tribalism

3   David Loy, *The Great Awakening: A Buddhist Social Theory* (Boston: Wisdom Publications, 1997).

4   David Loy, *Lack and Transcendence: The Problem of Death and Life in Psychotherapy, Existentialism, and Buddhism* (Boston: Wisdom Publications, 2018).

5   Ruben L.F. Habito, *Healing Breath: Zen for Christians and Buddhists in a Wounded World* (Boston: Wisdom Publications, 2006).

6   See James Marion, *Putting On the Mind of Christ: The Inner Work of Christian Spirituality* (Newburyport, MA: Hampton Roads Publishing, 2011).

7   This common preface is authored by Ewert Cousins. See Arthur Green, et. al., Eds, *World Spirituality: An Encyclopaedic History of the Religious Quest* (New York: Crossroads, 1989ff).

8   For an inspiring and empowering description of such a scenario, see Charles Eisenstein, *The More Beautiful World Our Hearts Know is Possible*. Sacred Activism Series (Berkeley, CA: North Atlantic Books, 2013).

MULTIFAITH ENCOUNTER AS SPIRITUAL PRACTICE
A PROJECT REPORT WITH A PANDEMIC POSTSCRIPT

Nancy Fuchs Kreimer

"I have a confession to make," said Roshi Enkyo Pat O'Hara, Abbot of the Village Zendo in New York City. It was the start of our 48-hour retreat, the first of our experiments in a new project, *Cultivating Character: A Conversation across Communities.* "I see the schedule tomorrow morning calls for our Catholic participant sharing her Centering Prayer for an hour before breakfast," she said. "That won't work for me." The other eleven participants tensed with anxiety. Was one of our band of spiritual leaders uncomfortable with what she had heard so far? Was she going to leave? The roshi continued: "I cannot pray until after I have my morning coffee."

Although this gifted Buddhist leader can give a brilliant dharma talk online to hundreds, she was the first to admit she was not ready for spirituality in the morning without caffeinated help. Although we were teachers of prayer, meditation, virtue education, and spiritual formation, we knew that we engaged in our spiritual disciplines because we needed them. We wanted to talk with one another about our common quests and our particular ways of addressing them. We each had spiritual practices and communities that nourished us. We were eager to explore what it could mean for the multifaith encounter *itself* to be a spiritual practice.

Therefore, during this time together, we answered an invitation to pull something out of our spiritual-practices toolbox (treasure chest, really), to explain why and how it worked, and to invite others to experience it. Some of these practices we had inherited from the traditions of our ancestors, others from traditions we had chosen as adults. Others were borrowed from different sources, even as we continued to locate ourselves in our legacy communities. The practices were the ways we kept trying to show up as our best selves—or at least better versions of ourselves. They were windows into what nurtured us. Their sharing would serve as a modality for multifaith literacy. Experiencing them together would be a way to create heart-opening connections. At least, that was the hope. Buoyed by the promise of early morning caffeine and a commitment to show up without pretense, we were ready to begin.

BEGINNING WITH NOT KNOWING

"What are your signature strengths?" we asked each other. "What are your growing edges?" Long before Brené Brown became a guru of "whole hearted leadership," I had been moved by Rabbi Abraham Joshua Heschel's teaching about the starting place for dialogue. When I entered the field in the late seventies, most Jewish-Christian encounters were based on a model of "what we want the other to know about us," and in those days, there was a great deal Jews wanted Christians to know about Jews and Judaism. We Jews were eager to help the Christians who, reckoning with Christianity's complicity in the Nazi Holocaust, were hard at work trying to help their community "get it right" with regard to Jews and Judaism. Heschel was a significant player in that effort. From Heschel (and later, from Brené Brown) I learned the importance of beginning in the place where we are most "embarrassed" (Heschel's word), most "vulnerable" (Brown's word). We begin where none of us has all the answers: the place where we need one another, as individuals and as communal traditions.

Many of us at the *Cultivating Character* retreat had been to multiple trainings: dialogue decalogue, appreciative inquiry, compassionate listening, civil conversations. We knew a dozen strategies for managing difference; but all came down to this wise advice: connect before you correct. We had seen how collaborating on shared projects of world transformation created connection. The modality we were exploring was another path to tread: one of actually participating in each other's spiritual practices of character cultivation.

The *Cultivating Character* program grew out of a previous encounter, also funded by the Henry Luce Foundation, for Jews and Muslims. It had taught us a great deal about the possibilities and limits of dialogue. Since both traditions had daily prayer practice, we had assigned separate rooms for the Jews and the Muslims to use as prayer space during our retreats and let the two communities work that out as they wished.

Contrary to our expectations, our fourth retreat (for women only) had turned out to be the hardest. Tensions roiled below and sometimes above the surface. Yet, powerful learning happened when a Muslim participant invited the others to witness her morning *dhikr* (vocalized repetition of divine names, phrases, or prayers). Among those who accepted her invitation, reactions varied. For some it was joyful, for others uncomfortable. We did not emerge from the room as one spiritual sisterhood; attending *dhikr* did not make the hard parts of our conversation any less difficult. But we did return to our encounters in a different spirit. We had reached down into a more profound place, the place that led each of us to engage in religious life in the first place. How could we capture that power and allow it to infuse our interreligious encounters? Were we risking creating a "New Age Soup" (a thin broth, at that)? How would we open widely and bond powerfully while also delving deeper into our gorgeous particularities?

LIVING SIDE BY SIDE

How might this work provide a way to become wiser about our own lives, even as we opened ourselves vulnerably to others? To me, a rabbi committed to the ongoing vitality of Jewish community, this question was most salient. Over the years, we learned to be clearer about what these retreats were about. For example, for the opening of our first retreat, each person had been asked to bring an object with personal spiritual significance (a Qur'an, a cross, a tallit, a leaf) to what we declared was our sacred space, our "altar," around which we sat in a circle for our conversations. Upon reflection, we realized that this had presumed a spiritual intimacy that was beyond the intention of the gathering. We had invited seasoned and grounded individuals to that first event; but as we opened our circle to younger, emerging leaders, some with weaker roots, some even a bit unmoored, such an opening made less sense. Therefore, for the second retreat, we made the sharing of these objects a learning session, not a communal ritual. We moved the objects to the back of the room. There, people explored them in pairs, describing them to each other, using them as pedagogical tools rather than as sacred objects.

In some ways, the program we created was itself a spiritual practice, an opportunity to cultivate traits such as humility and compassion that are the fruits of many religious disciplines. We were mindful that there has been a great deal of creative plagiarism happening in all our traditions for centuries. However, our goal was less about blending and borrowing and more about sending participants back to their wells with new insight and depth, thirsty for their own tradition's living waters. After all, says Rainer Maria Rilke, "even between the closest people infinite distances exist"; indeed, "a marvelous living side-by-side can grow up for them, if they succeed in loving the expanse between them."[1]

We thought our retreat would be a time for lively conversations about cultural appropriation, syncretism, and the proper role of "holy envy." In fact, those issues took a back seat to our own journeys of deepening in the practices we were sharing. The focus on character helped us to stay interested in seeing each other's traditions "whole against the sky" (to borrow Rilke's turn of phrase) while exploring how we could show up as our better selves.

TWO CONVERSATIONS

Two conversations stand out, which were both prompted by a teaching about *salat* (the Islamic canonical, daily prayers). At our first retreat, a professor shared that when she became a Muslim, she wondered how she would fit five-times-a-day prayer into her life. After years of living into the practice, her only question now is how to fit her life into five-times-a-day prayer. The conversation that ensued about obligation, structure, and the scaffolding of time reverberated in me for years. Later, one of the Christian participants wrote, "I journaled to God after that conversation and asked forgiveness for how sloppy I have become in my prayer life." For many of us, the session was an opening to think about the connection we had to a fixed prayer routine, its relationship to the dark and light of each day, to cycles of mealtime and rest time.

At a subsequent retreat with young leaders, a Muslim teacher showed us how to stand in a line shoulder to shoulder ("the devil slips in the cracks") and invited us to join in the experience (if we were comfortable doing so). Reflection followed. A young Buddhist practitioner remarked how he spent hours in a Zendo without ever making physical contact with the person next to him. How was that energy different? Jews and Christians then began to talk about their lives in communal prayer, about how they were impacted by the way their bodies did or did not connect with others. Theirs was a sharing of experiences rather than a debate about theology. The Buddhist priest-in-training left the conversation, not wanting to change his practice, but, rather, appreciating it from a different angle; wondering whether bowing to one another was, in its own way, touching. The Muslim presenter later noted how frequently she recalled that session while lining up with other women for salat. We had not essentialized these practices ("This is what Buddhists do; this is what Muslims do"). Rather, we all had found new insights into own practices.

WHY PRACTICES?

At the very beginning of the Muslim-Jewish project, we had brought twenty Muslim and Jewish emerging religious leaders to a small retreat center on the Hudson River. We learned about one another through personal and traditional storytelling, through text study, and through carefully planned dips into combustible issues. All the while, we were aware that in another corner of the dining room, a saffron-robed man, Matthieu Ricard, was engaging in a different conversation with a group of "happiness researchers." On the last day, the young leaders asked whether they could go sit with him. They wanted to know what he had been teaching the researchers. If our three days together had proven anything, it was that it is not that easy to be happy. What Ricard had been teaching was that "being happy" takes practice. Our young leaders, steeped in their Jewish and Muslim traditions, were all ears. Practice is working out at the gym, building the muscles; it is the preparation for the heavy lifting that life sometimes demands.

When we began our *Cultivating Character* retreats, I chose to invite participants into the retreat center kitchen to join me in one of my spiritual practices. While I do not observe many of the Shabbat restrictions, I have regularly opened my Friday night Shabbat table to guests. Serving my guests a meal, enjoying the interactions between friends old and new, nourishing ourselves at the table with food and companionship—all are powerful dimensions of celebration. But, for me, especially critical is the embodied routine of chopping and stirring, the creating of the meal. I call this a spiritual practice because I perform it in a ritual way each Friday, enforced by a schedule outside my personal whims, with an intention beyond the act itself. Hospitality, I have come to learn, is a disposition one cultivates—in my case in the routines of food preparation—that is meant to carry over into the way one presides in a classroom or a meeting or the way one greets life. Little did we realize when we left our last retreat in August 2019 that we would soon be in greater need than ever of all the virtues we had sought to hone.

PANDEMIC POSTSCRIPT

I began to shelter in place on Sunday, March 15, 2020. There would be no guests that Friday evening. Cooking would mean putting together a meal for my household of just two. It hardly seemed worth bothering. But, I can still make it special, I thought. We can still light candles. We can still welcome each other. It was soon apparent that other practices were no longer possible, among which were visiting a homebound friend and attending religious services. Cell phone calls and Zoom communal prayer services would have to stand in for previous practices of visiting and synagogue-going. Here was an opportunity to apply what I learned about spiritual practice, to let it guide me in reinventing my life. I recalled the conversation about the Muslim prayer line and the Buddhist sitting-practice. I realized that the energy of other people can be felt in different ways: not better or worse, just different. I could wrap my mind around Zoom services, Seders, support groups, even (with difficulty) Zoom funerals. I could reframe physical separation ("social distance") in a way that would both honor the aloneness and stretch into new ways of connecting. Once one lets go of expectations, new sweetness can be found.

What I missed most in this new life was service, activism, "healing the world—retail and wholesale." I remembered with special poignancy moments like driving with friends to Washington, DC, for rallies; attending and speaking at press conferences; risking arrest in Harrisburg with the Poor People's Campaign; showing up at my local mosque to pray with my friends when Islamophobic ads were placed on our city buses; serving dinner when our synagogue hosted families in transition from homelessness; walking the streets (always with a partner) on behalf of political campaigns; knocking on doors and talking with people face to face.

Because of COVID-19, most of this was no longer possible for me. Yet, at the same time I was overwhelmed by the volume of causes, all of them as dire as ever—if not even more urgent. Because it was all coming at me in email and text and social media, I felt flooded with the bulk of concerns, with what sociologist Barry Schwartz calls the "paradox of choice." Among the many emails and social media requests, one stood out. A rabbinic colleague reminded me each week on Facebook that he was fasting every Wednesday until Carmela and her four children were released from sanctuary. After being denied asylum, the family had made their home in a local church for the last two and a half years—one of fifty in the country to do so. Return to Mexico was not a safe option. My colleague was requesting us to place calls to our congresspeople and senators advocating for this particular cause. I knew from my years of talking about practices (and my own challenges with them) that joining this colleague in her cause would only work if I embedded it in a structure, a fixed time. I chose Tuesday mornings.

Obviously, there is no traditional Jewish commandment to call one's elected representatives; but there is an obligation to engage in morning prayers. There is also an obligation in our tradition to give *tzedakah* (often translated as charity, but whose literal meaning is justice). When should one give *tzedakah*? The *Shulhan Aruch* (Orech Hyyim 92:10), a sixteenth-century law code, says "It is a good thing to give *tzedakah* before prayer." I saw an opportunity to link these two obligations. I would commit myself to making my calls, followed by praying the morning service.

As with many Jews today, the duty to take action in the face of troubles in the world seems obvious to me. How to build it into the structure of my day is more of a challenge. The duty to pray in the middle of the week compels me less. And yet, I could see that linking it with the call to work toward justice would have the effect of bringing both prayer and this justice practice into a time-bound commitment. It would turn both into obligation, rather than option.

But why, I wondered: why give *before* prayer? Why does tradition suggest this order? One would think action would come *after* prayer, the result of prayer. If the true meaning of prayer is, as Heschel said, to be subversive, to be inspired by the godly encounter, to do the godly work, then, first, we fill our spiritual well and then, inspired by the prayer, we empty our pockets in the right spirit. So, I took the statement from the *Shulhan Aruch* as a challenge in crafting my own practice.

In following the *Shulhan Aruch*'s suggested order, I have found a way to understand both the phone calls and the prayers as spiritual exercises. I do this work as a humble, pragmatic response to evil that often feels like it is ascendant in our world. Clearly, this practice is more about my need to feel less useless than about solving the problem of asylum seekers in America. I recognize it as a spiritual practice primarily and only in very small measure about actual impact. By thinking about it is as a practice, I freely acknowledge it is minute, while raising up the intention that it be miniature. Rather than feeling proud of myself ("I have prayed with my dialing fingers!"), I often feel despair at the puny nature of my response. The fate of one family is emblematic of the larger problem of asylum seekers in our country at this moment, which itself is part of a larger morally bankrupt and broken immigration and refugee system that has grown even more perilous since the pandemic. I turn to prayer to connect my smallness with the Mystery that is also the Source of Renewal and Hope, then move on to the next way to intervene.

NOTES

1   Ranier Maria Rilke, *Letters to a Young Poet, 1899–1902,* translated with introduction and commentary by Reginald Snell (London: Sidgwick and Jackson, 1945), 107–08.

PART III

TEACHING INTERRELIGIOUSLY

"WE HAVE BEEN PRACTICING FOR THIS"
INTERFAITH ENGAGEMENT
RESHAPING THEOLOGICAL EDUCATION

Michelle Voss Roberts

During the early weeks of the COVID-19 pandemic, religious and spiritual practitioners felt their training kick in. "You have been practicing for this," said Master of Pastoral Studies student Andrea Taylor, leading online midday prayer at Emmanuel College (Toronto).[1] She observed that Buddhist teachings of wisdom and interdependence, and practices that cultivate equanimity and commitment to alleviate suffering, are well suited to the conditions of fear and loss created by the pandemic. People from diverse worldviews expressed similar sentiments as they set their faces toward an anxious new reality. Buddhist meditations on suffering and the causes of suffering, Christian withdrawal from a variety of comforts during Lent, Jewish observance of Sabbath, and the practices of other wisdom traditions had developed spiritual muscles needed to face the pandemic.

Something similar has happened with interfaith practitioners, whose disciplines of developing deep understanding across difference have prepared them to contribute positive leadership in divisive times. Even before the COVID-19 pandemic, they were navigating heightened xenophobic divisions. To combat Islamophobia after 9/11, interfaith groups created educational opportunities, organized visits to places of worship, and cultivated friendship through shared meals and service activities. To answer violent attacks, local religious leaders drew on their interfaith connections. They organized marches, rallies, and "rings of peace" to surround synagogues, mosques, and churches and demonstrate solidarity. Recognizing the unequal impacts of the pandemic, the same leaders are organizing neighborhood pods to assist people in need. Cultivated in relatively peaceful times, habits of interfaith engagement kick in when tensions rise.

INTERFAITH HABITS AND COMPARATIVE THEOLOGY

As interfaith habits developed among activists, social service and nonprofit organizations, and neighborhood religious communities, they have also trickled "up" into the institutions that train their future leaders. Action-reflection models, learned from the activist realm, have benefitted theological education greatly. Theological schools routinely partner with community organizations, including those with interfaith missions, for experiential and community-engaged learning.

Theological schools have different missions and different strengths from the institutions that their graduates will serve. They employ methods that are appropriate to educational contexts. As an educator and administrator at a multireligious theological school in Toronto, I look to the intellectual and spiritual habits of *comparative theology* to help transform theological education for deep interreligious understanding. Comparative theology claims deep understanding as its major goal. Harvard professor Francis X. Clooney, who can be largely credited with developing this method of study, titled his textbook *Comparative Theology: Deep Learning Across Religious Borders* (2010), and the same phrase appears in the title of his most recent book, *Reading the Hindu and Christian Classics: Why and How Deep Learning Still Matters* (2020).[2]

What does comparative theology entail? As "theology," it is the practice of seeking to understand the ultimate source of existence and all things in relation to that source. This search might include guidance from the sacred texts and wise teachers of one's tradition, as well as rational and affective reflection on them in relation to the community's experience. As "comparative," it extends this search to understand, as well, how people in other religious and spiritual traditions have grappled with questions of ultimate import. A comparative theologian does not treat other traditions at arm's length, with merely objective interest, but takes their wisdom seriously enough to engage in a prolonged, back-and-forth inquiry. This method can occasion "fresh theological insights that are indebted to the newly encountered tradition/s as well as the home tradition."[3]

Comparative theology's quest for deep understanding is well-suited to academic contexts, which offer different opportunities from the more episodic format of interreligious dialogue.

> The comparative theologian must do more than listen to others explain their faith; she must be willing to study their traditions deeply alongside her own, taking both to heart. In the process, she will begin to theologize as it were from both sides of the table, reflecting personally on old and new truths in an interior dialogue. Since comparative theology is ordinarily an academic theology, this reflection becomes eventually a somewhat specialized discourse that is different from the rightly broader and more varied conversations that characterize most dialogues.[4]

Students in theological schools gain prolonged practice in textual, historical, and critical methods. They benefit from the tutelage of instructors who challenge easy answers and unexamined views of self and other. By including comparative theological practices in their curricula, theological schools prepare their students for wise religious and spiritual leadership amid religious pluralism.

The practices of learning deeply from another tradition alongside one's own, and reflecting personally at this intersection, can become habits that religious and spiritual leaders draw upon when faced with conflict and division. Even so, comparative theology is typically practiced by individual scholars, pursuing their particular interests. How might the strengths of comparative theological method be translated to an institutional level?

ONE THEOLOGICAL SCHOOL

Religious stereotypes and prejudices can be replaced by accident, as it were, when friendships form across religious lines. They can be replaced intentionally, as when intrepid students enroll in a course in comparative theology. Both situations are even more effective if embedded in a cohort that regularly seeks deep understanding of the traditions present in the community. Emmanuel College has made the commitment that such engagement would be neither accidental nor optional in our curriculum.

Emmanuel College, a theological school of the United Church of Canada, is embedded in the ecumenical Toronto School of Theology in the University of Toronto. Our ecumenical commitments and our location within one of the world's most religiously diverse cities have fostered the development of our multireligious Master of Pastoral Studies (MPS) program. With formal programs for Christian, Muslim, and Buddhist students (and paths for students of other faith commitments), students training to become psychospiritual care providers interact with peers preparing for ministerial leadership, sacred music performance, and further academic study. To anchor this work, the Emmanuel College community has worked together to articulate the core values that guide this work, explicitly naming "interfaith engagement" and "contextual analysis" as part of our mission.[5]

The vision statement of the College reflects a comparative theological orientation: we prepare religious leaders and spiritual care providers to "become more deeply rooted in their own religious or spiritual traditions while engaging the beliefs and practices of people of other traditions." Learning about other traditions need not detract from learning about one's own. Rather, because religious diversity is a prominent feature of the contemporary context, it would be artificial to bracket the theological search for understanding from the faithful quests for meaning happening all around us. Theology always happens in a context, shaping the questions we bring to our own traditions. With good questions, sometimes inspired by the wise perspectives encountered in practices and ideas from other spiritual streams, one returns to the diversity of one's own heritage to inhabit it more fully. Held within a curriculum, this approach enables students and faculty to become "more deeply rooted." The ability to develop deep and appreciative deep understanding of others, while holding normative commitments, is particularly important in divisive times.

Some of the tangible steps toward the realization of the Emmanuel College mission include a first-semester course, *Introduction to Multireligious Theological Education and Leadership*, and a required elective in Religious Diversity, focused on a tradition other than their own. We have increased the religious diversity of our faculty and worked to connect our programs with resources in the University of Toronto. We have committed resources to spiritual and community life with spaces and programming for each tradition to explore their own practices and regular opportunities to come together. Our new community-based Supervised Pastoral Education units also facilitate practicums in a variety of religious communities as well as in the hospital settings afforded by traditional Clinical Pastoral Education programs.

LOCATING OUR PRACTICE

Being a relative newcomer to multireligious theological education (our first Muslim programs are now a decade old), we had the benefit of earlier models of interfaith learning and self-reflexivity in relation to what Rachel Mikva calls the "waves" of interreligious engagement. Comparing the development of the field with the waves of feminism, she notes that

> one wave does not end precisely as the next one begins. If we think of waves as forces within the ocean that have mass and momentum before they arrive on shore, and which continue to move in the waters after defining their particular outline in the sand, and if we recall that there is never only one wave moving at a time—then we can examine the sequential but not separate waves that emphasize 1) equality, 2) difference, 3) diversity, and 4) intersubjectivity.[6]

Similar to the emphasis on women's equality with men in the fight for voting and labor rights, the first wave of interreligious engagement in the twentieth century included Jews and Catholics on the basis of their similarity to mainline Protestants. The 1893 World's Parliament of Religions was a watershed moment for a universalist view of religion—but largely on Christian terms. An emphasis on commonality resulted in legal protections for some communities, but at the expense of recognition and representation of "lifestances" that "are not sufficiently 'like' the norm."[7] The next wave of the women's movement emphasized women's difference from men, with an essentialized view of "woman" that silenced differences of racialization, class, sexuality, ability, and religion. Similarly, the field of religious studies developed essentialized perceptions of "East" and "West," treated religions as bounded wholes, and continued to frame comparative inquiry in Christian terms. The third wave in each movement began to recognize the internal diversity of the categories. Individuals are no longer expected to represent entire traditions. Interdisciplinary, liberationist, decolonial, and queer methodologies are transforming the field. Hybrid identities and the intersection of religious and other embodied differences have become centered in new ways.[8]

A comparative theological approach centers the strengths of the third wave within theological education. It is content with neither the oppositional definitions of religious difference nor the well-meaning declarations of the sameness of all religions that characterized earlier waves. Rooted in particularity, this methodology preserves both the commitments of the theologian and the particular streams and voices encountered in other traditions. Schools might still assign overviews of religious, spiritual, and wisdom traditions in order to develop religious literacy. A comparative theological approach is an important next step that can introduce greater nuance, contextualization, and self-definition.

Some metaphors for comparative theological work, such as "crossing over" and "crossing back" between traditions, have implied that the boundaries between traditions and identities within and between them are less fluid that they are. The latest generation of comparative theologians are complicating this picture, joining what Mikva describes as a fourth wave. Transposed into the setting of a theological school, a comparative theological orientation will acknowledge how the actual people who arrive there are formed not only by home traditions but by the interaction and encounter with others as well. One of the emphases of the emerging fourth wave is intersubjectivity, which recognizes mutual formation, the intersections of identities within each person, and possibilities of solidarity and relation. Theological studies can thus expand to include a variety of sites of encounter: online, through media and the arts, and in families, as well as through texts and rituals.[9]

Deep understanding for divisive times requires a seriousness of study that fosters interfaith habits of listening, asking informed questions, self-reflection, and openness to transformation. When the waves of division come, it will be not only the longtime interfaith practitioners, but also the leaders emerging from theological schools who will say, "We have been practicing for this."

NOTES

1   Andrea Taylor, "Emmanuel College Midday Prayer—March 24, 2020," quoting Jack Kornfield, *No Time Like the Present* (New York: Atria Books, 2017). https://www.facebook.com/watch/?v=330170544630720. Accessed June 20, 2020.

2   Francis X. Clooney, *Comparative Theology: Deep Learning Across Religious Borders* (West Sussex: Wiley-Blackwell, 2010); *Reading the Hindu and Christian Classics: Why and How Deep Learning Still Matters* (Charlottesville: University of Virginia Press, 2020).

3   Clooney, *Comparative Theology*, 10.

4   Clooney, *Comparative Theology*, 13–14.

5   Emmanuel College. "Vision, Mission, Values & Strategic Plan." https://www.emmanuel.utoronto.ca/about-emmanuel/strategic-plan-mission-and-vision/. Accessed June 15, 2020.

6   Rachel S. Mikva, "Reflections in the Waves: What Interreligious Studies Can Learn from Women's Movements in the U.S.," in *Critical Reflections on Interreligious Education: Experiments in Empathy*, ed. Najeeba Syeed and Heidi Hadsell (Leiden, Netherlands: Brill Rodopi, 2020), 98–124, at 99.

7   Mikva, "Reflections in the Waves," 102.

8   Mikva, "Reflections in the Waves," 106.

9   Mikva, "Reflections in the Waves," 109.

"NOTHING OFF LIMITS"
PEDAGOGICAL REFLECTIONS BY A CHRISTIAN TEACHING CHRISTIANITY AT RABBINICAL SCHOOL

Soren M. Hessler

"I'm so sorry!" responded my friend and colleague the Rev. Dr. Kathryn House to a rabbinical school student. He had just relayed his experience of growing up in the American South, where Southern Baptists and Jehovah's Witnesses had come to his door every few months to ask if he and his family had invited Jesus into their hearts yet, and then harassed them about their mortal condemnation for failing to have done so. This account of a deeply personal, painful experience, shared in the context of a class called Introduction to Christianity (a required class for rabbinical students at Hebrew College) ended with a question: "How do you, as a progressive American Baptist pastor who grew up in fundamentalist and evangelical Southern Baptist circles, continue to relate to Southern Baptist friends and family who may continue to proselytize their Jewish neighbors?"

I had invited Kathryn to the class to talk about how Baptists organize themselves, not to respond to the anti-Semitic tendencies of some members of the broader Baptist community. Nevertheless, she listened patiently to the student's story, and she responded, not in defensiveness, but out of deep and sincere regret. She acknowledged that she might have been one of those people knocking on the student's door in high school, and she shared just how sorry she was for having engaged in that kind of proselytizing.

I spent the next several minutes of class moderating a deeply emotional conversation. Kathryn shared that she takes seriously the command to be reconciled with one another and with God. Therefore, an important part of her ministry life has been helping others understand why her actions had been wrong and inviting them to reflect critically on how they embodied their own Christian faith. She spoke further about the ways that staying connected to her family and the community of her youth engendered challenges and tensions but also provided many opportunities to share about another way of being Christian.

The student was startled by Kathryn's unfiltered and heartfelt response; it was the first time someone had apologized to him for what had happened so often when he was younger. For Kathryn, it was the first time she had directly apologized to someone who had been proselytized. That moment of reconciliation was powerful, but not only for that particular student and for Kathryn. It also changed the thinking of several students about the value of education for interreligious engagement. Several shared after the class and in later course evaluations that facilitating the conditions and creating space for encounters like this one caused them to reevaluate the potential importance of interreligious work in their future rabbinates.

In the summer of 2018, Rabbi Daniel Judson, dean of the Rabbinical School at Hebrew College, and Rabbi Or N. Rose, director of the Betty Ann Greenbaum Miller Center for Interreligious Learning and Leadership at Hebrew College, shared with me that the college, which had embraced Jewish pluralism from its founding, was transforming the rabbinical school curriculum to put religious pluralism more explicitly at the heart of rabbinic learning. As part of that transformation, Rabbi Sharon Cohen Anisfeld, the college's president and former dean of the Rabbinical School, with Or, would launch a new *Introduction to Pluralisms* course as a first-semester requirement for first-year students. January-term intensive introductory courses on Christianity and Islam would be required during the first and second years of rabbinical school. The school already had a robust program equipping students to engage in social and environmental justice and advocacy. These new courses were conceived as a way to better prepare students to engage across lines of religious difference, bridging the work of Jewish communities to broader religious networks. As a Christian minister who had worked for the Miller Center at Hebrew College for five years, who knew the community's values and understood the vocational ambitions and trajectories of its students, I was asked what a Christianity course for rabbinical students might look like.

Recognizing that my experience of Christianity was fairly narrow, especially as a White, heterosexual, cisgender male, ordained in the United Methodist Church, I pitched a course which would feature multiple classroom guests and site visits to represent a breadth of Christian expressions in the greater Boston area. Knowing the value that the Hebrew College community placed upon ordination credentials, I prioritized including a variety of Christian clergy, rather than simply academics or lay persons. My experience with the Hebrew College student body had taught me to expect that students will have had wildly uneven knowledge of, and experience with, Christians. Some may have grown up going to Sunday school at an Episcopal parish with their father, while others have only ever attended Jewish schools and have never set foot in a church. To help draw together these disparate experiences, I designed a "nothing off limits" classroom approach, attempting to provide foundational knowledge while also structuring the classroom for nuanced conversation. My not-so-secret goal was to make a real attempt to answer all the pent-up questions a rabbinical school student may have about Christians and Christianity while also trying to cover the fundamentals of histories, beliefs, and practices of different Christian groups that these students might encounter when working with various Boston Christian communities. Because space is important when teaching about liturgy, community practices, and architecture, I wanted the course's primary meeting place to be a church. That would enable me to lead different parts of the class in different parts of the building, i.e., to center embodied encounter, not only with texts, but also with people and space. Acknowledging the ambitious task of trying to cover Christianity in a week, Sharon, Dan, and Or supported the unusual course approach and provided a small pool of funds to bring guests to the class, which would be held in Boston

University's Marsh Chapel. Without doubt, offering this course has been one of the most meaningful teaching opportunities of my life; furthermore, the context has been more challenging than any other in which I have taught.

Leaning into the Miller Center's emphasis on personal narrative as a basis for building shared understanding and my own affection for the Rev. Dr. Howard Thurman's search for common ground, I begin the course by inviting students to share about their own backgrounds and experiences with Christianity, while sharing something about my own background. I also invite them to ask any initial questions they hope to have answered by the course. Then we break into their *havruta* pairs to read Rabbi Zalman Schachter-Shalomi's reflection on his initial encounter with Thurman in the 1950s from his piece "What I found in the Chapel," in *My Neighbor's Faith: Stories of Interreligious Encounter, Growth, and Transformation*. Most Hebrew College students are already deeply familiar with Reb Zalman, one of the founders of the Jewish Renewal movement; but few are familiar with the Rev. Howard Thurman who, in addition to being the civil rights leader, theologian, academic, and mentor to the Rev. Dr. Martin Luther King Jr, also co-founded the first intentionally racially integrated church in the United States in 1944. Fewer still know that these two important figures in Christianity and Judaism were friends. They learn the story of Zalman initially mistaking Thurman—who was, at the time, dean of Boston University's Marsh Chapel—for the chapel's janitor, Thurman creating space for Zalman to pray in the chapel before classes each morning, Zalman pondering whether his "'anchor chains' are long enough" to be Thurman's student, and Thurman insightfully asking Zalman, "Don't you trust the *ru'ah hakodesh*?" I reveal that the basement chapel where the *havruta* pairs have been discussing this text is the very same place where Thurman had removed a bronze cross and invited Zalman to pray some sixty years prior.

As we discuss Zalman's text, I invite students to name their concerns about the course. At this point in the conversation, someone usually will recount the long history of Christian persecution of Jews and perhaps question why they should be required to learn anything about Christians at all. I do my best to acknowledge the grave harm perpetrated by certain Christians on different Jewish groups over the last two thousand years. I explain that, as we move from introductions into the course content, I will be intentional about beginning at the beginning: for the next session of the day I bring in a New Testament scholar and Christian pastor to discuss the formation of the Christian canon and to contextualize the instances of anti-Judaism contained in the New Testament. The session includes everything from basics about what a "gospel" is, to details about ancient codices, pseudepigraphy, manuscript variations, Athanasius, and Christian theologies of scripture. Occasionally, a student is scandalized by the ease at which the guest and I acknowledge that, for example, several letters purported to be written by Paul probably are not, but remain important to our Christian communities, who also acknowledge that they are not likely written by Paul. Pre-readings for this session include Dr. Adele Reinhartz's "Reflections on My Journey with John," in which she discusses her struggles with the Gospel of John as one who is both a practicing Jew and a scholar whose career has been built on Johannine scholarship, and Dr.

Kwok Pui-lan's "Reading the Christian New Testament in the Contemporary World," which decenters the New Testament from White, Western, Protestant constructions of scripture.[1] It is an overwhelming amount of information, but by the time we break for lunch on the first day, I am pleased to have a student thank me for the "real talk" about the messiness of the Christian tradition.

If the morning goes well, then the stage is set for students to believe and live into my assertion that they can ask anything, that no question is off limits, and that the classroom guests and I will try to give them a straight answer. Over the course of the week, the students go on architectural tours of a neo-Gothic nave and an Orthodox cathedral. They get a crash course in basic Christian vocabulary, explore the typical parts of a Western liturgy, and discuss sacramental theology with a Roman Catholic comparative theologian. The students explore the role and work of a bishop with a bishop; they contrast that with a conversation with a Baptist minister, Kathryn. To consider religious expressions which have emerged from Christianity during the past three centuries, we read the Rev. Abigail Clauhs's particularly accessible and succinct introduction to Unitarian Universalism.[2] The students encounter the practices of hymn singing and journaling. They read "Baptism, Eucharist and Ministry," the landmark document produced by the World Council of Churches in 1982. While the average Christian may never have heard of the document, let alone have read it, I find that, for many rabbinical school students, it is a helpful consensus document conveying the shared beliefs of Orthodox Christians, Roman Catholics, and Protestants. On the last day, we discuss *Nostra aetate* (the Second Vatican Council's Declaration on the Relation of the Church with Non-Christian Religions) and contemporary Christian-Jewish relations.

Throughout the course, we discuss the role of women's leadership in different expressions of Christianity over time and the role of race in American Christianity. Students read selections from the journals of Frances Willard, arguably among the most influential Christian women of the nineteenth century. We discuss her partnership with another woman; we do not ignore the difficult reality of her use of racist, anti-black tropes to further the cause of women's suffrage. We think about depictions of Sojourner Truth's famous *Ain't I a Woman*? speech and her Christian identity, utilizing resources of the Sojourner Truth Project. I commend *Faithfully Feminist: Jewish, Christian, & Muslim Feminists on Why We Stay* and Kathryn's chapter, "Sometimes the Minister is a Girl," as an important source for thinking about finding professional colleagues across traditions who are committed to the role of women's leadership in their traditions.[3] And while my female colleagues are invited to join the class to discuss other topics, they inevitably address how they became women in ministry and the challenges they have experienced. The classroom guests speak honestly about their experiences, their challenges and triumphs, while also sharing their expertise, and often students make personal connections with the guests, recognizing in their Christian counterparts' experiences emerging into ministry aspects of their own rabbinical school journeys.

The students' final project is an essay addressing something about Christianity or a Christian community they believe they still need to know more about in order to be more effective in the rabbinical setting they are, or are going to be, working in. Their research must include an interview with a Christian about their chosen topic. Many class guests are willing to serve as interviewees for these papers, and ultimately some of those outside of the classroom conversations develop into professional relationships. This is one of the unexpected "course outcomes" of a class in Christianity at a rabbinical school: it seeds professional relationships among Jewish and Christian leaders in Boston.

How do I teach about Christianity as a Christian in a rabbinical school context responsibly? I speak openly and honestly. I rely on others to share their own stories. I create place for embodied learning. Most importantly, by looking to the example of treasured elders, Zalman and Thurman, I tread with humility.[4]

NOTES

1   Adele Reinhartz, "Reflections on My Journey with John," in *Ancient Jew Review* (April 11, 2018) https://www.ancientjewreview.com/articles/2018/2/24/reflections-on-my-journey -with-john-a-retrospective-from-adele-reinhartz; and Kwok Pui-lan, "Reading the Christian New Testament in the Contemporary World," *Fortress Commentary on the Bible: The New Testament* (Minneapolis: Fortress Press, 2014), 5–30.

2   Abigail Clauhs, "'The Cathedral of the World': Interconnection in Difference," in *Words to Live By: Sacred Sources for Interreligious Engagement*, ed. Or N. Rose, Homayra Ziad, and Soren M. Hessler (Maryknoll, NY: Orbis Books, 2018), 31–41.

3   Gina Messina-Dysert, Jennifer Zobair, and Amy Levin, eds., *Faithfully Feminist: Jewish, Christian, and Muslim Feminists on Why We Stay* (Ashland, OR: White Cloud Press, 2015)— particularly, Kathryn House, "Sometimes the Minister is a Girl," 188–93.

4   My deep gratitude extends to the Rev. Dr. Robert Allan Hill, Dean of Marsh Chapel, who has made it possible to use Boston University's Marsh Chapel as the home base for the course; it extends as well to the chapel hospitality staff, Mr. Raymond Bouchard and Ms. Heidi Freimanis-Cordts, who have handled so many logistical matters. Similarly, without the administrative support of colleagues at Hebrew College, Ms. Marilyn Stern and Mr. Thomas Reid, this course with its many guest speakers and several site visits would not have been possible in its current incarnation. Finally, this course would not be nearly as successful without the colleagues who have been classroom guests and who provided invaluable feedback. To my colleagues Very Rev. Robert M. Arida, Fr. David Barnes, Dr. Adama Brown-Hathaway, Dr. Jessica Chicka, Mr. Devin Harvin, Bishop Susan W. Hassinger, Rev. Dr. Kathryn House, Rev. Dr. Jennifer A. Quigley, and Dr. Axel Marc Oaks Takács, thank you for also engaging in this "nothing off limits" adventure.

THE ETHICAL TURN IN BIBLICAL STUDIES
ITS RELEVANCE FOR THE CLASSROOM AS AN INTERRELIGIOUS SPACE

Luis Menéndez-Antuña

Why study the New Testament? Although this question is hardly ever posed explicitly in the field, I would like to introduce it as the framing concern in the present essay.[1] Why should academics, ministers, Christians and non-Christians alike care to approach a 2000-year old text with renovated energies? Why, ultimately, care about it?[2] One could broach the subject in a myriad of ways; notwithstanding the lack of sources tackling the question directly, one can surmise that right under the surface of much scholarship exist hints about the reasons why we should be devoting attention to Early Christian writings.[3] As the answers go, we should care because it is important to understand the life and writings of early Christian communities. It is also relevant to appreciate these writings' literary significance or hear the divine whisper between the lines of these revelatory narratives. Historical, literary, and theological responses, respectively, mesh with each other and advocate for the ever-lasting relevance of the New Testament for our times. In theological programs, New Testament courses are usually designed to get students familiarized with the historical roots of the Christian faith while introducing the basic tenets of sound biblical exegesis.[4]

New Testament studies as an academic discipline has long been invested in historicism, particularly in the historical-critical approach. One of the main consequences of such investment is that the criteria that define sound biblical exegesis are based on understanding the original historical, cultural, and literary contexts of New Testament writings. To study the New Testament means to grasp the "original meaning," "the ethos of primordial communities," or "the theology of a certain book," in an attempt to capture authorial intention and its reception in the communities addressed. This historical and literary project, one of many manifestations of what Jonathan Sheehan has termed the "Enlightenment Bible," is indebted—as Stephen Moore and Yvonne Sherwood have argued so vehemently—to ways of performing biblical scholarship tied to enlightenment ideals of objectivism and value-free enquiry.[5] This monopoly of historical criticism has made anachronism the bête noire of biblical studies. Exegetical tools and hermeneutical methods have been particularly invested in fending off biblical scholarship from subjective, presentist, or even theological/confessional concerns. The goal is to bracket present readers' concerns from blemishing the interpretive outcome.[6]

THE ETHICAL TURN IN BIBLICAL STUDIES

Against such a backdrop, some developments in hermeneutical theory and New Testament studies suggest a different kind of ethos and ethics for fulfilling the task of interpretation. This is what I call the "ethical turn," by which I mean a host of approaches, methods, and tools that take contemporary concerns as the starting point for reflecting about the biblical past.[7] Whereas the "Enlightenment Bible" poses an abstracted, neutral, universal reader, the ethical turn pushes the agenda of real "flesh and blood" readers and specific communities of interpretation, each of them with their own ideological agendas. Such a way of performing criticism is particularly invested in addressing the relationship between reader and text, exploring the gaps between present and past communities of interpretation. Rather than being driven by questions about the fixation of the text, sources, composition, and reception in original audiences, the ethical turn focuses on how texts construct and categorize different areas of the human experience. Furthermore, the ethical turn assumes that such a task cannot be pursued without a proper contextualization of those very same concerns in the present. In sum, while traditional historicism fights off presentism, interpretations within the ethical turn take presentism as the springboard for critical hermeneutics. I should notice that this somewhat simplified mapping of the discipline does not imply that both approaches are antagonistic or incompatible. To the contrary, there is mutual fertilization and appreciation; therefore, it is most useful to think of this dichotomy more in terms of a continuum than in terms of a binary.[8]

The eruption of the ethical turn owes much to recent developments in historiography, literary studies, and cultural theory, but also to shifting demographics in the academy. Incorporation of ethnic minorities, women, migrants, and queers, to name just a few, in the production of knowledge has pushed the field to consider new research agendas and rethink previous theoretical and methodological assumptions. Although in the next section I will offer a specific example as it happens in the classroom, let me illustrate briefly how these renovated synergies inform the field. For instance, although the study of sexuality has a long tradition in New Testament studies, the ethical turn has brought attention to how contemporary sexual practices and identities inform both the theory and the analysis of texts. Whereas previously, ancient sexual practices were considered "completely other," the ethical turn proposes a more nuanced view by showing that we can only pose a break with the past if we essentialize the present. In other words, only by taking contemporary mainstream systems of sexuality at face value are we able to establish a break from ancient practices. When we take contemporary queer practices in their full range of possibilities, a new path to explore the connections between queerness in the present and queerness in the past becomes available.[9]

THE NEW CLASSROOM AND THE ETHICAL TURN

Demographics shifts do not only take place among faculty. At Boston University, where I am currently teaching, around forty percent of incoming students self-identify as a sexual minority. The number of women has slowly but consistently increased and so has the number of minoritized students, particularly Latinx and other migrants from the Global South. At a predominantly Methodist school, we also find Roman Catholics (among which I identify), Unitarian Universalists, Jews, Buddhists, and many who do not clearly identify with a denomination or a religious tradition. The vocations are equally diverse: traditional forms of ministry are giving way to chaplaincy, community organizing, and nonprofit work. I would also venture that even among those who are in more "traditional" career paths, their concerns about the Bible are as much doctrinal as ethical.

The Enlightenment Bible is poorly designed to address the kinds of questions such diversity brings to the class. Students, like scholars invested in the ethical turn, are reluctant to leave their embodied identities at the door. For instance, in a world where women's authority is still contested, women in the classroom seek to address how the biblical rhetoric conceptualizes gender but also what kind of arguments and theories enhance their agency and power. Queer students are no longer interested in whether the Bible accepts "homosexuality," but rather what ways are available to interpret the Bible queerly and what traces of queer sexuality we can spot in the biblical texts. In a world burning down around questions of racial inequity, the relevance of ethnic identity in Early Christianity takes new precedence and so do the contemporary political consequences of exploring those ethnic identities. The ethical turn is particularly well equipped here, not only to address such questions, but also to create bridges between contemporary and ancient identities and practices, and discover the modes of engagement that make these ancient texts lively, relevant, and politically responsible in the present.

The ethical turn's emphasis on theorizing the present offers a fertile ground to incorporate other religious traditions. For sure, courses in New Testament still attract mainly self-defined Christians, but it is less rare that we find Muslims, Jews, Buddhists, Unitarian Universalists, Pagans, and Humanists. Such increased diversity brings pedagogical and theoretical challenges. For instance, Jewish scholarship has a well-established trajectory in New Testament studies which has helped the field understand the key figures, Jesus and Paul, in their Jewish matrix.[10] When discussed in the classroom, this scholarship offers a template to avoid all too common supersessionist claims, allowing Christian students to appreciate the Jewish roots of the Christian faith while providing a platform for Jewish participants to express their own faith. Such dialogue not only contributes to a better understanding of contemporary religious identities, it also reframes the ways Christians look at their founding texts. Let me illustrate this ethos of doing biblical interpretation by mentioning a less common way of introducing interreligious dialogue.

Many students are particularly invested in gender equality and they resort to feminist methods and theories to approach biblical texts. Paul's injunctions on women's participation in the assemblies or Jesus' purported treatment of women as equals are some of the favorites.

There is a strong tendency, however, to understand agency and power in individualist terms. As the story goes, women hold power if they are named, are able to contest power, and subvert gender norms. This model assumes that emancipation is only possible when one contests oppressive societal and cultural forms. I am not opposed to these kinds of arguments, but I do think they tend to leave assumptions about personhood unquestioned. Furthermore, they ensue from individualistic, Protestant, notions of subjectivity and formation which are at odds with more community-based understandings of agency. In this case, I find it particularly illuminating to bring in some ethnographical research from the Islamic world. Sabah Mahmood conducted a detailed study of Muslim women in Egypt, and her research compellingly shows how these women construct their agency, not so much in terms of contesting patriarchal norms, but rather by fashioning themselves after a tradition. Mahmood criticizes "western secular feminism" for its "overwhelming tendency . . . to conceptualize agency in terms of subversion or re-signification of social norms, to locate agency within those operations that resist the dominating and subjectivating modes of power."[11] The subject here does not stand in isolation as a free-floating agent invested in contesting norms, but rather it is action and practice that shape agency. Transformation here is not a contestation of norms but a way of engaging norms in a manner that bridges the gap between religious belief and daily praxis. Mahmood's study is complex, and its details are beyond the scope of the present chapter, but her conceptualization of religious practice is most helpful to counteract abstracted, disembodied, and unexamined notions of power. Particularly, it offers students invested in exploring gender in the New Testament the possibility of centering Muslim women's experiences while bracketing liberal notions of resistance. This kind of intercontextual approach not only makes for better history (after all, this conceptualization of agency is closer to first-century anthropological notions), it also pushes against strands of feminism that situate the Muslim world as other.

This might only be an anecdotal example that illustrates ways in which resorting to other religious traditions benefits the interpretation of biblical texts. The ethical turn is particularly welcoming to such cross-fertilization, but proper interreligious hermeneutics is still missing in the study of New Testament. Although it is only natural that theoretical investment in Christian worldviews informs biblical interpretation (after all, most academics and students of Scripture self-identify as Christian), the ethical turn creates a framework where other concerns and perspectives could be incorporated. This is not a call for more traditional topics such as the "synoptic problem" or "the theology of Paul's justification" to be dropped out of the discipline; but it is an invitation to redefine the discipline beyond the constraints of historical-critical understandings and to approach New Testament texts in light of today's global diversity.

NOTES

1   Wayne Meeks' presidential address at the Studiorum Novi Testamenti Societas annual meeting (2004) and Fernando Segovia's presidential address at the Society of Biblical Literature annual meeting (2014) constitute rare exceptions, both examples advocating for quite divergent views on the purpose, task, and telos of the discipline: Wayne A. Meeks, "Why Study the New Testament?" in *New Testament Studies* 51, no. 2 (2005): 155–70; Fernando F. Segovia, "Criticism in Critical Times: Reflections on Vision and Task" in *Journal of Biblical Literature* 134, no. 1 (2015): 6–29.

2   There are also voices claiming that we actually should not care about it. See Hector Avalos, *The End of Biblical Studies* (Amherst, NY: Prometheus Books, 2007).

3   Elizabeth Schüssler Fiorenza, "The Ethics of Biblical Interpretation: Decentering Biblical Scholarship" in *Journal of Biblical Literature* 107, no. 1 (1988): 3–17; Robert J. Hurley, "The Ethics of Biblical Interpretation: Rhetoricizing the Foundations" in *ARC: the Journal of the School of Religious Studies*, McGill University 33 (2005): 384–400.

4   Dale B. Martin, *Pedagogy of the Bible: An Analysis and Proposal* (Louisville: Westminster John Knox, 2008).

5   Jonathan Sheehan, *The Enlightenment Bible: Translation, Scholarship, Culture* (Princeton, NJ: Princeton University Press, 2005); Stephen D. Moore and Yvonne Sherwood, *The Invention of the Biblical Scholar: a Critical Manifesto* (Minneapolis: Fortress Press, 2011).

6   For a compelling critique see Fernando F. Segovia, *Decolonizing Biblical Studies: a View from the Margins* (Maryknoll, NY: Orbis Books, 2000).

7   The bibliography here is too extensive. I offer some references as samples of what I consider works that epitomize this approach: Musa W. Dube, *Postcolonial Feminist Interpretation of the Bible* (Nashville: Chalice Press, 2000); Musa W. Dube, *Other Ways of Reading: African Women and the Bible* (Atlanta: Society of Biblical Literature, 2001); Jin Young Choi, *Postcolonial Discipleship of Embodiment* (New York: Palgrave Macmillan, 2015); Jacqueline M. Hidalgo, *Revelation in Aztlán Scriptures, Utopias, and the Chicano Movement* (New York: Palgrave Macmillan, 2016); Sharon Jacob, *Reading Mary Alongside Indian Surrogate Mothers: Violent Love, Oppressive Liberation, and Infancy Narratives* (New York: Palgrave Macmillan, 2015); Gay L. Byron, *Symbolic Blackness and Ethnic Difference in Early Christian Literature* (London: Routledge, 2008); Erin Runions, *The Babylon Complex: Theopolitical Fantasies of War, Sex, and Sovereignty* (New York: Fordham University Press, 2014); Teresa J. Hornsby and Ken Stone, *Bible Trouble: Queer Reading at the Boundaries of Biblical Scholarship* (Leiden: Brill, 2012); Lynn R. Huber, *Thinking and Seeing with Women in Revelation* (London: Bloomsbury T & T Clark, 2013); Tat-siong Benny Liew and Fernando F. Segovia, *Colonialism and the Bible: Contemporary Reflections from the Global South* (Lanham, MD: Lexington Books, 2018); Gay L. Byron and Vanessa Lovelace, *Womanist Interpretations of the Bible: Expanding the Discourse* (Atlanta: SBL Press, 2016); Candida R. Moss, *Disability Studies and Biblical Literature* (New York: Palgrave Macmillan, 2011).

8   There are, of course, as in most families, bitter rifts. See John J. Collins, *The Bible after Babel: Historical Criticism in a Postmodern Age* (Grand Rapids, MI: Eerdmans, 2010); George Aichele, Peter D. Miscall, and Richard Walsh, "An Elephant in the Room: Historical-Critical and Postmodern Interpretations of the Bible" in *Journal of Biblical Literature* 128, no. 2 (2009): 383–404; Ronald S. Hendel, "Mind the Gap: Modern and Postmodern in Biblical Studies" in *Journal of Biblical Literature* 133, no. 2 (2014): 422–43; Peter D. Miscall, George Aichele, and Richard Walsh, "Response to Ron Hendel" in *Journal of Biblical Literature* 133, no. 2 (2014): 451–58; Stephen D. Moore, "Watch the Target: A Post-Postmodernist Response to Ronald Hendel" in *Journal of Biblical Literature* 133, no. 2 (2014): 444–50. One can sense in some recent work compelling attempts to incorporate the ethical turn into more traditional approaches: Michal Beth Dinkler, *Literary Theory and the New Testament* (New Haven: Yale University Press, 2019); Laura Salah Nasrallah, *Archaeology and the Letters of Paul* (Oxford: Oxford University Press, 2019).

9   See Luis Menéndez-Antuña, "Is There Room for Queer Desires in the House of Biblical Scholarship?: A Methodological Reflection on Queer Desires in the Context of Contemporary New Testament Studies" in *Biblical Interpretation* 23, no. 3 (2019): 399–427.

10   Geza Vermes and Stefan C. Reif, *Jesus the Jew: a Historian's Reading of the Gospels* (London: SCM Press, 2001); Paula Fredriksen, *Jesus of Nazareth, King of the Jews: a Jewish Life and the Emergence of Christianity* (London: Papermac, 2001); Mark D. Nanos, "Paul—Why Bother?: A Jewish Perspective" in *Svensk Teologisk Kvartalskrift* 95, no. 4 (2019): 271–87.

11   Saba Mahmood, *Politics of Piety: The Islamic Revival and the Feminist Subject* (Princeton, NJ: Princeton University Press, 2011), 14.

TEACHING PLURALISM AND RAISING CONSCIENCE
LESSONS FROM A HIGH SCHOOL CLASSROOM

Celene Ibrahim

What if getting an education were about more than learning to think critically about the nature of the world? What if education were about learning frameworks for *critical introspection* about the nature of *ourselves*? If we, as educators, can commit to equipping teens with this skill, perhaps we, as global citizens, can benefit from a rising generation that has truly committed to seeing dignity in all human lives. Conveying basic literacy is indispensable, but the true potential of the classroom in our divisive times lies in discovering fresh ways to make meaning, in facing our limitations and shortcomings with integrity, and in consciously examining how experience conditions us to make sense of our lifeworlds. This experiential learning is valuable at any age, but it is especially deep and impactful for teenagers whose brains are in a profound stage of neural restructuring.

Intellectual spaces designed for negotiating conflicting moral philosophies and navigating divergent political and religious values enable teens to hone their capacities for empathy and self-awareness. Teens grow in analytic capacity, gain social-emotional maturity, and hone the conflict-negotiation skills needed to navigate the divisiveness, biases, and bigotries they will inevitably encounter in their lives. Drawing on my experiences teaching comparative religion, global religious history, and moral philosophy in an institution that is actively grappling with its own identity and relationship to diversity, I offer strategies for inviting conversations on sensitive issues as a means to engender transformative learning.

FACING OUR LEGACIES AND REASSESSING CORE VALUES

A high school that could easily be mistaken for a small liberal arts college, Groton School (est. 1884) is a storied New England boarding school. This is an institution rooted in classical studies with an emphasis on education as a means for character formation. Episcopal in heritage, Groton's curriculum has transformed over the past decades to include less of an emphasis on transmitting Christian mores to teaching a plurality of worldviews and the histories of religious and philosophical encounter, ranging from ancient Mesopotamia, through antiquity, to the contemporary world. We still have time for religious practice built into communal life, a requirement incumbent upon even the most secular-minded and religiously unaffiliated of students—now more than a quarter of our student body—who

120

tend to find a guest home in the burgeoning Buddhist community. Like many of her sister schools, Groton once catered exclusively to White Protestant boys of America's economic elite. This legacy remains, but a different legacy is simultaneously taking root, one that is—were we to be honest—in notable, if not productive, tension with the first.

I am told that the year 1952 marked the admittance of the first Black student, nearly seventy years after the School's founding by the Reverend Endicott Peabody (d. 1944). Fast forward another nearly seventy years from this first Black student, and the incoming cohort is closer to fifty percent students of color, a number that is bolstered by robust recruiting in Asia and a growing presence of African and African-heritage students. A successful effort to make the Groton experience accessible to students of all socioeconomic backgrounds has been a flagship priority of the school's board and current head, Temba Maqubela, the first non-White head of school, a South African with close family connections to Nelson Mandela and the anti-apartheid movement and with longstanding commitments to racial, ethnic, and socioeconomic school integration. With a student body of fewer than four hundred, the School has a hefty endowment of approximately that same number in millions and is backed by a donor base that has gallantly taken up the charge of expanding financial aid.

The large marble busts of great Western figures lining the schoolhouse walls is now short Columbus, who was doused in red paint one fateful night and never reinstated. Word is that the collection of White men is soon to be augmented, thanks to unrelenting student efforts, by the company of Rosa Parks, Nelson Mandela, Mahatma Gandhi, and former US First Lady Eleanor Roosevelt (whose family counts a dozen or more Groton graduates). The busts collection is a physical reminder of the gargantuan task of achieving equity of representation alongside the veneration of tradition. From racial inclusion, to the integration of more international students, to non-Protestant identifying students, to young women (and now non-cisgender students), to students who come from middle- and lower-income backgrounds, student-body demographics today offer quite a different picture from the early twentieth-century photos hanging on its walls. The tensions latent in this transformation cannot be captured as obviously in a photograph.

For my part, I am very aware of myself as a Muslim faculty member in these spaces, especially one who is rendered visible by my headscarf. My own daughter is likely the first Groton School hijabi (now there is an item of embossed apparel missing from the school store!). Almost every morning, faculty and staff attend worship in the School's impressive Gothic revival chapel, a service that includes gorgeous organ preludes, prayers, and traditional hymns, but notably absent communion and most talk of Christ. In lieu of a sermon, the service features reflections on moral themes and questions of life purpose by a rotating cast of students, faculty, alumni, trustees, and occasionally an outside guest. The whole experience is reminiscent of a TED-style talk overlaid on Protestant worship. "Where High Episcopalian Liturgy Encounters Secular Humanism," could easily be our chapel's tagline. We may be located in a town that insists on maintaining "Crusaders" as its moniker, but even as we remain peripherally grounded in a Christian identity, the school is necessarily reorienting toward this heritage in the name of inclusion. Still, peculiarities remain: for instance, all faculty (irrespective of personal religious commitment) are required to attend the school's Christmas worship "Lessons and Carols," a festive service I might well attend of my own volition, were it not already a job expectation.

Such expressions of the School's historic identity are kept alive by a strong alumni presence and the living memory of the many faculty who have served the school for decades. As with many institutions, national conversations have given momentum to the diversity and inclusion work that was previously happening on a smaller scale, driven by faculty and students of color and allies. As faculty cohorts, we have begun plugging into national conversations on White supremacy more vigorously by discussing how to relate to the legacy of our institution in honest and open ways and how to help ourselves and our students address issues of equity. What would Rev. Peabody think of *me* teaching biblical history or the work of Audre Lorde in my ethics courses? Yet, what better place than my ethics and religion classes to examine systems of oppression and delve into the tandem work of increasing religious and cultural literacy?

TEACHING WHEN "LIFE" IS THE TEST

In my first year in this institution, I have been experimenting in my classroom with teaching and dialogue techniques, many of them passed down to me by cherished mentors and colleagues, that have worked particularly well in opening up spaces for authentic exchange and transformative learning across the differences of identity and experience. I want students to become invested in issues of public value, to be sensitive to the ways in which global issues impact individual human beings, to have confidence discussing topics that are taboo because of their potential to cause conflict or shame, and to learn to craft their personal views, narratives, and identities in ways that consider both their own social location and the experiences of those in drastically different situations.

Working as I do with academic high-achievers who are often left stone-faced and exhausted from too great an emphasis on extrinsic forms of achievement, teaching for me is about developing skills for deep listening and promoting introspection. It is not only about teaching how to engage multiple perspectives on philosophical and moral issues, but it is also about discovering the aptitude to engage our gut and emotional responses to such issues. In addition to mastering how to select the correct multiple-choice bubble, I want to teach my teens to walk away from their high school experience knowing that it is okay to not have all the answers. One of my favorite answers to an end-of-term survey this spring that elicited meta-reflections on their personal course takeaways was: "I learned how much I didn't know."

The students overwhelmingly appreciate the spirit of this approach. Most, although not all, students really do want to grapple with notions of privilege and equity and to think about how their perspectives on issues are contingent upon their particular set of life experiences. I often find myself prompting, "Do you still think you would have that view if you were. . . ."

This approach leads to moments in which students can appreciate how their prerogatives are not necessarily normative to the larger human experience. This may seem somewhat obvious, but many assumptions about what is normative must actually be unlearned, and this process of encountering philosophical or identity difference can be disorienting. The analogies that come to mind are someone operating a car with the steering wheel on the opposite side for the first time, or someone who has not been raised multilingual realizing that an object has a vast array of names. I regularly witness my students encountering epistemic difference and then having to either account for it within their preexisting intellectual frameworks or shift their frameworks significantly. Part of why I love teaching is that I am also regularly having these growth moments, too.

In my classrooms, I draw upon the "theme-center interaction" pedagogical model by social psychologist, psychotherapist, and educator Ruth Cohn (d. 2010), as introduced to me by feminist theologian Elisabeth Schüssler-Fiorenza. Cohn put forth dynamic, non-hierarchical models for groups to relate to knowledge creation and transmission. In practical application, this means that I may be the designated instructor for the course, but I am not the gatekeeper of all knowledge. Similar insights can be found too in the reflections on teaching of the prolific writer and educator Parker Palmer, who speaks frequently about holding the tension and sitting with paradox. This model requires conscientious vulnerability and co-created learning. Rather than seizing too much time to pontificate, sometimes a more generative moment is opened by prompting gently with thorny questions and then unpacking together the elicited reactions.

I guide my students to become content creators, and sometimes they choose areas of focus that stretch my horizons too. We work on projects such as peer-edited op-eds and podcasts as a way of thinking about public voice. Such projects require meta-cognition and attention to intended real-world audiences and communities of accountability. I see our class conversations on contentious issues continuing passionately in lunch lines and in dorm check-in times. I worry sometimes that I will be seen by my colleagues or administration as stirring a pot, but as one forty-year veteran teacher of the School reassured me: "It's *your job* to make them think—you're not going to get fired for doing it." I am reminded of a lesson from Katie Orenstein, OpEd Project founder: "If you say things of consequence, there might be consequences. The alternative is to be inconsequential." I do not want to be an inconsequential teacher.

Contentious issues need a strong holding container. I teach and try to model non-violent communication methods, including ways of speaking that convey ownership of our emotions, nonjudgmental descriptions of situations, and proposals for mutual commitments to resolve conflicts. I ask students to brainstorm different conflict-generating scenarios, we role-play them, and we think about how to communicate to tease out workable resolutions. We discuss how to know when we should stand firm in our values and when and how to compromise. We need to practice navigating practical relationships before we delve headfirst into Kant or Confucius.

The lines of the poem "An Invitation to Brave Space," by racial justice advocate Mickey ScottBey Jones, are my starting place:

> We amplify voices that fight to be heard elsewhere,
>
> We call each other to more truth and love.
>
> We have the right to start somewhere and continue to grow.
>
> We have the responsibility to examine what we think we know.

Following this framework passed on to me from the Reverend Jennifer Bailey, I invite students into a "brave space"; this invitation to take intellectual risks is accompanied by my request that we be generous and patient with one another. If we are unsure about the intentions behind someone's statement, rather than assume intentions—good or bad, we commit to using language that opens up conversation in a non-defensive way: "Help me understand why...." Giving a chance for clarification is sometimes helpful: "I heard you saying that...; did I understand you correctly?" Another question for the back pocket, one I first heard masterfully used when co-teaching with interfaith educator Jennifer Howe Peace, can be a powerful invitation for the sharing of personal experience: "What in your life experience has led you to that belief?"

To build empathy and situational intelligence, in both my religion and ethics courses we work on case studies—a teaching method introduced to me by Diana Eck and Ellie Pierce at Harvard's Pluralism Project. We even write and play out fictional case simulations. In my religion course, we discuss what wisdoms the stories in the traditions we study hold for us, as individuals and as a learning community. This way of engaging traditions allows students to intellectually step in and out of perspectives while thinking about the personal relevance of the new knowledge. For instance, after we had studied some Daoist philosophy and practice, my religion students implored me to start our classes with a bit of qi gong, which was led by a young man from Beijing who recalled his grandmother's practice. The text of our books becomes intertwined with the text of our lives.

After a term of these kinds of exercises, I can see that students have a greater ability to empathize with people from different identities and life situations and can see issues from more angles. To me, a vibrant classroom is one where peer networks are strong, where difficult and controversial subjects are regularly raised, and where intellectual risk-taking is encouraged and affirmed. This requires regular reflection on our own stereotypes, misconceptions, limits, and biases. I still have a note from a young woman of color who was a force on the basketball court but who was noticeably reticent to speak in class. However, partway through the year—and to the initial visible surprise of her peers—she began jumping in with perspectives grounded in her unique life experiences. "Thank you, Dr. Ibrahim," reads the note, "I feel like I have found my voice...."

For many of our "Generation Z" students, moral reasoning is not about analyzing totalizing abstract theory, and religion is not about blind allegiance to dogma. Morality and spirituality are about trying to figure out how to show up in the world with integrity and authenticity. As I jest with my interminably grade-conscientious students: "Life is the final exam."

THIS EMERGENT OCCASION
ON STUDYING INTERFAITH LEADERSHIP
IN TIMES OF CRISIS

Lucinda Allen Mosher

In 1623, the great metaphysical poet John Donne composed an extended theological reflection on a grave illness from which he had come close to dying. He called this multi-part prose work *Devotions on Emergent Occasions*; and, given his fondness for wordplay, it is reasonable to presume that in his use of the term, "emergent" carries the sense both of "budding or developing" and of "being an emergency." In both senses, it is a term that well described Hartford Seminary's circumstances in March 2020. Due to the rapid, global spread of the novel coronavirus, we were in the midst of a situation that was extremely fluid and evolving; an occasion that truly was an emergency. The writing was on the wall in big letters: all Summer Term courses would need to be online; it was morally imperative that one of those courses address the sensitive nature of this unique moment in history. I had copious experience in online instruction. Would I be willing to develop and teach such a course? Could it deal with mass casualty situations of all sorts? Could it incorporate the literature of lament? Could it somehow include lessons about and from monastic traditions for this season of pandemic lockdown? Could we post a preliminary syllabus by tomorrow? Sometimes, an "emergent occasion" is nothing if not the budding and developing of new possibilities. I was being offered an opportunity that would make fresh use of my decades of extensive research, practical experience, writing, and teaching about religious manyness, leadership, and chaplaincy. Of course, I said "yes." What follows here is an explanation of design, implementation, and outcome of *Interfaith Leadership in Times of Crisis*.

As an asynchronous, online intensive course, *Interfaith Leadership in Times of Crisis* would run for six weeks (May 18–June 26, 2020), with each week meant as equivalent to a bit more than two weeks of a typical semester-long course. It would be thorough, demanding, concentrated! (Indeed, the metaphor of drinking knowledge from a firehose would be apt: students could expect to be drenched with information and activities.) Given the imposition of a pandemic lockdown as my planning began, it would require e-books only. I chose two: my own *Personhood, Illness, and Death in America's Multifaith Neighborhoods: A Practical Guide* (2018) and *Disaster Spiritual Care*, Second Edition, edited by Willard W. C. Ashley Sr. and Stephen B. Roberts (2017). As for content-organizing principles, the calendar provided the first: six instructional modules, one for each of the six weeks. I then had a choice to make. One approach would have me cordon off each topic, allotting a week to each. Accordingly, we might spend a week on multifaith literacy without mentioning leadership or disaster preparedness; monasticism would have a module of its own. Another approach would require each module to be multi-dimensional. I would take this latter option: a multi-textured, multi-hued module for each week:

1. *Overview* (a first look at the course's key terms, themes, topics, resources, and methods);

2. *Interfaith Leadership and Collaboration* (characteristics, skills, concrete strategies, principles, obstacles; religion-based rationales; religion-informed attitudes toward healthcare);

3. *In Times of Crisis* (death in multifaith perspective, spiritual caregiving in times of great stress, disaster response);

4. *At a Distance* (physical distancing and the social contract; mourning, lament, complaint; solace)

5. *Making the Most of Blue Sky Time* (disaster preparedness, remembrance, lessons learned from trauma, cultivation of hope);

6. *Resilience* (its connection to creativity, divergent thinking, entrepreneurship, and courage).

Under each of these headings, the course website offered a page of navigation instructions, an introductory lecture by me, other things to watch or read, informal and formal discussion-forums, and a short video (posted on Sunday night) in which I would comment on the week's progress.

In each module, each of the course's three essential categories—interreligious studies, leadership studies, "times of crisis" studies—were present and often tightly intertwined. Further, just as multifaith literacy (its development or improvement) was a concern in every module, so too would self-care (its rationales and methods). Relatedly, every module provided prayers, scripture, poetry, or music for reflection and inspiration—plus at least one lesson about "practitioners of solitude" (that is, Jews, Christians, Muslims, Hindus, and Buddhists who embrace "alone-ness" as a spiritual discipline).[1]

The close of Module Two coincided with the eruption of widespread civil unrest in reaction to the murder of George Floyd while in Minneapolis police custody.[2] What had already been true was now blatantly obvious: we were in the midst of—not one pandemic, but two. We were dealing, not just with the pervasiveness of the novel coronavirus, but also with the insidiousness of systemic racism and White immunity. Immediately, the syllabus pivoted. It was an easy move; for this course had never been only about COVID-19. In fact, the original design of the third module served the moment precisely, needing only modest adjustment to study materials (chief among them being Hartford Seminary panel discussions and chapel sermons) and retooling of some discussion prompts.[3]

Over six weeks, more than forty enrollees on four continents took in nearly two dozen lectures (mostly by me, but also by several other scholars—whom they received graciously and enthusiastically). They dug into our two textbooks. They attended to journal articles, blogs, multi-media objects, poetry, scripture, and devotional literature. They commented on a formal case-study that, at intervals, they analyzed from different angles.[4] Over the six weeks, music (song, especially) played an important role. I opened some of my lectures by singing. I posted compositions that somehow commented on the themes of the moment.[5] Each had its fans. However, grabbing students' hearts more so than any other piece was the profoundly moving five-cello arrangement of Henry Purcell's "Dido's Lament" performed by Yves Dharamraj in tribute to George Floyd and other victims of police violence.[6]

Module upon module, the class had explored numerous intertwining topics in pursuit of answers to questions such as these:

- In times of great stress, to what spiritual resources do we and our neighbors of other lifeways turn?

- What are we to do when access to those resources is disrupted?

- How can faith-based leaders provide comfort, hope, and cautious wisdom with integrity when anxiety, grief, fear, or demands for physical distancing threaten to overwhelm or isolate?

- When great loss exacerbates bigotry and blaming, what actions can we take?

- What sorts of interfaith collaboration have proven effective?

- How does intentional practice of solitude differ from imposed isolation, and what lessons for our current situation can we draw from its exemplars?

During our six weeks together, we did entertain answers to all of these and more. The use of VoiceThread as a delivery tool provided students with a means for immediate response, in the moment, to my lectures. (Think of the chat option in use during a webinar or Zoom call.) Questions could be posed as they arose. The discussion forum tool encouraged deeper reflection before speaking. Whether it was a low-stakes query or a complex request for an essay summarizing an entire module, many of students laid out their ideas and analyses time and again in elegant prose, then responded to their classmates' posts with substance and clarity. (Think of Facebook at its best.) Use of such tools are typical attributes of online courses. What distinguished this course was the degree of engagement with prayers, poetry, and examples of the practice of solitude alongside textbooks, journal articles, blogs, documentaries, and scholarly presentations.

Each module included a prayer or poem meant both as a spiritual resource generally and a comment on that module's theme. Some modules had several. In their reflections on the course as a whole, it was clear that a number of these prayers and poems were now treasured spiritual care resources. Among them was Jan Richardson's "Blessing When the World Is Ending," penned in response to the Pulse night-club shooting.[7] This poet's emphatic refusal to offer "false comfort" rang true for many class participants; but so did the pronouncement of Julian of Norwich, in her book *Showings of Divine Love,* that "Sin is behovely, yet all shall be well, and all shall be well, and all manner of things shall be well." It would seem that not just a few of them have joined me in inhabiting the dynamic tension between the wise words of these two women.

Mention of Julian provides opportunity to reiterate that a constant claim throughout this six-week term was that, during this season of pandemic-induced lock-down, we have something to learn from representatives of Christian, Islamic, Jewish, Buddhist, and Hindu hermit traditions who have chosen isolation, separation, alone-ness. As the course neared its end, some students expressed the truth of this, whatever their circumstances during the pandemic lockdown. While among us were individuals who had been isolated (or nearly so) for many weeks, others, as parents of toddlers or school-aged children, were enduring too much togetherness. Those in the latter category were heartened to discover that some of our exemplars modeled the creation of solitude in the midst of a busy community.

A final unifying factor in this course was a direct product of my initial educational design decision not to silo the core themes, but rather to let each have a life of its own throughout the course: every module was replete with serendipitous intersections. For example, one student mentioned watching two visually compelling videos back-to-back. In the first, the esteemed Thich Nhat Hanh commented on Buddhism's Great Bell Chant while the camera panned the Himalayas in their spaciousness and grandeur; in the second, Amina Chaudry documented houses of worship that had been shut down by efforts to control the novel coronavirus.[8] Whereas the first portrayed cosmic presence and super-abundance but almost no people, the second portrayed interior spaces deemed "sacred" yet now proclaimed empty by virtue of the lack of people in them. He had found the juxtaposition was fascinating!

To cap their learning during this six-week intensive course, enrollees were to create and share something relevant to leadership in times of crisis that was meaningful to themselves personally or useful to the community they serve. The results were stunning! Among them were illustrated lectures, case studies, a training manual, meditation-guides, poems, musical performances, paintings, photography, collages, videos, liturgies. Several students designed (and even conducted) memorial services for COVID-19 victims. Many created art with a Black Lives Matter theme. One student constructed a multi-media resource for a twenty-minute exercise of lament for use by individuals or groups. Using the six stages of the "disaster life cycle" as her framework, another student composed a set of poems, reflections, and writings in other genres. She envisioned this as a series of discussion-starters when working with a group; but it could also facilitate a self-guided meditation. A rabbi made a video in which she demonstrated the ritual of Havdalah that concludes the weekly observance of Shabbat, reworked as a rite of re-entry into ordinary life when pandemic restrictions finally end.

Having bonded within the first few days of the course, this learning community of academics, physicians, and schoolteachers; military personnel and people working in the corporate, small-business, and not-for-profit worlds; imams, rabbis, and Christian clergy; chaplains or chaplains-in-training in hospitals, assisted living and hospice facilities, prisons, universities, and schools; retirees, first-career people, and folks in-between now delighted in each other's offerings by posting supportive and substantive comments that were a pleasure to read. Indeed, it had been that way for the entire six weeks. As they (a Buddhist, a Hindu, a Quaker, a Baptist, a Methodist, a Catholic, an Orthodox Christian, several Unitarian-Univeralists, many Congregationalists, at least as many Episcopalians, Muslims, and Jews—plus others) interacted with each other and with me, they had been consistently congenial, insightful, determined. This course had been about multifaith literacy. Indeed, most reported increased fluency with the ideas, practices, and vocabulary of other religions; but they could also see that, as one woman put it, development of multifaith literacy is a lifelong enterprise. This course had been about leadership. However, just as this course had been asynchronous, so too had been our relationship as a group to "leading" (especially "interfaith leading"). As the course ended, several—empowered by our lessons on asset-assessment and team-building—set out on new trajectories. Yet it had also proven important to affirm that not everyone who studies "leadership" need be or aspire to be a "leader" per se. One woman found that assurance liberating. This course had also been about self-care. In their final reflections, many noted how surprised they had been by that emphasis—and how grateful. "I am nearing graduation," one said; "this is the first course I've taken that I did not want to end."

The uniqueness of the strange season during which this course took place was not lost on this community of learners. "We normally study these things after the fact," one student noted. Instead, "we're reading about social distancing while socially distant; as we're studying the literature of lament, I'm recognizing my own desperate need for solace." Another called the course "an amazing opportunity to study about interfaith leadership *for* times of crisis *in* a time of multiple crises." After six demanding weeks, it was clearer now: this course may have been born out of a pandemic lockdown, but it had never been only about COVID-19; it was also about justice and safety, high risk versus immunity, privilege and lack. Clearer now as well was that the foreseeable future would be one in which multifaith fluency, competency in disaster preparedness and response, and access to a range of approaches to spiritual care would indeed be useful. The next emergent occasion would find us better prepared.

NOTES

1   Our exemplars included practitioners of the Hindu sannyasin tradition; the Desert Mothers and Fathers of the third through fifth centuries, Julian of Norwich (c. 1345–c. 1417), and others of the Christian hermit tradition; Rabbi Nahman of Bratslav (1772–1810) from the Jewish contemplative tradition; Buddhists Thich Nhat Hanh and Jetsunma Tenzin Palmo; and Muslims Rabi'a of Basra (c. 714–801) and Bediuzaman Said Nursi (1877–1960).

2   Evan Hill, et al., "How George Floyd Was Killed in Police Custody," *New York Times*, May 31, 2020, https://www.nytimes.com/2020/05/31/us/george-floyd-investigation.html.

3   The Hartford Seminary offerings addressing systemic racism were:

•   Professor Shanell T. Smith's HartSem Chapel sermon, "Show Me Your Hands!" June 3, 2020, https://www.youtube.com/watch?v=UPcLdp6eM0Y&fbclid=IwAR3Tag1JU0Oq 4kSkVxHKtQ-vBLQp70tcsz_q9qBxvzcLXg_Axkd2yBZdrIE.

•   *Where Do We Go from Here: A Conversation for Faith Leaders* with the Rt. Rev. Dr. Benjamin Watts, Director of the Black Ministries Program at Hartford Seminary, and an interfaith panel speaking about racial justice, posted June 5, 2020, https://www.youtube .com/watch?v=IRsD86GRKew/.

•   *A Discussion Around Chaplaincy, Racial Violence and Healing – A Community Crisis Response*, posted June 10, 2020. https://www.youtube.com/watch?v=jeZs84j4oc8.

•   Hartford Seminary Chapel Sermon by Professor Benjamin Watts, June 10, 2020, https://www.youtube.com/watch?v=j_Wf3xEsOBE.

•   *Conversation with Beverly Daniel Tatum: Where Do We Go from Here?* moderated by the Rt. Rev. Dr. Benjamin Watts, Director of the Black Ministries Program at Hartford Seminary, posted June 12, 2020, https://www.youtube.com/watch?v=R_ OvgfUwt5U&feature=youtu.be.

To these I added the sermon preached by the Rev. Dr. William J. Barber II at the Washington National Cathedral on June 14, 2020: https://www.youtube.com/watch?v=eviTAayTGT4.

I had already provided a link to Trevor Noah, "George Floyd, Minneapolis Protests, Ahmaud Arbery & Amy Cooper" from *The Daily Social Distancing Show,* May 29, 2020, https://www .youtube.com/watch?v=v4amCfVbA_c&feature=emb_title.

4   We used *Showing Up for Shabbat*, about a mass shooting at Pittsburgh's Tree of Life Synagogue (October 2018), written by Ellie Pierce for the Case Initiative of Harvard University's Pluralism Project: https://pluralism.org/showing-up-for-shabbat.

5   One example: "Resilience," words and music by Abbie Betinis (St. Paul, MN, 2017), as performed by the University of North Florida Chamber Singers, posted January 21, 2018. https://www.youtube.com/watch?v=jB6c6aOGEGY.

6   "I Can't Breathe: Cellist Performs Dido's Lament for Black Lives Matter Protest," posted June 5, 2020. https://www.youtube.com/watch?v=JMSuKqLYsgI&feature=share&fbclid=I- wAR0yXqWIB2D8kKGZuQwUAAisjZcoNl2wi8RAf5DM8HZkOwrZNWO0rjHAQI0. Also receiving high marks was Drew Drake's performance of his "Lament: Searching My Rage," Posted June 8, 2020. http://www.ifyc.org/article/lament-searching-my-rage./

watch?v=JMSuKqLYsgI&feature=share&fbclid=IwAR0yXqWIB2D8kKGZuQwUAAisjZ-coNl2wi8RAf5DM8HZkOwrZNWO0rjHAQI0.

7   Jan Richardson, "Blessing When the World Is Ending," from *Circle of Grace: A Book of Blessings for the Seasons* (Orlando, FL: Wanton Gospeller Press, 2015). https://paintedprayerbook .com/2016/07/18/blessing-when-the-world-is-ending/.

8   Thich Nhat Hanh, The Great Bell Chant (The End of Suffering), posted October 28, 2012, https://www.youtube.com/watch?time_continue=6&v=F1ZwaEzMtJw&feature=emb_title; Amina Chaudhry, Emptying Sacred Spaces. https://vimeo.com/401158817/ff89587a9a. Accessed July 25, 2020.

INTERFAITH PLACE-MAKING IN THE ACADEMIC LANDSCAPE
RELIGION AND CONFLICT TRANSFORMATION

Judith Oleson

Many Schools of Theology have established an Interreligious Study Center in order to conduct research, teach, share religious practices, and develop interreligious initiatives in the larger community. Although not an Interreligious Study Center *per se*, the mission of The Tom Porter Program on Religion and Conflict Transformation (RCT) is to "prepare religious leaders to become a resource for peace in a multi-cultural, multi-faith world." An understanding of pluralism is foundational to peacemaking. RCT is a program within Boston University School of Theology (STH), which is ecumenical and is associated with the Methodist Church. RCT collaborates with many of its faculty across disciplines, but few faculty members at STH represent diverse religious traditions. Thus, several years ago, RCT invited five scholars/practitioners (from outside the University) representing Buddhist, Jewish, Islamic, and Christian religious traditions to serve as Visiting Researchers.

In the Summer 2015 edition of *Journal of Interreligious Studies*, Diana Eck, Director of the Pluralism Center at Harvard Divinity School, wrote:

> If pluralism is about relationship-building across lines of difference, it is also about placemaking, that is, creating a new sense of place in a diverse and changing landscape. Whitney Barth explores this aspect of pluralism: the importance of the local, of place and context in relationship building. . . . What are some of the ways in which the relationship building that is critical to interfaith initiatives can also be "place-making"?[1]

What follows here documents a form of "place-making," a consultation model that was developed not only to advise the RCT program from an interfaith, inter-cultural perspective, but to practice pluralism in a local context. It was the desire and intent of RCT's leadership to create an interreligious and intercultural "new sense of place" within their academic landscape.

Officially invited to campus by the Academic Dean, the scholars of the "Visiting Researcher" program conduct research, and research-informed practice, from outside of the University. Historically speaking, Visiting Researchers have a loose association, entailing a photo and bio on a department website and occasional opportunities to interact with faculty and students. Initially, the RCT Visiting Researchers were invited to meet together once each semester. After one session, this group chose to gather monthly to share their work as it intersects with their respective faiths and core values around conflict transformation. They agreed to utilize a peer consultation model, where one person would present in depth and then seek feedback and suggestions from the group. For the past two years, they have met monthly to share their research, theologies, spiritual practices, convictions, and actions in their respective communities.

The RCT program was founded almost twenty years ago to equip religious and community leaders in addressing deep divides in our institutions and larger systems. Utilizing the term "conflict transformation," the RCT program assumes that conflict is normal and that it can be transformational. The RCT program acknowledges religion as both a source of conflict and a powerful resource for peace. Learning from leaders of diverse religious traditions is essential to RCT's mission. Teaching skills such as dialogue, mediation, dispute resolution, and restorative justice methods prepares graduate and doctoral students for the concrete work of transforming conflict. The Visiting Researchers were invited by the RCT program for religious and cultural diversity, but also for their unique capacity to facilitate conflict transformation both within their traditions and in their larger communities.

> *Fatehmeh Haghighatjoo* is a Shia Muslim, reformist and a former member of the Iranian Parliament. She is a leading advocate for a civil, democratic society in Iran, one that grants freedom of speech and human rights, including women's rights, academic freedom, and a free press. Before entering politics, Dr. Haghighatjoo was a psychologist, holding professorships at Tehran University and Shahid Beheshti University. She has authored a book entitled *Search for Truth* (published in Persian in 2002), and is a co-founding chair of the Nonviolent Initiative for Democracy, Inc.

> *Duncan Hollomon* has been a psychotherapist for the past twenty-five years, integrating spiritual practice and mindfulness. A student of Buddhism most of his adult life, Dr. Hollomon is currently exploring the Christian faith. Previously, he was a professional actor/singer and attorney. He has taught theories and practices of psychotherapy for more than seven years, as well as leadership, mindful communication, and dialogue. His current research is on "relational knowing," drawing on spirituality, neuroscience, and developmental psychology. He is an adjunct professor at Antioch College.

Rabbi David Jaffe is the Principal and Founder of Kirva Consulting, which makes Jewish spiritual wisdom accessible to leaders, change-makers and seekers to build healthy, sustainable communities, organizations and relationships. Rabbi Jaffe's current focus is the Inside Out Wisdom and Action Project, which helps social change leaders integrate applied Jewish ethics and applied Jewish mysticism to the work of social justice. He is the author of *Changing the World from the Inside Out: A Jewish Approach to Personal and Social Change* (Trumpeter 2016), winner of the National Jewish Book Award.

Rev. Irene Monroe is an ordained Christian minister, motivational speaker and African American lesbian feminist theologian. She is a *Huffington Post* blogger with a syndicated religion column and describes her columns as an interdisciplinary approach drawing on critical race theory, African American, queer and religious studies. Rev. Monroe is a founder and now member emeritus of several national LGBTQ+ black and religious organizations. Her papers are at the Schlesinger Library at Radcliffe College's Research Library on the History of Women in America. She co-hosts the podcast and WGBH standing segment, ALL REV'D UP.

Bob Stains maintains a private conflict transformation practice, serving organizations in the US and around the globe. He is also a Senior Associate at Essential Partners (formerly, Public Conversations Project) and for twenty-five years has created constructive conversations on sexual orientation, religion, race, abortion, social class, gender, firearms, and other divisive issues within and between local, national, and international organizations. He has trained over 30,000 people in dialogue, conflict resolution, and communication skill-building and has worked with clients from across the US and seventeen other countries. Stains is an active Episcopalian with Roman Catholic and Evangelical roots.

From a theological perspective, the study of religion and conflict transformation emphasizes relationships. Creating space for relationship building as well as intellectual exchange among the Visiting Researchers was essential. RCT draws on the circle process,[2] one of several tools that facilitates respectful, honest speech and deep listening. The skills of appreciative inquiry and creating collective ritual are often included. Utilizing aspects of the circle process, RCT Visiting Researchers moved beyond academic performance to a dialogue that permeated mutual inquiry, empathy, and respect.

The commitment of these Visiting Researchers raises the following questions: What are the more nuanced connections that invigorate and challenge scholars of different faiths to come together on an ongoing basis? What motivates busy leaders/scholars in their own respective traditions, to take time for interfaith conversations? What have these participants experienced together that has created a "new sense of place?" Here are responses from the Visiting Researchers to similar questions about their experience together.

In what ways has the group been meaningful for you?

- The qualities I have seen manifested in the group are generosity and kindness. The Visiting Researchers are there for each other when they ask help in their journeys as scholars and activists.

- I have deeply appreciated having a group of kindred spirits as colleagues with whom to gather in a sacred circle. We all "walk the talk" in our own particular ways.

- I appreciate getting the chance to learn with and from such a brilliant and accomplished group of spiritual seekers and leaders. The fellowship among the group has been the most meaningful thing. I feel like I could call on anyone in this group for personal or professional needs.

- I appreciated the rich dialogue across different faith perspectives. The group has been affirming in my doing public theology.

- I am deeply grateful—and honored—to have been part of this group. While I am involved in other interfaith activities, in none of them am I co-wrestling with important issues like we do in our group. Nor do I get the chance to be with people who are deeply involved in the complexities of scholarship as well as practice.

In what ways has interacting with colleagues from a faith different from your own, been instructive?

- I have enjoyed being part of a very diverse experiential faith-based group which has enriched me in many ways. The group members' main qualities are authenticity and openness, allowing themselves to dive deeply in exploring relationships with Allah/God/Source, self and others and devote themselves in this triangle.

- Having the opportunity to learn from folks of other faiths has provided a larger context for religious belief and spiritual practice. Being in close proximity to those who are sophisticated and diligent about their religious practices challenges me not only to expand my understanding, but also to empathize, to feel kindredship beyond what I might have imagined. The diversity of the group has been a bonus—in terms of background, personality, ethnicity, and gender, to reference some of the more obvious areas of uniqueness and difference.

- So much of my time and life is spent immersed in Jewish community. It is both refreshing and challenging to confront Christian paradigms of thought and practice. I need to do some translation into my own faith's language, but more striking is when I need to acknowledge that a concept or way of being is simply different and doesn't completely translate. This is a difficult yet enriching experience.

- All have given me a deeper insight of the similarities and complexities of their callings guided by good faith principles.

- I've probably learned the most actionable faith-based things from David, from his teaching of the Baal Shem Tov and the social implications of mystical Judaism.

How has the group process of presenting, listening, and feedback been helpful to you?

- The structure of monthly presentations allows for "breathing room," a spaciousness for contemplation, listening and mutual learning.

- This has been incredibly helpful. I was able to share my desires and hopes and concerns with our group and get such helpful feedback about how to design an interview process for my leadership cohort that helped it successfully launch last year. I also learn so much from others' presentations.

- The group has been, for me, the most instructive and engaging when projects were presented

- Really, really rich. Each and every time, I find myself wishing for more time. It feels like we just get going and then we have to leave. I take notes, re-read them and do the reading that others suggest.

Has your spiritual practice been expanded by learning from others in the group?

- Yes. I've been inspired to take my own spiritual practice more seriously; indeed, to take my own truth more seriously.

- Definitely. I can think of a way that each person's sharing and questions have impacted my spiritual life. Duncan's teachings about the nervous system and spirituality stands out, as does Irene's public theology as a modality of opening up spiritual wisdom to more people.

- Yes, especially deepening my exploration of Judaism. Even though I was already involved in Judaism my interest has grown in Jesus as a Jew, the early church as Jews who were later expunged by Constantine and all that was lost in the process that should be reclaimed. I have brought this to my church and have been consulting with a local rabbi about what could be incorporated into our worship and observance without it being appropriation. I have also been looking more at Buddhist/Christian practices of contemplation.

How has your specific research or practice been impacted by the group interactions?

- I would say that's the greatest value I have received from being in the group— the opportunity to focus my research as I came to see more clearly how my background and expertise might be useful to others. My efforts here have been fairly isolated, both in terms of research as well as clinical practice and teaching. Being in the group has provided multiple portals through which I can see the relevance of what I might have to offer, particularly in the realms of theology and trauma. I have consulted with Fatemeh for instance, about the impact of trauma on women in Iran, and have been a presenter at an interfaith conference where I spoke about trauma and theology.

- Definitely—the kinds of questions I ask my participants in the fellowship group that I lead, and how I created a container for managing conflict in my cohorts were direct outcomes of our group.

- My research project has been informed by the group suggestions in finding the right balance in presenting scholarly topics for the news.

- I just wrote a journal article that was inspired by our group; now starting on another for a different journal that comes right out of the questions Duncan has raised and his expertise on trauma. In my training and consulting practice, I have broken down the difference between "conflict resolution" and "conflict transformation" for potential clients: churches, businesses, relationship/communication coaching. I have been thinking more deeply about multi-race conversations about race; wrestling with how to approach the different levels of risk taken on by participants and how to create environments that encourage the taking of responsibility while discouraging shaming.

This "new sense of place" that the RCT Visiting Scholars inhabit has also been fertile ground for new initiatives in conflict transformation. Participants have applied for grants together, assisted each other in planning difficult dialogues, and advised the RCT program on critical questions to prioritize their research agenda. They have also contributed to the larger STH community: holding forums, speaking in classes, and participating on faculty panels. Most significant, the Visiting Scholars embody the RCT mission, "to prepare religious leaders to become a resource for peace in a multi-cultural, multi-faith world." Through the mutuality of their relationships, they have become the "we" essential to pluralism process that Diana Eck has so clearly described:

> But as in any relationship, it is strongest in its mutuality, and it is weakest when one incorporates the other.… The most important of our two-letter words is "we." Who do we mean when we say "we?" As scholars, in our analysis of what "we" see happening in the world, we need words to describe the range of new initiatives and relationships that are cropping profusely in cities and towns, colleges and chaplaincies. Pluralism is such a word. It is not a doctrine, but a process.[3]

NOTES

1   Diana L. Eck, "Pluralism: Problems and Promise" in *The Journal of Inter-Religious Studies* 17 (Summer 2015): 54–62, at 58.

2   The Circle Process is an ancient Indigenous tradition that that has been reintroduced through the writings and teachings of Ann Linnea and Christina Baldwin of PeerSpirit, Inc, as well as others.

3   Eck, "Pluralism: Problems and Promise," 62

PSALMSEASON
FROM GRADUATE THEOLOGICAL SEMINAR TO NATIONAL VIRTUAL INITIATIVE

Or N. Rose

Listen to my words, YHWH, consider my lament.
Hear my cry for help. (Psalm 5:1–2)

For the last three years I have had the privilege of co-teaching a course on the Book of Psalms with Dr. Andrew Davis of the Boston College School of Theology and Ministry. The course is designed as an interdisciplinary exploration of this time-honored biblical book and the many Jewish and Christian interpretations of it throughout the ages. We welcome graduate students from across the Boston Theological Interreligious Consortium (BTI)—the association of religious studies departments, divinity schools, and theological institutions of higher learning in the Boston area plus Hartford (Connecticut)—to participate in the class. The majority of the students have been from Jewish, Catholic, Protestant, and Unitarian Universalist communities.

We undertook the third iteration of the course in the spring of 2020. For the first several weeks of the semester, we met in person—a two-hour session once weekly. Then, of course, with the onset of the pandemic, we moved online, meeting for ninety minutes weekly through Zoom. While we all struggled somewhat to find our virtual footing, the learning experience took on greater urgency for many students, as well as for Andrew and me. After all, the Book of Psalms has served as an important spiritual resource to countless numbers of Jews, Christians, and other seekers for centuries, particularly in times of pain and suffering. And while we do not know the specific circumstances of the writing or editing of most of the psalms, it is clear that the ancient poets were often responding to dramatic experiences of joy or sorrow—individual and communal—in their own lives.

For the members of our course, our sessions became a kind of grounding ritual in the midst of great tumult and uncertainty. Each week, we focused on a single psalm, exploring the original text in Hebrew and English, using literary, historical, and theological tools to unpack it. We would also share with students how various ancient and modern interpreters have understood these sources, and the different ways the psalms have been performed or presented in liturgical and artistic settings. As one student from Hebrew College put it, "the pandemic changed so much in my life all at once. The Psalms course has become a sacred space in which to explore my thoughts and feelings in conversation with a diverse group of peers and mentors. It has become a key part of my weekly spiritual routine."

Underscoring the connection between the content of the course and the moment we found ourselves in, a student from Boston College remarked: "Knowing that previous generations of Jews and Christians recited these sacred poems when they were experiencing pain and loss, or unexpected moments of joy in the midst of illness and death, make me feel supported by my ancestors and grateful for the resources they handed down to us in this frightening time."

Several class participants also spoke about the power of grappling with some of the more difficult psalms—texts that include caustic statements about the sinfulness of "enemies" and the desire for God to take revenge on those who had hurt the psalmists and their communities. As one adult education student auditing the class stated, "I understand why the poet is so angry and why he might have needed to express that anger. My challenge is to ask myself how I want to respond to my own anger. Do I want to act violently or pray to God to avenge my losses and punish my enemies, or are there other ways to move forward?"

As the course wound down, I was inspired to share some of the riches of the experience with a broader audience. And so, I began reaching out to entrepreneurial colleagues from a few different organizations across the country, asking how we might engage more people in such a conversation. My dear friend Rev. Paul Raushenbush, Senior Advisor for Public Affairs and Innovation at the Interfaith Youth Core (IFYC), expressed immediate excitement and offered several key insights; we quickly forged an organizational partnership between Hebrew College and IFYC and launched *PsalmSeason: An Online Encounter with the Wisdom of the Psalms.*[1]

The *PsalmSeason* initiative had an eighteen-week horizon—the numerical equivalent of the Hebrew word for life, *chai*. This choice symbolized our yearning for the renewal of life amidst so much illness and death. It was also inspired by various existing Psalms-related rituals in different Jewish and Christian communities, thus linking our efforts to past generations of practitioners and ritual-makers. One key difference between this project and most earlier work on the Psalms is that *PsalmSeason* (like the Boston College–Hebrew College graduate seminar) was intentionally interreligious. While it is true that for centuries Jews and Christians have turned to this collection for guidance and inspiration, there have been far fewer opportunities for members of these two communities and others to explore these sources *together* as fellow seekers. What do we share in common? Where do we differ? How might reading these texts through the lens of the "other" impact our understanding of life and our struggles at this time? The goal of the *PsalmSeason* project was not to collapse our distinct traditions, but to share resources thoughtfully in a profoundly painful moment in human history.

As in the graduate seminar, we focused on one psalm per week, offering several different forms of commentary: music, poetry, personal reflection, and visual art. In addition, we invited reflections on major themes in the Psalms or significant cultural creations inspired by these legendary texts. We also hosted live events periodically on topics related to the Psalms and our contemporary situation. We are deeply grateful to the more than fifty contributors—religious leaders, cultural critics, musicians, poets, artists, and activists—from several different countries who lent their talents and skills to the project.

In inviting our colleagues to contribute, we asked them to keep in mind the following insight from Dr. Ellen Davis of Duke University, who wrote the introduction to the project: "The Psalms speak directly from and to the human heart." Further, as Davis notes, "The book of 150 Psalms speaks with the most consistently personal voice in the Bible, often in the first person ('I' or 'we')." Following the model of the ancient Hebrew poets, we asked our contributors to read and respond to the original texts and various commentaries on them from a personal perspective. What do you hear, see, or feel *now* as you engage these sources? How do they land in the midst of the pandemic and in light of the more recent social uprising?

Among the first pieces we published was a commentary on Psalm 23 by Katherine Gergen-Barnett, a physician at the Boston Medical Center (BMC) responsible for training forty primary care doctors. In her essay, "The Valley of Deepest Darkness," she weaves her thoughts around several key verses from this iconic text. For example, in reflecting on the fourth verse, "Though I walk through a valley of deepest darkness, I fear no harm, for You are with me; Your rod and Your staff—they comfort me," she writes:

> In the first weeks of the outbreak, our hospital was turned into a bunker, with many doors now either locked or guarded by men and women in HAZMAT-like suits; outside those doors the number of homeless people swelled, IV needles strewn on nearby sidewalks. . . . During the day, food tasted like sawdust in my mouth and, at night, I battled my own nightmares. The darkness had eclipsed the days and I was overcome with a gnawing, ravenous fear. Fear for my life; fear for the lives of those I love; fear for the hundreds of patients who call me their doctor; fear for our city; fear for our country.

Dr. Gergen-Barnett proceeds to walk the reader through her experience of the next few weeks, describing how she and her colleagues managed to temper their fears and lean on one another as they learned more about this mysterious virus, received crucial supplies, and began to quell the first wave of the outbreak. Using the language of the shepherd's staff from the psalm, she speaks of the power of compassion among the BMC staff as the key instrument that "guides and binds us."

Gergen-Barnett does not try to tie up her reflection neatly, but asks what she and her colleagues have learned from this agonizing experience: "When all of this is over, will we be able to continue to walk together on this path of fellowship? Will we remember the ever-present shadow of death and still face down our fears?" Conjuring the image of frontline medical workers wearing face masks, she closes with one final question: "Can we continue to see into each other's eyes without looking away?"[2]

A few weeks later, in a reflection on Psalm 133, Jennifer Howe Peace, a scholar of religion, wrote with great fondness about her visits to a Benedictine monastery as a younger graduate student. It was there that she first witnessed a community reciting this psalm on a nightly basis. Deeply moved by this rite even years later, she feels compelled to ask if the words "How good and pleasant it is for siblings to dwell together as one" (133:1) could still be recited with integrity in the midst of the pandemic and social uprising:

> What does this ancient rite still performed at the Abbey and in many other monastic communities have to do with us in these days— these days when COVID-19 has thrown into question the wisdom of dwelling together, without masks and six-foot buffer zones. What relevance does it have in these days following George Floyd's murder, when protesters have taken to the streets demanding an end to police brutality against black and brown people and to structural violence 400-years in the making? The psalmist's vision of unity, in which people dwell together as siblings, safe and secure, is not easy to hold even in the best of times. During a global pandemic and in the midst of an uprising, it seems almost naive.

In response to this question, Dr. Peace states,

> But what strikes me when I read Psalm 133 today and think about the nuns gathering in their choir stalls, is the importance of regular reminders that dwelling together in unity, should be our daily goal and aspiration. Whether we pull it off or not on a given day, we need rituals that invite us to really see one another. . . . Such moments of true recognition are, as the psalmist states so eloquently, like being anointed with fine oil [verse 2]; like dew coming down on parched mountains [verse 3].

She ends her reflection by explaining to the reader that the words of Psalm 133 are the last the nuns sing to one another before they retreat for the night. The image of these devotees going into the "Great Silence" with this hope in their hearts seems like a most fitting picture for us to hold in our hearts in this time of widespread illness, polarization, and reckoning with racial injustice.[3]

Addressing the issue of racism and misogyny directly, Reverend Leslie Callahan describes how the imagery of exile in Psalm 137 resonates with her experience as an African American woman in the United States: "The complex emotions of exilic texts mirror my own complicated relationship with the United States—the way that I am aware on a cellular level that *this place* is simultaneously both home and not home." Speaking with prophetic passion, Callahan voices her pain as a successful public figure working to transform entrenched systems of oppression that have been in place for centuries and whose destructive consequences have been on public display in recent weeks:

> I am a U.S. citizen by birth. I know the pledge of allegiance and the Star-Spangled Banner by heart. I have earned degrees from premier institutions, gotten good jobs with benefits, and bought a house. But history and current events are replete with reminders that my people—Black and Woman—have only provisional welcome and entree in this society. We are so often embraced only on the terms and for the purposes of the captors' culture.[4]

Refusing to succumb to these pernicious social maladies, she uses the psalmist's language of longing to return to Zion to inspire her ongoing work in the long walk to justice.

I share these three examples from our *PsalmSeason* website, as they illustrate several of the key issues the contributors addressed during the project. Through poetry, visual art, music, and personal reflection, they simultaneously created a contemporary multifaith commentary on the Book of Psalms and an historical record of spiritual yearning from this unprecedented moment in human history.

In inviting viewers to engage with the weekly selection of materials, we encouraged them to take three simple actions:

1. **Reflect** quietly on the biblical texts and interpretations offered on our site. What are the key insights or questions that emerge for you as you read today?

2. **Share** your insights and questions with at least one other person. Who might be a helpful companion on this journey? Who might benefit from such a conversation?

3. **Create** your own commentary on the *PsalmSeason* materials you explore, be it in the form of poetry, music, dance, or drama. How might this process help you grow as an individual and contribute more deeply to a world in dire need of healing?

While we learned that thousands of people were opening and exploring the *PsalmSeason* resources, we did not know how many of them engaged in these or other related activities. Further, although many religious leaders and educators shared with us that they were utilizing the materials in their teaching, preaching, and counseling, we still had much to learn about how they did so, and which resources they found most helpful (or most helpful in a given context). Hence, we began gathering more information on these questions with the intention of creating a digital curriculum (perhaps with a parallel print edition) for use by houses of worship and similar study groups. We look forward to sharing our learning as we delve further into these pedagogic questions.

In closing, I wish to share a brief teaching on Psalm 27:4, which reads as follows: "One thing I ask of YHWH, this do I seek: to dwell in the house of YHWH all the days of my life, to behold the beauty of YHWH, to frequent God's temple." Centuries after this piece was composed, a Hasidic master named Rabbi Yehiel Mikhel of Zlotchov (d. 1786) asked the following rhetorical question: why does the psalmist state the words "this do I seek" having just stated that he has a request of God? The *rebbe* (master) explains that what appears to be a mere literary flourish is, in fact, a profound lesson on humility. By adding the seemingly extraneous phrase, the biblical poet is urging us to remember that even when we "behold the beauty of YHWH" or feel at home in God's presence, we must understand that the journey is not over. The words "this do I seek" are intended to guard against spiritual arrogance or complacency.

I have thought of this teaching often throughout the *PsalmSeason* experience. This project provided me with the opportunity to meditate anew on the grandeur and mystery of life with a diverse group of thoughtful teachers, peers, and students— all of whom were searching (often groping) for meaning and purpose in the midst of significant loss, pain, and upheaval. Their contributions helped me to behold glimpses of divine beauty that I otherwise would not have seen.

NOTES

1   https://hebrewcollege.edu/community-learning/professional-development/ interreligious-engagement/an-encounter-with-the-wisdom-of-psalms/.

2   Katherine Gergen Barnett, M. D., "Medicine in the Valley of Deepest Darkness," on *PsalmSeason* website June 8, 2020. https://ifyc.org/article/ ps-23-medicine-valley-deepest-darkness.

3   Jennifer Howe Peace, "Psalm 133: The Power of Ritual to Inspire Change," on *PsalmSeason* website June 15, 2020. https://ifyc.org/article/ps-133-power-ritual-inspire-change.

4   Leslie Callahan, "Psalm 137: Exilic Emotions," on *PsalmSeason* website, July 27, 2020. https:// ifyc.org/article/ps-137-exilic-emotions.

PART IV

ACTING INTERRELIGIOUSLY

DIALOGUE TOOLS FOR BUILDING A GLOBAL COMMUNITY

Judith Simmer-Brown

In the clear vision of 2020, a time of a global pandemic, unparalleled cries for racial justice, economic collapse, and the looming climate crisis, it is clear that our challenges as a global community demand that we find fresh ways to work together for the common good. Interreligious studies has an opportunity to offer perspectives and skills beyond the realms of religious studies and theology to alleviate the fears and hopelessness of our time. It is especially in the subfield of interreligious dialogue practice that we may bring compassionate intention to the divisions that permeate the public square, making contributions through many different activities, initiatives, and vocations.

Probably the most promising contributions come from the practice of dialogue itself. While dialogue surfaces as a topic of discussion in interreligious studies, too often the word is applied to activities that are anything but dialogue. For example, I have often been invited to participate as a Buddhist on a panel in which I might have seven minutes for presentation, and then be available to the audience for a question-answer period. I leave those events feeling that the promised dialogue has never occurred. The academy often substitutes theoretical discussion for real-life experience, meaning that our students are unprepared to enter actual interreligious exchange. The notion of practical training never comes up.

The most significant experiences I have had in dialogue have been extended exchanges with religious or spiritual others that were genuine encounters. At the Gethsemani Dialogues in 1994,[1] I was paired with a young Benedictine monk for breakout dialogue sessions. In the years since, those sessions have extended into a long friendship, a dialogical relationship that has lasted more than twenty-five years. We have learned deeply from each other across differences of age, gender, religion, and lifestyle. In my decades in the Cobb-Abe Buddhist-Christian Theological Encounter (1984–2004), a small and committed group of theologians met roughly every eighteen months for five days of dialogue that profoundly affected each of us.[2] Opportunities like these are rare in our divisive, fragmented, and speedy world.

Realizing the importance of the engagement in actual dialogue, fifteen years ago I made practical dialogue training an integral part of my graduate dialogue seminars. Bringing dialogue practice into the classroom was natural for me at our Buddhist-inspired university, where we commit to integrating "theory and practice" into every one of our academic fields and disciplines. It is not enough to think about dialogue or to intend it. We need to train in it, practice it, and experience the impact of actual dialogue. These encounters have the potential to transform our lives.

How do we train in dialogue skills? Contemporary initiatives in dialogue have come from diverse sources, from Jewish philosopher Martin Buber and the Second Vatican Council, to Russian literary theorist Mikhail Bakhtin and Brazilian philosopher Paulo Freire, founder of the critical pedagogy movement. I have been especially influenced by the work of the American quantum physicist David Bohm, who developed a form of dialogue in which groups of people "think together" in an exploratory way, without a pre-established agenda or objective. Bohm was influenced by twenty-five years of conversation with philosopher Jiddu Krishnamurti and became intrigued by parallels he observed between human interactions and the principles of quantum physics he discovered in his groundbreaking work. He developed dialogue as a social practice, steeped in contemplative principles, and spent his later years experimenting with dialogue communities.[3]

The Center for Organizational Learning at the MIT Sloan School of Management, home of Bohm's work, has shaped a broad range of fields and forged a whole new generation of dialogue aficionados who are rethinking previous paradigms in organizational development, innovation, and change. Systems scientist Peter Senge remarks that "team learning starts with 'dialogue,' the capacity of members of a team to suspend assumptions and enter into a genuine 'thinking together,'" the actual definition of the word dialogue.[4] Senge says this brings greater capacity to understand complexity and especially to embrace new perspectives. These are skills necessary in our contemporary world, interreligiously, interpersonally, and as a global community.

Bohm protégé William Isaacs has argued for the importance of actual dialogue training in his book *Dialogue and the Art of Thinking Together*. He argues that in Western culture we have learned to think alone, and this habit brings problems of abstraction, individualism, dogmatism, and territoriality. When we try to address these problems individually, our habit of solitary thinking merely reinforces the very problems we are trying to address. Under duress, "human beings do not come together well to solve their problems."[5] He argues that dialogue, the "art of thinking together," provides creativity, inclusion, and openness that make it possible to freshly address the systemic problems of our world.[6]

While Isaacs' book is not so much a workshop text, I have found it a powerful basis for training my students in the practice of dialogue. He speaks of the importance of building a ground of trust before beginning to dialogue—that is, creating a "container" that is neutral and trusting. While we cannot manufacture trust and openness for dialogue, we can build the conditions that maximize the likelihood of authentic connection.[7] Conducive conditions relate to both time and space. He speaks practically here. The physical setting needs to be a neutrally supportive one, encouraging peer conversations and quiet so that listening is possible. It helps to have dedicated time for the encounters, so that all participants settle in for the duration, resisting the temptation to race off to another event or meeting. Conference or retreat centers provide optimal conditions for dialogue, and so can the classroom. Isaacs emphasizes nonhierarchical arrangements like circles of chairs without tables that can create barriers between people. And it is helpful to have ground rules for the conversations. Without these conducive conditions, it is hard for the magic of genuine dialogue to ignite.

The foundational skill of any dialogue is *listening*, sometimes called "deep listening."[8] This requires staying close to the actual words that are spoken by the other person, refraining from jumping to conclusions about what we think is being said. This is nonjudgmental listening, and requires attentive presence related to mindfulness. It is important that we also actually listen to ourselves, and our tendencies to plan how we are going to respond rather than paying attention to the spoken words and body language of the other person.

The practice of deep listening has tremendous potential to change our relationships with each other. In an interview with Oprah Winfrey, the Vietnamese Zen master Thich Nhat Hanh speaks of deep listening in this way:

> You listen with only one purpose: to help him or her to empty his heart. Even if he says things that are full of wrong perceptions, full of bitterness, you are still capable of continuing to listen with compassion. . . . For now, you don't interrupt. You don't argue. If you do, he loses his chance. You just listen with compassion and help him to suffer less. One hour like that can bring transformation and healing.[9]

This kind of listening is called "listening to understand" rather than "listening to respond." This important foundation sets the stage for real shift in human communication.

The second and third skills relate closely to one another.[10] *Respecting* requires us to see the person from their own side, acknowledging the integrity of their needs and wishes apart from how we want them to be. This also suggests seeing the humanity and wholeness of the other person. Suspending supports our attending to the other person, noticing when there might be some reaction on our own part that causes us to react prematurely to what the other person is saying. It is also helpful for us to open inquiry into what is being said, allowing ourselves not to know the answer rather than assuming we know.

The fourth skill is *voicing*.[11] Dialogue includes our being able to speak personally and freshly in the present moment, rather than relying on scripts, habitual thoughts, and dictates from the past. In dialogue, we may be hearing ourselves for the first time expressing new discoveries that arise in relationship. The greatest generativity of dialogue is not unlike musical improvisation, responding creatively in an environment of "thinking together" developing perspectives and solutions that have never been imagined before. We also recognize the novel ideas of the other person.

Isaacs shows that as our dialogue skills grow, we can progress through four quadrants over time, changing the flow of communication and discovery. We begin with shared monologues (entitled "politeness"), to shifting emphasis from "me" to "we" ("shared experience"), to inquiry and analysis ("reflective dialogue"), and making meaning together ("generative dialogue").[12] It is common for us to begin with shared monologues, the most common of human interactions and the foundation for the development of trust that can lead to further genuine communication. Without learning dialogue skills, many relationships can get stuck there, even in close friendships and marriages.

Eventually, the habit of "debate," arising when individualistic habits dog our work, gives way to "dialogue," which brings more open-ended encounters to the fore.[13] Every year, my dialogue students first learn these specific dialogue skills in a three-week workshop in my graduate seminar. They report that they discover that most of the time they have not really listened to others—classmates, spouses, teachers, friends. They have been much more used to defending an idea they have, and they have merely been waiting for a chance to reply. They realize in retrospect that often they are talking past each other, with no real communication occurring. Dialogue skills are helpful in interreligious dialogue, but they have also enabled them to deeply listen nonjudgmentally to another person and to speak from the heart sharing personal experience.

MIT's dialogue movement has also interfaced with Otto Scharmer's "Theory U" work, which has presented a new paradigm for organizational change. Scharmer maps how organizations that commit to change can transition from pyramid power dynamics that freeze and harden against innovation to living organisms from which collective vision can arise. When organizations come alive, they go through a transformative process of letting go of current structure that can be terrifying and threatening, down to the bottom of the "U." If they stay in connection and process with each other, organizations can find a core of mutual creativity and vision that births new possibilities for structure, communication, and action.[14] This team approach to leadership has influenced corporations, nonprofits, and governments worldwide. The foundational skill of Scharmer's work is dialogue.

All of this may seem like a stretch for academic, religious, and spiritual communities. But all of these communities are in crisis. Academia is challenged by the current pandemic and economic crises to provide a relevant, affordable, safe, and stimulating education for our young people. Religious hierarchies are under scrutiny, as their conservatism and self-preservation tendencies seem to override their abilities to compassionately alleviate the anguish of our time. Millennials and their younger cohorts question whether membership in organizations makes sense at all for pursuing a spiritual life, as they turn to the internet and social media for connection and counsel. Yet, social isolation and lack of intimacy have brought on an epidemic of loneliness across diverse demographics. Dialogue skills and practice have the potential to begin to build fresh connection to others, and could create the ground for new paradigms in organizational creativity and social change.

NOTES

1   Proceedings were published as Donald W. Mitchell and James Wiseman, O.S.B., eds., *The Gethsemani Encounter* (New York: Continuum, 1997).

2   Rita Gross, "The International Buddhist-Christian Theological Encounter: Twenty Years of Dialogue," *Buddhist-Christian Studies* 25 (1): 3–7, 2005.

3   David Bohm, *On Dialogue* (London: Routledge, 1996), Chapter 2.

4   Peter Senge, *The Fifth Discipline: The Art & Practice of the Learning Organization* (New York: Doubleday, 1990), 10.

5   William Isaacs, *Dialogue and the Art of Thinking Together* (New York: Doubleday, 1999), 52.

6   Isaacs, Chapter 2.

7   Isaacs, 242, Chapter 10.

8   Isaacs, Chapter 4.

9   Conversation with Oprah Winfrey, *O: The Oprah Magazine*, March 2010. https://www.oprah.com/spirit/oprah-talks-to-thich-nhat-hanh/5.

10 Isaacs, Chapters 5 and 6.

11 Isaacs, Chapter 7.

12 Ibid, 259–62.

13 Isaacs, 41.

14 Otto Scharmer and Peter Senge, *Theory U: Leading from the Future as It Emerges*, Second Edition (Oakland: Berrett-Koehler Publishers, 2016), Chapter 2.

MUSLIMS IN AMERICA
LIVING UP TO THE IDEALS OF THE GREATEST

Amir Hussain

In the "new normal" of the coronavirus, and the religious questions and challenges that it brings to faith communities (Will a public Mass be celebrated? Is it still required for Muslims to pray the Friday afternoon prayer in congregation? How do you have a *minyan* in a time of social isolation, etc.), I think back to the life of the most famous Muslim in America (and perhaps the world), the blessed Muhammad Ali. My academic work for the past twenty-five years, as well as own life as an American Muslim during that time, examines the reality of American Muslim life and shows how Muslims have helped to make America the country that it is.

I was born in Pakistan and came to Canada in 1970 when I was four years old. At that time, there were fewer than 34,000 Muslims in all of Canada. I grew up in Toronto, educated there from kindergarten to PhD. My parents' generation were not the pioneers of Islam in Canada. The first Canadian census in 1871 (the modern country came into existence in 1867) listed thirteen Muslims. But when my parents came to Toronto, there was only one mosque in the city, and only one small store near that mosque that sold halal meat. One of my mother's oldest friends told me that she met my mother around 1972, when my mother crossed a major city street because she heard this woman and her husband speaking Punjabi. My mother was so excited to hear a language from her native land from someone that wasn't in her family that she crossed a busy street to talk with strangers. Since then, the number of Muslims in Canada has grown tremendously: by 2001, it was 579,600, and the last Canadian Household Survey in 2011 counted over one-million Muslims. Now, one hears Urdu everywhere and there is a Punjabi broadcast of Hockey Night in Canada, something I would have never imagined in 1970.

In those days, when racism was more common, I saw very few non-White people on television, and almost no Muslims. The only ones I remember were African American athletes, such as Kareem Abdul-Jabbar, and the Greatest of All Time, Muhammad Ali. Those were my childhood Muslim heroes, and over forty years later, they remain models for me of how to be a Muslim.

At the age of thirty-two, I moved to Los Angeles, where I've lived for the past twenty-five years. American Muslims, it should be pointed out, are very different from European or Canadian Muslim communities, other places where we are also minorities in a Western context. Canadian Muslims do not have the same history that American Muslims do. So while there was a small Muslim population in Canada at the end of the nineteenth century, it was nothing like the number of Muslim slaves that were present in America generations earlier. There is no comparable component in Canadian Muslim life that resembles African American Muslims, who represent at least one-quarter of American Muslims. African American Muslims—as Americans—have, for centuries, been part of the history of the United States.[1]

In Europe, the situation is markedly different, both among the Muslim and non-Muslim populations, which each tend to be much more homogeneous than they are in the United States. So in Britain, the majority of Muslims have their origins in South Asia. In France, Muslims are mostly from North Africa. In Germany, Muslims are usually Turks or Kurds. Contrast that with the American situation, where Muslims are equally African American, South Asian, or Middle Eastern (to take only the three largest groups). There are also narrower definitions of what it means to be French or English or German than what it means to be American, which incorporates all of those European identities and many others.

There is also a socio-economic difference. American Muslims are often an American success story, solidly middle class and mostly professional. There are thousands of American Muslim physicians, for example, perhaps as many as 20,000 if one looks at information from the Islamic Medical Association of North America. While there is also a large percentage of working class Muslims in America, European Muslims by contrast are more marginalized, often in a much lower socio-economic class with much higher rates of unemployment. Sometimes, as is often the case in Germany, they are in the status of migrants or guest workers, not citizens.

Finally, there is a difference between American-style secularism, which doesn't seek to abolish religion but to give all religions an equal seat at the table, and various kinds of European disestablishment of religion, which seek to make the public space non-religious. In the United States, America's seven million Muslims are free to live out their Islam in the public space. And there are so many American Muslims who do this, none who did it better than my childhood hero, the Greatest of All Time.

Muhammad Ali was born Cassius Clay in Louisville and gained national fame when he won a gold medal at the Rome Olympics in 1960 as a light heavyweight boxer. That same year, Clay turned professional, and he became known as much for his verbal as well as his boxing skills. The poetry that he and his cornerman Drew Bundini Brown created has had lasting significance in American culture.

In 1964, the 22-year-old Clay, by his own admission, "shook up the world" in his six-round defeat of Sonny Liston, becoming the world heavyweight boxing champion. A few years earlier, Clay had gone to Nation of Islam meetings. There, he met Malcolm X, who as a friend and advisor was part of Clay's entourage for the Liston fight. Clay made his conversion public after the fight, and was renamed by Nation of Islam leader Elijah Muhammad as Muhammad Ali. When Malcolm X left the Nation of Islam because of his issues with Elijah Muhammad, Ali broke with his old friend.

Ali was no saint. He could be cruel, with an arrogance to match his unmatchable skill. He prolonged a fight with Floyd Patterson; and when Ernie Terrell would not call Ali by his new name, he kept punishing him for the full fifteen rounds of a fight he could have ended much sooner, repeatedly asking Terrell "what's my name?" However, Ali also had a conscience. When he was reclassified as eligible for induction into the draft for the Vietnam War, Ali refused on the grounds of his new Muslim religious beliefs. Famously, he said that "war is against the teachings of the Holy Koran. I'm not trying to dodge the draft. We are not supposed to take part in no wars unless declared by Allah or the Messenger [Elijah Muhammad]. We don't take part in Christian wars or wars of any unbelievers." Even more famously, reflecting on the racism he had experienced in America, Ali said, "I ain't got no quarrel with them Viet Cong—no Viet Cong ever called me Ni**er." This conscientious objector status was rooted in the teachings of the Nation of Islam, and Elijah Muhammad had been jailed for his refusal to enter the draft in World War II.

On April 28, 1967, Ali refused induction into the draft. He was arrested, and his boxing titles were stripped from him. Ali never went to prison, but he couldn't box for over three years. Think about that for a minute. There was Ali, age twenty-five and at the height of his athletic prowess, three years into his undefeated reign as world heavyweight champion. Ali also might not have faced danger in Vietnam, so it wasn't about any kind of cowardice. Almost a decade earlier, Elvis Presley had been inducted into the United States Army. Elvis refused any kind of privileges with special services, but with no war being waged at that time, he also didn't have to serve on the front line. Elvis was instead assigned to a US Army base in West Germany. The Champ most likely would not have been put on the front lines. He might have been a celebrity, giving exhibitions for the troops to boost morale. But for him, as a Muslim, as a Black Muslim, the Vietnam War was wrong. In 1967, that was not the popular stance that it is today, and Ali paid dearly, unable to make a living at the trade for which he was eminently qualified, at the peak of his talents.

Ali's case went to the United States Supreme Court, which ruled unanimously on June 28, 1971, to overturn his conviction. The Court did this on a technicality, since the appeal court had never given a reason for why Ali was denied conscientious objector status. But Ali was free, and able to resume his work.

His later boxing history is well-known to sports fans. The loss to Joe Frazier in 1971 (his first professional loss), the loss to Ken Norton in 1973 (fighting the full twelve rounds despite a jaw broken by Norton), the rematch win with Frazier in 1974, the regaining of his heavyweight title later that year against Foreman, the conclusion of the triptych with his second win against Frazier (what Ali famously called "the closest thing to dying that I know"), becoming the first three-time heavyweight champion in his rematch with Leon Spinks in 1978, and the brutal beat down at the hands of Larry Holmes in 1980 that effectively ended Ali's career as a boxer.

But there he was, an American Muslim who changed America. In 1975, he followed Warith Deen Mohammed, who took his father's Nation of Islam into Sunni orthodoxy. He became a proselytizer for Islam, giving out pamphlets inviting others to Islam, autographed so that he knew they would be kept by those who received them. And as people began to see what Ali had done in the 1960s, he became a hero not just for his athletic prowess, but for his work on civil rights. Who can forget in 1996, when the opening ceremonies were held for the Olympics in Atlanta? There was Janet Evans, one of the most decorated American swimmers, the last athlete to hold the torch, who we all thought would light the Olympic cauldron. And there she was, passing the torch to Ali, who held the torch aloft in his right hand, but whose left hand was shaking with Parkinson's Syndrome. In the hush of the crowd, it was Ali who would light the cauldron, something that he would repeat at the Winter Olympics in Salt Lake City in 2002.

Ali's funeral showed the outpouring of love and support for him. This was a beloved American hero returning home, a beloved American Muslim. The public funeral was held during the first week of Ramadan, on June 10, 2016, in his hometown of Louisville, Kentucky. The funeral was by Ali's own design an interfaith event, featuring remarks by religious leaders, family members, celebrities, and politicians, concluding with a eulogy from former president Bill Clinton. The service was arranged by my friend Timothy Gianotti, who was the religious advisor to Muhammad Ali and his family. I first met Timothy when we were both graduate students at the University of Toronto, and it was lovely to see the service that he had coordinated after years of working on it with Ali and his family. The service began with a procession through the streets of Ali's hometown to his Muslim burial in the Cave Hill Cemetery. However, the day before, Ali had also had a traditional Muslim funeral service, or janazah. At his passing, his body was washed and shrouded and prayed over in accordance with Islamic customs. Muslims across America and around the world were encouraged to hold janazah prayers for our deceased Muslim brother.

The *janazah* prayer for Ali was extraordinary, held on June 9, 2016, at the Kentucky Exposition Center in Louisville. This was next to Freedom Hall, where Ali had fought Tunney Hunsaker in his first professional fight on October 29, 1960. I watched the funeral service online from Los Angeles, on a YouTube feed from Fox 10 News, the Fox-owned and -operated television station in Phoenix, Arizona. The irony was rich. Here was a television station, Fox, not noted for its sympathetic coverage of Muslims, covering live the full Islamic prayer service for Muhammad Ali. On the drive home, I heard part of the Qur'an recitation from the funeral on CBS radio, the first time I ever heard coverage of a Muslim funeral on the recap of the daily news.

The service was led by Imam Zaid Shakir, a noted American imam from California and the co-founder of Zaytuna College, the first accredited Muslim liberal arts college in the United States. The coffin was brought in by pall-bearers that included Shaikh Hamza Yusuf (another co-founder of Zaytuna College), and international recording star Yusuf Islam (the former Cat Stevens). Imam Zaid explained to the crowd what would happen, as the *janazah* prayer is unique in that there is no bowing or prostration, only four cycles of prayer where the congregation remains standing. The funeral prayer was performed, followed by a Qur'an recitation and a translation of the words recited by Shaikh Hamza. Then three people were invited to give short sermons to the crowd. They were Sherman Jackson, a professor at the University of Southern California and one of the most important Muslim scholars in the US; Dalia Mogahed, the former director of the Gallup Center for Muslim Studies; and Khadija Sharif-Drinkard, a lawyer who oversees business and legal affairs for the New York offices of Black Entertainment Television (BET). That two of the three were Muslim women (who were also successful businesswomen) was important to show the leadership roles that many American Muslim women have in American society.

Sherman Jackson is one of the most important American Muslim scholars, a mentor and friend for years. Professor Jackson's short sermon was brilliant, and a few lines from it captured the intertwining of American and Muslim identities in the body of Muhammad Ali:

> As a cultural icon, Ali made being Muslim cool. Ali made being a Muslim dignified. Ali made being a Muslim relevant. And all of this he did in a way that no one could challenge his belongingness to or in this country. Ali put the question of whether a person can be a Muslim and an American to rest. Indeed, he KO'd that question. With his passing, let us hope that that question will now be interred with his precious remains. . . Ali helped this country move closer to its own ideals. He helped America do and see some things that America was not quite ready to do or see on its own. And because of Ali's heroic efforts, America is a better place today for us all. And in this regard, Ali belongs not just to the Muslims of this country, Ali belongs to all Americans. . . . If you are an American, Ali is part of your history, part of what makes you who you are, and as an American, Ali belongs to you, and you too should be proud of this precious piece of your American heritage.

At another funeral service over fifty years earlier, on February 27, 1965, Ossie Davis gave the eulogy for Malcolm X. There, he famously said, "Malcolm was our manhood, our living, black manhood! This was his meaning to his people. And in honoring him we honor the best in ourselves." Ali, as Professor Jackson pointed out, was not just for *his* people, but for all people. If Malcolm was our manhood, then Ali was our humanity, with a life lived for all the world to see. A life lived in complexity and contradiction, triumph and tragedy. A life of change and metamorphosis. A life which gave the lie to F. Scott Fitzgerald's line about there being no second acts in American lives by living out its successful second and third acts. A life which showed us, in the old cliché, that it's not about how many times you get knocked down, but if you get back up, and what you do when you get back up that truly matters. An iconic American life, lived by an iconic American Muslim.

One often hears talk of "Islam *and* the West" or "Islam *and* America." This brings up an image of two mutually exclusive realities. If we change one simple word, we get instead "Islam *in* the West" or "Islam *in* America." That simple change makes all the difference. Instead of posing two warring factions, "Islam" and "America," we see the reality of their interconnectedness. Islam is, of course, a "Western" religion, sharing deep roots with Judaism and Christianity. Muslims are much closer religiously to Jews and to Christians than we are to "Eastern" religions such as Hinduism and Buddhism. Muslims are also a strong presence in "the West." Islam is the second-largest religion in Canada, Britain, and France, and may well be the second-largest religion in the United States. "Islam in the West" recognizes the entwined heritage of Islam and the West. The West as we know it would not be what it is without the contribution of Muslims. Think quickly of our number system, for example, and ask yourself if it is easier to do multiplication and division with Arabic numbers or with Roman numerals. To be sure, the number system came from India, but it was the Arabs who named it. Yet we often don't see our connections, and people here in America often have a fear or hatred of Muslims.

American Muslims have served in the United States military since the Revolutionary War. There were some three-hundred Muslim soldiers who served during the American Civil War. That's not a large number, certainly, but it also gives the lie to the oft-repeated claim that Muslims are newcomers to the United States. At the end of 2015, ABC News reported figures from the US Department of Defense that some 5,896 Muslims were serving in the military. That number may be higher, since some 400,000 service members did not self-identify their faith. So almost 6,000 American Muslims serve in the armed forces, helping to defend our country.

I think that Muhammad Ali represents our best ideals as a country. American Muslims need to live the legacy of Muhammad Ali. We need to continue to stand, as he did, for justice. "Service to others is the rent you pay for your room here on earth," Ali would often say, and we need not only to remember that saying, but also to act on it. In this way, we can live out the best of our ideals, both as Americans and as Muslims.

NOTES

1   For more information, see Kambiz Ghanea Bassiri, *A History of Islam in America: From the New World to the New World Order* (New York: Cambridge University Press, 2010).

HANDS ACROSS THE HILLS
APPALACHIANS AND NEW ENGLANDERS BUILD BRIDGES OF UNDERSTANDING AND CARE

Paula Green

In Whitesburg, Kentucky, county seat for a coal-mining region, there are fourteen churches for a population of 2000. Most are Evangelical, including varieties such as Primitive Baptist, Old Baptist, and Southern Baptist. Seekers must travel out of town for a Catholic Church; and should anyone wish for a synagogue, the closest is about four hours away. In Leverett Massachusetts, also with a population of 2000, there are three churches, one Quaker Meeting, two Buddhist communities, and a small Sikh community. By driving for about thirty minutes, one can reach any of three synagogues or a mosque.

For the 2016 election, Whitesburg voters chose Trump by about eighty-five percent, while Leverett voters chose Clinton by the same percentage. A group of progressive voters in Leverett, seeking to comprehend how our country had become so divided, searched for a Trump-voting population with whom they could dialogue and deepen their understanding. Through a community organizer working in Whitesburg and publishing online, Leverett discovered the Kentucky city and a partnership was proposed, struggled over, and eventually accepted. This article is a tale of two cities, towns actually, where some residents came together across deep chasms of distrust and suspicion. Although our purpose was not interreligious, our spiritual beliefs and practices are embedded in both our differences and similarities. Three years later, with three weekend visits exchanged and a fourth planned, approximately thirty participants are in relationship with each other, stretching and growing.

I am a member of the Leverett community that proposed the idea of bridging divides and am also a professional dialogue facilitator and international peacebuilder. Over the past several decades, I have led dialogues across differences in race, religion, ethnic identity, gender, geography, history, culture, and just about every other imaginable division, in countries intent on preventing war, engaging in war, recovering from war, or seeking healing and wholeness across boundaries and perceptions. I am a believer in the power of structured dialogue to shift prejudices and stereotypes, but I am way too experienced to be naïve about easy outcomes and long-term impact. The Leverett group, which named itself *Hands Across the Hills*, invited me to be its chief organizer, project designer, and facilitator, which I have been doing since its inception in early 2017.

Most attempts to create bridging activities in the US since the Trump election have developed half- or full-day events for dialogue or a combination of work projects, meals, and conversations. From my international experiences, I learned that one-day and one-off encounters are too brief to support substantial change. Additionally, our two groups are a thousand miles apart, so the long trip to meet each other necessitated more time together to justify the journey. We settled upon three-day weekends, the first in Leverett, with the Whitesburg group arriving on a Thursday night after a fifteen-hour van ride and returning the same way on Monday morning. This model offered us the luxury of three full days to be with each other within and beyond our formal dialogues.

In order to create intimacy and also to keep our expenses minimal, we elected to offer our guests homestays rather than hotels. This decision became a major contributor to the building of relationships and, in fact, much of the bonding that continues arose from the guest-host pairs. Staying in someone's home, meeting their family, and drinking coffee at their kitchen table is a perfect vehicle for knowing the other. There is not much hiding; the intimate setting offers an opportunity for stepping into the life of the other, if not into their shoes.

Another lesson learned in my decades of dialogue practice is that we cannot develop relationships through dialogue alone. It's too exhausting, too concentrated, and leaves out too much of life. In *Hands Across the Hills,* we engaged in structured dialogue for three to five hours a day, leaving ample time for music, art, theater games, dance, sightseeing, walks, meeting each other's communities, and endless potlucks. It's also true that we each learn differently, some through verbal forms like dialogue and others through these different means of expressing our humanity. I know that participants bonded deeply through the various activities on offer, opening their hearts to each other as they danced, sang, hiked, and broke bread together.

We were unlikely soul mates. The differences between a predominantly progressive and privileged community in Western Massachusetts, where college education is the principal regional business, and an economically impoverished community in Eastern Kentucky, where mining coal is the only business and one that is fast disappearing, are pretty stark. Group members delved deeply to find common ground despite the differences in educational opportunities, income levels, political outlook, health indexes, life experiences, religious practices, family relations, and more.

I wondered how to design the first encounter, seeking an entry point that would reduce the host of fears I assumed everyone was silently carrying. I selected family stories as the initial topic, since all of us, for better or worse, have families. I thought this might offer us a base of commonality upon which to later explore differences. It did not take long, however, to discover that family stories from these two communities are pretty dissimilar. In Leverett, most families are small and live scattered across and beyond the country. None of our group members, in fact, had been raised in Massachusetts and none of their grown children live permanently in Leverett. In Whitesburg, most families are large, live close to their parents, and everyone in the dialogue group came from that region and had their adult children living nearby. Folks in coal country generally remain there, as their Scots-Irish ancestors have done since arriving perhaps two-hundred years ago. Folks in Leverett are more frequently second or third generation descendants of Europeans and quite mobile.

Despite the differences, family sagas created a great deal of bonding. As it turned out, two of our women members were first-generation Holocaust survivors, one with a parent who escaped from Germany in 1938 and the other with a parent from Paris who also fled the Nazi occupation. The women shared intimately and emotionally, leaving many group members in tears. Our Kentucky counterparts had never heard direct Holocaust stories and in fact had limited historical knowledge of the Nazi era. Afterwards one confessed that she had never met a refugee or immigrant but would no longer oppose their human rights because these two group members were also immigrants and she liked them already. The Kentucky stories, focused on the endless tragedies of coal mining accidents and diseases stripping families of fathers and sons, husbands and brothers, were equally emotional. Our group members on both sides had a fulsome and memorable experience of empathy and compassion, a wonderful way to acknowledge their different realities and build connection with each other.

Over the three days of this first encounter, and again when the Leverett group went to Whitesburg six months later and yet again when the Kentuckians returned to Massachusetts a year and a half later, we dialogued about provocative issues, and we made time to sing, dance, walk, chat, and feast. We talked politics and hot button topics like guns and immigration, we explored gender roles, North/South history, racism, religion, xenophobia, injustice, perceptions, media choices, and more. The group members disagreed a lot. We promised early on that we were not in this initiative to change each other, but to understand and to honor the truths of each other's lives and challenges. Although keeping that promise was often challenging, violating it would have harmed a tenuous trust.

Over time, group members came to appreciate each other's life journeys. I began to hear the language of love. Emails and Facebook messages affirmed the other, who was no longer "other" but was a complete individual with a biography and a heart. I call this humanization. Its opposite, dehumanization, operates almost universally as an essential component of psychological preparation for armed conflict. For me this shift in perceptions and stereotypes becomes the foundation of protection, inclusion, and concern. Not only can participants perceive each other differently, they can also extrapolate that shift to accommodate those who resemble the new friend in religious, cultural, or political orientation. If I care about you, the story goes, I can also affirm those who are similar to you, who vote the way you did, who worship the way you do, who look and think like you. And if I care, I can defend your right to be you and to hold your values, even when those values compete with mine.

What are the lessons learned from this experiment in intergroup relations? We have learned that:

- We have the internal capacity to dethrone the prejudices and stereotypes we have accrued throughout our lives

- Changes in beliefs about others prefigures changes in attitudes and behaviors

- Attitudinal and behavioral changes are slow and require reinforcement over time

- A carefully crafted dialogue creates a container of safety in which cherished values and beliefs can be explored and adjusted to conform to new sensibilities

- Communication guidelines and practices are essential for creating a safe dialogue container

Intergroup or interfaith dialogue provides the opportunity for the kind of "aha" moment described above whereby a woman from Kentucky met first-generation descendants of immigrants from Massachusetts whose stories and presence touched her heart. If that moment of awakening is reinforced with future contact and positive encouragement, her behavior toward other immigrants may shift. My own experience of *Hands Across the Hills* gave me the opportunity to meet women and men whose male relatives without exception worked in the mines for generations. While familiar with US stereotypes about "hillbillies" and "hicks," I had never known coal mining families personally. Now I find myself not only speaking up against prejudices about rural Kentuckians, but also about other conservative Trump voters, acknowledging that each person has a history, a social and religious community, and a media environment, all of which profoundly impact their voting choices.

A successful dialogue, especially one called upon to bridge sharply divided group members, is neither casual nor accidental, but rather a specifically designed format led or co-led by trained facilitators. My experiences confirm that informal attempts at bridging quickly derail, with participants blaming each other for starting a war, voting ignorantly, or somehow being irresponsible. Guidelines for dialogue, presented and agreed upon by group members, control inappropriate and blame-based communication, require significant verbal discipline, and eschew arguments, interruptions, side comments, cell phones, and dominance. Questions for the dialogue, shaped by facilitators, encourage new and unexplored responses, allow for ambivalence, encourage fresh thinking, and take participants deeper than the level of opinion or position. Dialogue is discovery, both within the self and with the identified "other."

We are challenged to sustain the gains made during dialogue. Participants frequently leave encounter groups of all sorts with a "high" born of our longing to see and be seen, to be affirmed for our authentic selves, to feel the joy of community. Sustaining such rare feelings is impossible; we are called to come down from the mountain back into the marketplace where we live. But we can take some of our insights with us, expressing our solidarity by educating others and widening the circles of awareness. Without reinforcement, we gradually slide back into the communal norms we left behind in this journey, norms filled with stereotypes and prejudices born of ignorance of our fellow travelers.

In *Hands Across the Hills*, we reinvigorate our relationships and commitments through full group and individual communications, especially in times of ill health or political crises. We currently have shared committees promoting online youth exchanges and a joint speakers bureau. Interreligious and intergroup dialogue members in geographic proximity have even more opportunities for exchange and reinforcement. Research shows the positive results of enlarging the conversation to include more members and key members, such as leaders of communities who can widely facilitate changes in attitudes, behaviors, and structures using media and political outreach. Dialogue is an essential step, but only a step, in the process of social change, one with transformative outcomes that in the best of times builds communities across so many divides that "division" ceases to be operative. We are then on the way to honoring, celebrating, and treasuring our multiple diversities and common ground, creating safe passage for each valued life.

INTERFAITH YOUTH INITIATIVE FELLOWSHIP
A COMMUNITY OF PRACTICE MODEL FOR TRANSFORMATIVE INTERRELIGIOUS AND INTERCULTURAL EXPERIENCE

Shelton Oakley Hersey

Among the most profound and transformative experiences of my adult life sits the Interfaith Youth Initiative and my tenure as its Program Director. An immersive fellowship program for high school youth, IFYI recruits a diverse representation of approximately twenty strangers with varied religious, racial, socioeconomic, gender, and ethnic identities. Through experiential learning and interactive facilitation, as well as the roles of peer leadership, autonomy, creativity, and mentorship from a trained team of graduate theological students, participants are shaped by the *community of practice* pedagogical model as much as they are the content. The high school age population is often underdeveloped in terms of interreligious engagement and leadership; yet, intentional interreligious and intercultural exposure at this early life stage might perhaps have the most long-lasting impact. Developing effective youth leaders requires a balance between empowering dialogue and teaching, agency and accountability, autonomy and direction.

This chapter will examine the efficacy and virtue of the *community of practice* learning model when engaging youth in interreligious and intercultural activities. Taking a deep dive into the Interfaith Youth Initiative as an illustration of this model, the specific nature of the audience, ethos, and program structure will be explored as well as the identification of the IFYI's *community, domain, and practices*. Many youth and graduate student Mentors share my transformative experience, attributing IFYI to their long-term personal and spiritual development and deeper sense of interconnectedness with others.

THE IMPORTANCE OF ENGAGING YOUTH

The Interfaith Youth Initiative has a long history of life-changing impact with alumni citing their IFYI experience for the reason they pursued a religious commitment or a clergy vocation in later years. Other younger alumni report a notable shift in their worldview toward a greater sense of interconnectedness, hospitality toward "the other" and personal agency for collective change. This program is successful for two principal reasons. First, its cohorts are groups of adolescents who are therefore at a unique and formative stage of development;

second, it takes advantage of this developmental stage by employing peer learning. Youth at this age are ripe and yearning to receive from older mentors and role models as well as their peers in a mixture of structured and unstructured spaces. They are in their final key formative years—developmentally speaking—and beginning to name, choose, and internalize core values that will shape their own future choices and worldview. Peers and mentors provide the greatest influence at this age, and this supports why IFYI youth Fellows leave with increased confidence and connection to their own stories and values as well as the stories and values of others. One youth from 2018 remarked, "The discussions I had at IFYI on faith, privilege and social change are not the ones I regularly have with peers my age, and I learned not only about, but how to deeply listen, create safe spaces and advocate for inclusion with humility and authenticity." In 2019, another youth shared, "Do not underestimate when I say this week has been literally life-changing…stretching me to engage those who are different and giving me tremendous hope for our collective future and my part in securing it." More than ever, the possibility of a more interconnected future, along with the skills to see such a future come to fruition, are becoming increasingly dire; therefore, we need youth with informed and practiced leadership experience in a diverse setting who are also grounded in the wisdom of our great faith traditions and collective values.

UNIQUE PROGRAM ELEMENTS

It may prove helpful to illuminate several of IFYI's unique program elements. Rather than open applications, targeted recruitment allows for a greater equitable representation of identities in terms of religion, race, and gender. The Fellowship framework grants higher expectations of the youth Fellows to act and contribute as selected leaders of their various communities. Furthermore, since the Fellowship is free and provides a stipend for full participation, it diminishes the unavoidable power gap between youth from different economic stratifications.

The weeklong, residential setting provides the intrinsically transformational experience of immersion. The built-in spaces to eat, drink, play, travel, and "do life" together should not be undervalued. This is where many youths report their having engaged in the most honest and transparent conversations about all manners of life. Continuity reinforces the value of these relationships, so by revisiting the IFYI community through monthly fall activities and another immersive mid-year retreat, peer-leadership opportunities increase.

Over the many years of its existence, IFYI leaders identify a recurring community arc that can best be described by educational psychologist Bruce Tuckman's model of group formation: forming, storming, norming, performing, and adjourning.[1] The community would experience understandable discomfort upon arrival in this initial stage of forming: there was need of increased guidance and direction, clearly stated expectations, safer discussion topics, opportunities for socialization and focus on group identity and purpose. Invariably, specific signs of storming would arise such as conflict, high emotions, resistance, and power struggles. Understanding this framework of community dynamics meant embracing this difficult stage as an invaluable time for learning (rather than an interruption). Norming came next and involved reconciliation through honest and respectful feedback, higher levels of member engagement and motivation, consensus and greater cohesion and personal responsibility.

At this point in the immersive program, the IFYI community had become a healthier system—shifting its attention to small group collaboration and balancing task and process orientation. At the end of the program, participants described feeling a mixture of pride and recognition with great sadness that they cannot go on living so closely within this unique community. Shifting fully to process orientation, the final hours focus on personal internal changes, the arc of the communal journey, and what participants will bring home with them, thus leading the group through the fifth stage of adjourning.

The program consists of community building activities, workshops by the trained Mentor cohort and external facilitators, small group artistic expression, religious site visits, collective service, Reflective Structured Dialogue, and personal and group reflection.[2] There is an equal balance of learning from outside sources and experiences and learning from the harvested experience and wisdom of the IFYI community. Local graduate student Mentors add a great deal to this intragroup wisdom. Designed as a model cohort for the youth to observe and emulate, the Mentors undergo intensive training on subjects such as narrative-sharing, interactive facilitation, and mentorship through inquiry. Resisting the pedagogical model of "teaching unto," Mentors learn and practice the art of facilitating learning through experience, reflection, and dialogue. The program uses the age-old concept of apprenticeship as a learning model, learning by doing with Mentors as guides.

A COMMUNITY OF PRACTICE

IFYI mostly closely aligns with the *communities of practice* pedagogical model. "Communities of practice are groups of people who share a concern or a passion for something they do and learn how to do it better as they interact regularly."[3] Three characteristics are central to communities of practice: the domain, the community, and the practice.[4] The domain can be described in different ways: the shared mission, the learning goals, group values or just generally what a group of people collectively cares about. Clarifying the domain creates shared identity, meaning, purpose, and values, thus inspiriting participation and mutual exploration. The community is a group of people who pursue interest in their shared "domain and where members engage in joint activities and discussions, help each other and share information. They build relationships that enable them to learn from each other; they care about their standing with each other."[5] A community like this "creates social fabric of learning, fosters mutual respect and trust, willingness to share, ask, listen, be vulnerable and courageous."[6] The practice is defined by how and what we do to practice the domain, as well as the specific knowledge, activities, and experiences helping us explore our shared interest and values.. It is the union of these three components that compose a community of practice. And it is by cultivating these three components in concert that such a community is formed.

THE INTERFAITH YOUTH INITIATIVE (IFYI) COMMUNITY OF PRACTICE

The IFYI domain can be summarized as the development of transformative leaders in a globalized world who foster understanding across lines of difference in their own lives and communities. This shared vision is founded upon the program outcomes of mindset development and identity formation. The former seeks to reinforce the valuing of diverse perspectives and recognizing interdependence as a strength while the latter focuses on increasing one's understanding of identity constellations of self and others. The domain is achieved by the community through various experiential learning practices, described in greater detail later on.

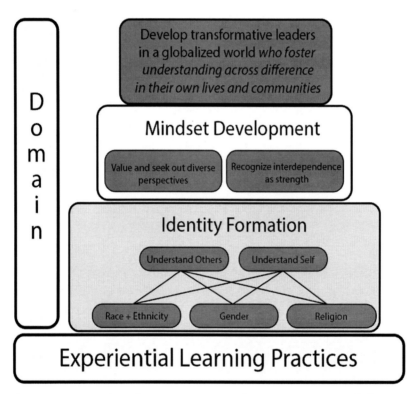

The community involves all core participants in the IFYI experience, including Program Director, graduate student Mentors, and youth Fellows who interact through experiential practices in the pursuit of their mindset development and identity formation. It is a relational cohort focused on an individual's and a group's way of being with one another. As one youth described IFYI: "We are a community, we live together, we're in this work together, we describe ourselves as the IFYI community, we cocreate Community Commitments, we work through conflict together, and so on." An exhaustive list of practices is beyond the scope of this chapter; however, the outline below will give the reader a glimpse into the IFYI program, which places more emphasis on practicing *how* the community relates to one another than on what the community accomplishes.

Exposure to (and engaging across lines) of difference

- Diversity training: owned versus perceived identity
- Workshop: understanding bias, stereotypes and power dynamics
- Skills practice: conflict and mediation, participant observation and sacred curiosity—the power of asking questions
- Reflective Structured Dialogue
- Site visits: Jewish Shabbat, Muslim Jummah, and Sikh Sangat
- Mentor theology and spiritual panel
- Mentor workshops on spiritual practices
- Collective service and advocacy
- Day of service and advocacy
- Workshop on structural racism and justice reform
- Workshop on how to use your voice for change
- Community Projects: empowering youth to take this back to their home community

Community building through informal and formal life together

- Ice cream social and evening fun
- Open mic night: participants share a different side of themselves
- Ice breakers and games
- Meals and travel together
- Living in dormitories with strangers
- Cocreation of Community Commitments: focusing on accountability and intrinsic motivation

Collaboration across lines of difference

- Reflection cohorts: nurture vulnerability and practice storytelling
- Expression cohorts: workshop on team styles, feedback, and conflict; focus on youth autonomy and creativity; Closing celebration and community projects: complete ownership by youth with Mentors as guides

MAKING THE CASE FOR YOUTH

A 2014 study on the phenomenological impact of interreligious engagement at Interfaith Youth Core's annual conference found the following: "Results demonstrated that the lived-experience of interfaith dialogue was characterized by: (1) the role of the environment, (2) the value of individual relationships through sharing and storytelling, (3) holding an ecumenical worldview, which led to the (4) strengthening of the individual's faith or non-faith tradition."[7] Interfaith Youth Initiative's program history fully supports these findings. A youth from IFYI 2014 shared about the deepening of her Muslim identity: "Not only did I learn about other religious traditions, I learned about my very own and will become a stronger Muslim because of it. It basically moved me to tears to know that people of other faiths honestly want to understand mine and how they prayed with us (the Muslims). I will never forget it." Another youth from IFYI 2017 wrote a year after her participation citing IFYI as the reason for her decision to pursue a relationship with God, within her Christian tradition, and the source of inspiration behind a six-month journey of exploring various Christian denominations to learn and find her place of belonging. Interreligious and intercultural engagement and relationships do not create identity confusion; rather, experience testifies that the result is quite the opposite. More youth personally identify with their religious community and belief/value system with a greater sense of desire and ownership.

Community of practice programs focused on pre-college youth, such as IFYI, provide a rare chance to experience a different kind of community, an experience of belonging not dependent on total sameness or geographical or social conveniences. These programs are indeed transformational and uniquely invaluable in shaping a more interdependent world. Youth daily live an intensive process of becoming, and who they become depends largely on their experiences and the people with whom they journey. Following up on past IFYI Fellows, the long-term impact remains clear: youth exit with a different way of thinking about and interacting with others, expanded skills of empathy and inquiry, inclusive language development and capacity building, confidence and motivation to take on more leadership positions, and practice with how to be a guest in someone else's space. Their self-esteem grows, and they find themselves more rooted in their own intersection of identities, with a greater balance of humility and confidence. Nearly all past Fellows communicate an increased commitment to befriending people across differences for their own personal flourishing and the flourishing of the greater good.

Understanding that our lives, words, thoughts, and choices impact others either positively or negatively, never neutrally, remains one of the most significant collective takeaways from this experience. Youth who arrive tending to dehumanize people they perceive as different emerge from the program with a more refined worldview and identity grounded in a greater sense of "we." These youth are catalysts for the change so desperately needed in our world, and their impact—by sheer measurement of years left on this earth—need not be undermined or undervalued. When the impact on a young person is positive, the total collective impact is multiplied. Nurturing change agents for a world in which every person can be more fully themselves because of the reverence by which we engage with one another is the work; and the work is messy and hard-won. The work is IFYI and other youth programs like it. The work is the intentional facilitation of lived experiences that teach youth by creating teachable moments. When the lives of youth are changed, the future changes with them.

NOTES

1   Bruce W. Tuckman, "Developmental sequence in small groups," in *Psychological Bulletin,* 63, no. 6 (1965): 384–99.

2   Reflective Structured Dialogue is a dialogue model created by Essential Partners in Boston, MA, https://whatisessential.org/.

3   Etienne and Beverly Wenger-Trayner, "Introduction to Communities of Practice: a brief overview of the concept and its uses," *BE*, 2015, https://wenger-trayner.com/introduction-to-communities-of-practice/.

4   Etienne Wenger, Richard McDermott, and William Snyder, *Cultivating Communities of Practice* (Boston: Harvard Business School Press, 2002).

5   Etienne and Beverly Wenger-Trayner.

6   Tommy Brewer II, Mary Jo Ginty, and Michelle Perrenoud, "Taking It To The Next Level: Expanded Learning Leadership" presentation, *BOOST Conference* (Palm Springs, CA: May 3, 2018),

7   Stephanie R. Krebs, "Voices of Interfaith Dialogue: A Phenomenological Analysis," PhD diss., Colorado State University, 2014.

SEIZE THE CHALLENGE
DISCERNING SHARED VALUES AND
BUILDING FRAMEWORKS FOR ACTION

David Rhodes & Thomas A. Mitchell

When people recognize and seize the opportunity, challenges can define the character of an institution, illuminating deep questions at the heart of operationalizing a mission. The following two stories are about leveraging the potential of these sorts of challenges to create applicable principles of discernment that support frameworks for institutional action. As conversation partners, we offer these stories to illustrate our respective involvement in organizational discernment processes that stem from our personal interests in bridging divides and including others.

THE FIRST STORY: MOVING BEYOND POLARIZING QUESTIONS
Thomas A. Mitchell

"We know better than others that every attribute of their character fits them for dependence and servitude." Those words were spoken by the Rev. Dr. Benjamin Morgan Palmer during his infamous 1861 Thanksgiving Day Sermon that precipitated the secession of Louisiana from the United States. They are also the words that raised questions and conversations surrounding race, inclusion, belonging, and memorialization on the campus of my alma mater, Rhodes College, which had been named after former faculty member and president Peyton Nalle Rhodes. Rev. Palmer, an influential and significant figure in the Presbyterian Church in the Confederate States of America (later PCUS), was a similarly important figure in the history of the College. Upon its organization as a Presbyterian institution, Palmer, though he would decline the nomination, was selected as the first chancellor. Several decades later, when the school moved to Memphis, the administrative building was named in Palmer's honor. More than ninety years after that decision, the cover story of the student newspaper confronted the majority White liberal arts college sitting in the middle of a majority Black city with its most contentious conversation about the building's name. The article reduced the questions at hand into a single one that was deeply polarizing: "Keep the name or change it?" The story dominated campus life for days, resulting in a plethora of social media posts, campus demonstrations, and even a late-night meeting between campus administrators and student leaders. Although the question and conversation focused on the building's name, the real stake lay in the articulation and illustration of the College's values. And it is that stake that centers this discussion. How does an institution that is more than 170 years old identify and make clear its values in a moment of deep polarization? Moreover, how does an institution create a process through which those values can be articulated, so that interested parties have access to the same contexts and definitions necessary for a more holistic and resolvable conversation? And, finally, how might this be understood in the context of origin narratives?

A mission and vision are helpful tools in understanding how an institution defines its values; however, they are aspirational rather than operational. As a result, an institution may commit to diversity and inclusion, yet fail to have structures in place to facilitate and actualize said commitment. This was the situation at Rhodes. Opposing sides concentrated on different parts of the same statements. Those who supported changing the building's name tied their position to the language of the College's vision that uplifted and committed to diversity. Advocates for leaving the name unchanged referred to the same statement's assurance of "freedom of thought" and the desire for a tolerant and respectful environment for difficult conversations. In both cases, despite a seemingly clear articulation of ideals and beliefs, there were competing ideologies and understandings of the praxis of those ideals that created a nearly impassable cleavage. As a result, the College embarked upon a process to establish "Principles for the Process of Discernment" that could better facilitate the various conversations.

The process of establishing principles necessarily sidestepped the question of a building's name. Although the controversy of the name was the catalyst for the principles' needing to be established, it was clear that simply discussing the name would never address the deeper questions and conversations that lay beneath the surface. Throughout the spring of 2018, a small committee of students, faculty, staff, and trustees met to review the mission and vision of the College and develop principles with an eye toward ensuring that the product of their work could inform future conversations.

This process resulted in six principles: Alignment, History, Discernment, Inclusion, Hospitable Environment, and Transparency. These principles had the distinct purpose of creating a more objective foundation upon which difficult conversations about naming and memorialization could take place. Yet, the principles also quietly lent themselves to a more complete articulation of shared values and beliefs for the College community. It was through this articulation that once polarized ends were brought more closely together.

As a result of the articulation of (and agreement on) these principles, the conversation was refocused. More abstract conversations about the history of the College and the Confederacy were replaced by the intentional exploration of the life and legacy of Palmer through faculty lectures, a panel of Presbyterian ministers, and conversations with the contemporary leadership of the church that Palmer once led. Broader conversations about race and belonging were reoriented to focus on the role and impact of the building in campus life, as illustrated through surveys and a review of the building's purpose. Perhaps most importantly, for the first time, works authored by Palmer or written about him were made publicly available in the same space. This provided an opportunity for individuals who had, perhaps, already staked a position on the naming issue on account of their own biases or ideologies, to more closely examine their thoughts in concert with the historical record. All of these community-oriented actions occurred in tandem with the work of a specially authorized committee that was charged with utilizing the now established principles to recommend action on the name of the building. Ultimately, the decision was made to rename the building. Palmer was replaced by the College's old name, Southwestern, which was selected as a nod to alumni who still associated themselves with that name, and had the effect of highlighting an era that saw the admission of women and Black students, a marked growth in enrollment, and the development of a national identity. It was quite literally a refocusing of the institution's origin narrative from its older, more polarizing past towards its more recent and inclusive history. No decision would have been possible without the earlier development of the Principles for the Process of Discernment.

THE SECOND STORY:
BUILDING FRAMEWORKS FOR ACTION WITH THE "OTHER"
David Rhodes

In December 2015, I was living in Ithaca, New York, and working as a middle school social studies teacher. One day, I received a message from the pastor of a local Presbyterian church. She was inviting community members to an open meeting to discuss a collective response to the global refugee crisis. I felt compelled to respond to the call.

During the meeting, people from all faiths and backgrounds expressed a willingness to dedicate energy and resources to take action, and our collective challenge was to determine a path forward from the ground up. In seeking that path, a steering committee coalesced to explore the next steps. I was nominated to be one of two co-conveners of Ithaca Welcomes Refugees (IWR).

My initial responsibility was to facilitate a process that would illuminate a shared purpose and vision. This involved seeking to understand and leverage the wisdom of multiple communities, including communities of people who had previously sought refuge in the Ithaca area. As a nascent organization, we also felt an acute need to learn from what was already being done, within and beyond our region, to welcome people coming as refugees. Such information would enable us to be more effective in furthering our goals.

The narrative at the heart of our work was simple: we were placed on this earth to care for one another; when individuals and families are fleeing persecution and violence, it is our responsibility to come together to create a fair and welcoming community as best we can. While nothing in its mission statement suggested that this was an interfaith organization, in reality its work involved the collaboration of many faith-based communities in support of a common cause. This was reflected in the leadership of the organization: I am Jewish, my co-convener was a Muslim woman, and the founding board president was a Christian who was raising her family within both Hindu and Christian traditions. There was religious diversity among the volunteers in the organization; and diversity within faiths was represented as well. This allowed us to build bridges with various congregations and expand our calls for support, since each of us could translate the story of welcoming the stranger into the language and values of our religious communities.

As the organization coalesced, we all benefited from the opportunities to connect across lines of religious difference, developing appreciation for the complexity of individuals, cultures, and faiths involved in the collective effort. This connection would happen on the front lines of the mission, when diverse teams were formed with language skills, cultural understanding, and areas of expertise that would be most relevant in a particular context with new members of our community. There were also opportunities to build relationships behind the scenes, where volunteers would run different aspects of the organization from communications to development, and teams would engage in activities such as coordinating the donation, pick-up, and storage of furniture and other household items. There were events, from potlucks in the park to a co-sponsored Karen-Burmese cultural evening, where people could meet and break bread together. As we faced new challenges and hard decisions, it became clear through conversation that creating space for connection was an essential aspect of our work to build a welcoming community that respected the dignity of all its members, and we needed to model that space in the practices of the organization. This came to the fore whenever we received invitations to partner with other organizations in sponsoring events or launching new initiatives.

IWR sought to welcome people without efforts, on its end, to impose an agenda or encourage allegiance to any particular faith or complete worldview. We were also committed to recognizing the dignity of the "other" in all aspects of the organization and to fostering opportunities for learning and connection across differences that affirmed the infinite complexity of individual and cultural identity. If an organization sought to partner with us for an event or initiative with an agenda that explicitly conflicted with this core principle, we would decline the invitation. Even when such an agenda was not explicit, we would avoid collaborative endeavors that could be understood to demonize or dehumanize a group of people across any lines of difference or conflict. For example, the broader community was deeply divided in relation to the Israeli-Palestinian conflict, and while explicit vitriol was not uncommon, events more often contained implicit messages that affirmed or aligned with dehumanizing views of the opposing camp. We were careful not to associate IWR with these messages. Rather, we worked diligently to create space for members of opposing camps to join in the work of IWR. In all aspects of our work, we sought to bridge rather than divide. We grounded our efforts in the compassion and curiosity that follows from the idea that our categories are inadequate to capture the many aspects of identity and that we cannot grasp the infinite nuance of how even a single aspect/category actually relates to the lived experience of an individual.

With clarity around core values of dignity and connection, our goal was to ensure that, so long as people were committed to these values and dedicated to welcoming people seeking refuge, there would not be other ideological barriers to participation in IWR. This stance was subject to criticism because it limited possibilities to join coalitions focused on other social justice issues. While our approach could be perceived as an abdication of responsibility to define and stand up for a more comprehensive set of values, our core commitment opened possibilities for people with opposing worldviews to stand side-by-side in welcoming and being welcomed. Through our shared work, stereotypes were challenged, nuanced narratives emerged, and genuine relationships of trust and understanding were forged. While deep divides in worldview still persisted, there were also new bonds of connection that could provide a foundation for learning and understanding even when we might advocate for opposing paths in other spheres of our lives. On individual and collective levels, the stranger was less strange and more complex. As we experienced the dignity and humanity of the "other," preconceived notions and stereotypes were replaced with nuance and curiosity. In our reaching out across divides with compassion and warmth, the spoken and unspoken message of IWR was that, in the face of a global refugee crisis, we can come together.

REFLECTION

In the first story, Thomas A. Mitchell showed how transformation of a contentious debate regarding the name of a building at his alma mater created space for the establishment of shared values and ideals. In the second story, David Rhodes explained the decision-making related to building partnerships with a grassroots organization that coalesced to help welcome people coming as refugees to the Finger Lakes region of upstate New York. Both stories shed light upon a process of discerning institutional values that can then strengthen efforts to foster deep understanding and connection across differences. These narratives offer useful guides for groups and organizations to establish their own processes for determining the values at the heart of their work. Moreover, the processes described in these stories may be most useful for organizations that place community at their center, as they will undoubtedly need a structure for effective dialogue across differences.

BRAVE LISTENING AND PASSIONATE SPEAKING
ENGAGING STRONG EMOTION
IN INTERFAITH DIALOGUE

Robert R. Stains Jr

What does it take, in a group, for people to listen to what is hard to hear from others? What enables someone to speak their truth in ways that others can take in? It takes bravery: the courage to take that journey from head to heart. Bravery that can be encouraged and supported by creating a fitting, "safe-enough" container through meeting design, facilitation, and helping participants prepare themselves for a new encounter.

Conversations across religious differences can raise powerful emotions when they move beyond polite exchanges about faith and practice traditions to exploring how one's beliefs and practices may affect others. Feelings of fear, pride, shame, anger, sadness, affection, and others may come to the surface. Those feelings carry the dual possibilities of injury and intimacy depending on how they are valued, invited, and engaged. Facilitators can unwittingly discourage the expression of emotion or allow its unbridled display in ways that silence or wound both the speaker as well as listeners. Neither alternative will result in deeper mutual understanding. Instead, self-silencing, enhanced vigilance, fear, attack, and future avoidance are likely.

Emotion is what makes connection authentic. The challenge is in how it is expressed by the speaker and whether and how it will be taken in by the listener. Emotion can be expressed in ways that are abusive, shaming, traumatizing, and self-demeaning, or in ways that are reflective, regulated, self-disclosing, and spark curiosity in the listener. Yet many dialogue and conflict transformation practitioners are shy about what to do when participants express strong emotion. When I recently asked a group of one hundred seasoned mediators with decades of experience with the hardest cases—cases I would be terrified to touch—what they feared most or what they felt they needed the most help with was, they said, "What to do when emotion is in the room." Many facilitators of conversations across differences feel this way.

The challenge for the facilitator is to prevent suppressing or venting and promote connecting expression as much as possible. This is a tricky proposition. As DeTemple and Sarrouf have noted in their paper on teaching religion in a multi-religious classroom,

To change the old pattern takes attention and intention—attention to what has been the old pattern that we want to prevent and intentional choices to "foster the new" (Chasin et al., 1996). Every choice we make as facilitators and teachers will invite one way of being together and discourage another. We need to make wise choices.[1]

For many people, religion or spiritual practice is at the core of their identity; it is deeply woven into who they consider themselves to be. Because of that, conversations across religious lines can easily create and amplify feelings of threat. Stone, Patton, and Heen have demonstrated the special challenge that "identity threat" poses to conversations and relationships: how people avoid discussing it in unpacking a conflict or when they do approach it, doing so can make things worse.[2] Participants usually feel safe in interfaith conversations as long as their religion is neither challenged nor denigrated, i.e., when conversation stays at the level of theology, description, and shared values. When it veers away from those precincts, however, the heat can rise pretty quickly. Offense can be given and taken. Safety can be eroded, and people may feel threatened. Fear and anger may grow; people may become defensive and revert to attacks to keep the "feared other" at arm's length. These behaviors will most likely provoke a similar response in others. Understanding this sequence of feeling and response can help facilitators plan and facilitate interfaith conversations that provide the heat and light of emotion without burning the house down.

Here is an example of how things can go awry quickly in the absence of a "safe-enough" container for conversation.

> *In an unstructured, multi-faith conversation focused on Israel/Palestine, a non-Muslim woman expressed sympathy and sorrow to Muslim women in the room, Muslim women in general, and Palestinian women in particular for how they are treated by men in their religion. One of the Muslim women stood up and said, "Who do you think you are to have sympathy for me? You know nothing about me or the men in my world!" The first speaker, of course, thought she was doing a good thing and was offended by the blow-back. Trying to explain herself, she only inflamed her listener more. The exchange briefly escalated with voices raised, then stopped. The speakers faded into the background, silencing themselves. The group moved on, but the impact of their speaking hung in the air like the smoke of a smoldering fire. The facilitator was handicapped by a murky role description, the absence of shared purpose, clear communication agreements/ground rules, a lack of participant preparation and a totally open meeting format. There was little to do but watch as the unbridled expression of anger hijacked the process and left people feeling wounded, misunderstood, and distant. People who had come to this multi-session program for the purpose of deepening*

*understanding and relationships left the process feeling more separated
than when they had begun.*

This was a classic example of how the absence of participant preparation, meeting structure, agreed-on ground rules, guidelines for questions, and a hobbled facilitator created "unsafe" space that left people feeling vulnerable and threatened and invited venting, attack, and defense rather than brave speaking and listening.

It is important to understand what happens to perception and communication when people feel threatened, and how their response can be connected to previous experience of trauma. Trauma researcher and clinician Bruce Perry discusses the similarities between traumatized children's responses to threat and our own:

> When threatened, a child is likely to act in an "immature" fashion. Regression, a "retreat" to a less mature style of functioning and behavior, is commonly observed in all of us when we are physically ill, sleep-deprived, hungry, fatigued or threatened. During the regressive response to the real or perceived threat, less-complex brain areas mediate our behaviors.... the traumatized child will have a "sensitized" alarm response, over-reading verbal and nonverbal cues as threatening. This increased reactivity will result in dramatic changes in behavior in the face of seemingly minor provocative cues. All too often, this over-reading of threat will lead to a "fight" or "flight" reaction—and increase the probability of impulsive aggression.[3]

It need not be this way. We can invite and hold strong emotions that can be taken in and understood when we create the right conversational milieu. One of the great innovators in psychiatric care, Maxwell Jones, sought a fresh approach to helping people with intractable psychiatric problems. He created "milieu therapy": the intentional construction of a social milieu surrounding and involving the patient that enables them to regulate their emotions, overcome their symptoms, and engage others in constructive ways.[4] Margaret Wheatley also speaks of the power of social milieu as energy "fields" that characterize groups and organizations; how they call forth certain thoughts, feelings, and behaviors and discourage others.[5] Drawing on the understanding from Wheatley and the example of Jones, we can create and maintain positive relational and conversational fields that support the brave speaking and listening that deepen understanding and relationship.

According to Perry, one must "regulate" before one can "relate" when managing strong emotion, and that the external social milieu plays a big role in enabling internal self-regulation in moments of perceived threat.

> The social milieu, then, becomes a major mediator of individual stress response baseline and reactivity. . . . The bottom line is that healthy

relational interactions with safe and familiar individuals can buffer and heal trauma-related problems, whereas the ongoing process of . . . creating an "us" and "them" . . . is a powerful but destructive aspect of the human condition that only exacerbates trauma in individuals, families, and communities attempting to heal.[6]

Here is an example of how things can go right when religious identity is threatened and feelings run high:

> *"How can you say you love me when the God that you serve says that I will burn in Hell? And you believe that I will, too! Do you know how offensive and hurtful that is to me?" So said a Jewish person—with a mixture of anger and sadness—to a Christian person near the end of an interfaith retreat. This exchange could have been a threat to the gathering, but it was a profound moment of deep honesty that had been waiting for years to be spoken and reflected the unsaid feelings of many in the group. With the group's permission the two continued their exchange, lightly moderated by the facilitator. People left the gathering satisfied that they had fulfilled their purpose of "going deeper."*

In this group, there was a shared understanding of purpose; the design was co-created well in advance with a representative planning team; communication agreements were clear, enforceable, and committed to; and participants had been prepared through an interview with a facilitator, advance reading, and questions for reflection. The meeting design was tight, with frequent, time-limited turn-taking interspersed with open discussion but amenable to modification, as in this vignette. The facilitator's role was clear and authorized by all present. People were able to speak and listen from and with the heart. In order to do that, they had to recognize and moderate their emotions or, in more clinical language, "self-regulate."

The milieu of dialogue, when done well, breaks down factional, divisive walls and enables people to hear the "sound of the genuine" in one another through the honest expression of feelings.[7] It is a holding environment, a liminal space or a container within which some things are called forth and protected and some things are discouraged, especially reactivity, listening to judge or win, and speaking to convert or condemn. The Reflective Structured Dialogue model from Essential Partners is a good example and a terrific resource for creating this kind of dialogic space.[8]

As facilitators, we can help people navigate the journey from head to heart. We can help them meet at deeper levels of emotion and meaning. By thinking and planning in advance, we can create and maintain the conversational and relational vessel that makes it easier for people find the courage to speak from the heart with feeling about what most deeply matters to them and to listen with curiosity, resilience, and empathy in return. By bringing our human, empathetic and boundaried presence into the room, we can help people feel brave enough to hang in when it may be hard to listen and to speak without reactivity.

NOTES

1   J. DeTemple and J. Sarrouf, "Disruption, Dialogue, and Swerve: Reflective Structured Dialogue in Religious Studies Classrooms," in *Teaching Theology and Religion* 20 (2017):283–292. https://doi.org/10.1111/ teth.12398. The authors cite R. Chasin, M. Herzig, S. Roth, L. Chasin, C. Becker, C., and R. Stains, Jr, "From Diatribe to Dialogue on Divisive Public Issues: Approaches Drawn from Family Therapy" in *Mediation Quarterly*, 13:4 (Summer 1996): 323.

2   D. Stone, B. Patton, and S. Heen, *Difficult Conversations: How to Discuss What Matters Most* (New York: Penguin, updated edition, 2010), 109–28.

3   Bruce D. Perry, "Understanding Hyperarousal: the 'Flock, Freeze, Flight and Fight' Continuum." Child Trauma Academy/Bruce D. Perry, 2007–2017. Retrievable at: https://www.pcaaz.org/wp-content/uploads/2019/07/B21-Insightful-Caregiving-Hyperarousal.pdf.

4   Maxwell Jones, *Beyond the Therapeutic Community: Social Learning and Social Psychiatry* (New Haven, CT: Yale University Press, 1968).

5   Margaret Wheatley, *Leadership and the New Science: Discovering Order in a Chaotic World* (San Francisco: Berrett-Koehler, 2006), 49–60.

6   Bruce Perry, "Sequence of Engagement" from *Neurosequential Model Core Slides: "Best Hits" Package* (Neurosequential Network, 2004–2019). https://8888cf92-fc69-4812-b8a8 -1049afbcc7cf.filesusr.com/ugd/5cebf2_6b9a260d654f4e3dbf0118dcbd971742.pdf.

7   Sound of the genuine" is a turn of phrase from Howard Thurman's Baccalaureate Address at Spelman College (May 9, 1980), reprinted in University of Indianapolis, *The Crossing Project: Crossings Reflection #4* (2004) http://eip.uindy.edu/crossings/publications /reflection4.pdf.

8   M. Herzig and L. Chasin, *Fostering Dialogue Across Divides: A Nuts and Bolts Guide from the Public Conversations Project* (Watertown, MA: The Public Conversations Project, 2006). Available at www.whatisessential.org.

GETTING OUT OF OUR OWN WAY
MAXIMIZING OUR COLLECTIVE POWER
IN SERVICE TO JUSTICE

Wendy von Courter

"When I saw you join us, my heart calmed and I could breathe again," said Maria. Thirty minutes earlier we had been sitting together, cross-legged, arms linked with others, chanting "Sí, se puede" as we awaited arrest. She said she was reminded in that moment that God was present. There were one hundred women, blocking the intersection outside of the US House of Representatives. A quarter of the women were undocumented. We were protesting the Representatives' refusal to pass comprehensive immigration reform that would treat women and children with respect and justice. I was one of five clergy in the hundred. As requested by the organizers of the action, I wore a clerical collar and religious stole so I would be visibly identifiable as a clergy person.

Earlier in my ministry, I might have felt the need to clarify my nontheist identity. Lacking a God or Goddess figure in my theology, let alone Christology, I might have offered a clarifying response: "Yes, the God of our many understandings is present." Or perhaps I would have simply nodded, smiled, and moved on to my well-oiled internal translation: "Okay, she is saying God is present, but what she really means is that it is great that religious leaders are here." Either would have been a disservice to her, to me, and most importantly, the action. Her words and intent did not need interpretation, translation, or manipulation. Rather, they called me to attention. Attention to the depth of connection each of us felt to the action. Like the call to join Dr. Martin Luther King Jr. in Selma, the injustice called Catholics, Muslims, Jews, Pagans, pantheists, atheists, secular and religious humanists, and more. We were all there because each of our core beliefs made it clear we had to be present. We diminish the power of our presence when we fail to acknowledge the power of what called us. Each of us.

Today, it is essential we unite more effectively for justice: maximize our power to stop the rise of fascism, call out racism and oppression, and insist upon a future in which all Creation's children are welcomed and treasured. This is not a new call. Our siblings of color and those with marginalized identities have long been the targets of rhetoric, injustice, harm, and danger. They and their ancestors, have led the resistance for generations. Some White-identified people have been present too. We have arrived from many faith traditions and belief systems. Sadly, it is not uncommon for us to squander our power and the power of the collective because of self-limiting behaviors. We will not collaborate with other groups because of positions on marriage equality or women's reproductive rights. We have felt excluded because we are laity and only clergy are valued. We have excluded others because our vision for religious identity is too narrow. We have disengaged and caused others to do the same. This is what I risked in that moment—disengagement, if even only within my own mind. Thankfully, some generous souls, primarily from communities of color, and experiences have taught me the spiritual practice of getting out of my own way.

Participating in group civil disobedience offers an intense learning environment. Everyone who participates shares a bond reflected in their willingness to put their body on the line for a specific justice objective. Because of the controlled, and at times abusive, settings, senses are heightened. There is a mix of people who have been doing this for years and those for whom this is a new experience. Acts of solidarity, large and small occur throughout: an offer of exact change for bail, a courageous yell out to loosen someone's too-tight zip-tie cuffs. As bodies are patted down fully in view of others, a forced intimacy arises. As a tall, White, 63-year-old clergywoman who easily passes as straight, the odds of me being singled out for harm are quite low. That is not the case for many I protest beside, for whom there are additional levels of risk that require additional levels of courage, vigilance, and solidarity.

In that setting, across theology, race, class, gender identification, affectional orientation, and how we move through the world, a bond is made instantly. With that bond come two opportunities. The first is collective power. The second is individual spiritual maturation. When the second takes place, the collective power increases exponentially in that action and those that will follow. In a way, our own spiritual maturation is a contribution to the momentum of the movement.

My own spiritual maturation, at times reluctant and often clumsy, has been most impacted at justice actions, including the risk of civil disobedience. The settings have been diverse: blocking a county jail entrance in Maricopa County, AZ; marching through Lafayette Park to the White House with the Poor People's Campaign; putting my body in the pathway of ICE officers and immigrants in a New England courtroom; recruiting clergy to be part of a 100-mile trek for immigration justice; carrying a child-sized coffin bearing the pictures of children who died because of our immigration policies; and on the steps of the Supreme Court of the Unites States in protest of a threat to LGBTQIA rights. Although the settings differed, in each case I needed to let go of something or things I held dear—a wish to know exactly what would happen next and what my role would be, a preference to work solely alongside people who would affirm my marriage to a woman, a belief that my layers of privilege were not a positive thing. Differently put, in each case, I needed to get out of my own way. Each of these experiences gave me an opportunity to do so.

An early lesson helped me let go of my own beliefs about privilege and learn to leverage that privilege in service to justice. Let me set the scene: I was in Phoenix, AZ. I was there in response to the call by local immigrant justice groups to protest the roll-out of SB1070, a bill that legalized the racial profiling that was already taking place. I was not new to racial justice work but was just beginning to learn how broken our immigration system was and that

Arizona was being used as a test lab for racial profiling efforts across the country. I sat with arms locked with other activists. The press was six or seven deep in front of us, being pushed almost on top of us by the growing crowd. Behind us were officers with shields, weapons, and dogs. Within minutes we were dragged off, across the cement, without even being given the chance to stand. It was startling, frightening, and painful. In the midst of it all, the focus was placed on me rather than the seasoned activists to my left and to my right. The same focus continued in the days that followed. I did not know why. In the wee hours of the night, in a cold and filthy jail cell, in conversation with one of the Latina activists I got my answer. "Don't you get it? It's because you're White the press are paying attention. It's why we wanted you here." The conversation was formative and helped me realize that with the privilege gifted to me by the very system we were trying to dismantle, came the power to tell the story. It was a gift that came with the responsibility to use that power. I left, bringing that story back to the East Coast, where, indeed, it was easy to get it in local papers and the *Boston Globe*.

This experience, and others like it, moved me from a textbook understanding of White privilege to a commitment to use privilege in service to justice. That commitment means saying yes to offering my body to acts of civil disobedience because it is safer for me than it is for others. That commitment means being willing to be a driver for those who are targeted by police or the ICE, knowing I am less likely to be stopped or violated asserting my right to deny them access to those passengers. That commitment means using the full power of my clergy garb and body to seek different outcomes in courtrooms and ICE check-ins. That commitment means showing up where my identities as clergy and/or White make a difference. That commitment means remembering fourteen frightening hours in a filthy jail cell are a far cry from the constant harm being inflicted on those without my layers of privilege.

But privilege is a two-sided sword. Far more common than the instances of using privilege to serve justice is the need to leave privileged-born behaviors at the door. I come from a faith tradition steeped in White supremacy culture, a tradition in which followership is not taught or valued. My experience in Arizona taught me to be clear on what was being asked of me. That lesson also taught me to seek out actions that were being led by communities most impacted by the injustice and oppression. My experiences fighting for justice with groups like Puente, We Belong Together, Faith In Action, and Cosecha taught me something ministry formation had not: to follow. In 2014, We Belong Together, a group founded by Pramila Jayapal and Miriam Yeung that centered immigrant women in leadership and valued collaboration, held a two-day fast. Over one hundred women, many undocumented, fasted while demanding an end to deportations, and compassionate immigration reform. Throughout the forty-eight hours, congressional representatives and other leaders holding key roles impacting immigration were invited to the tent into a set-up of three concentric semi-circles. In the past I would have been eager for a front row seat and equally ready to raise my hand with a question. However, I was invited to this precious space not to lead, but to follow. Following meant letting go of those old patterns, birthed in privilege, and finding my place in the outermost circle. Unless I was asked to do otherwise. Following meant letting go of the need to have any role other than to show up ready to do what I was asked to do, even if it changed. Most of all, following meant refraining from offering "different approaches," "yeah, buts," and "I was thinkings." Following meant following. Period.

I have been given many opportunities to follow since that event. In 2015 I was invited to recruit a team of clergy to accompany one hundred women walking one hundred miles to bring a message about compassionate immigration reform to Pope Francis. The nine-day march began at a detention center in Pennsylvania and ended in Washington, DC, where the Pope was meeting with government officials. In recruiting fellow clergy, someone offered to make a list of UU congregations along the way. I knew I needed something different. I needed to create a list of fellow clergy who knew how to follow. Another opportunity came in Layfayette Park when the Secret Service constructed a barricade turning a misdemeanor into a felony should the three hundred protesters proceed. While a number of protesters, safe in their privilege, shouted out, "knock it down," the Rev. William J. Barber, founder of the Poor People's Campaign, was clear in his decision. We left the petitions—calling on the White House to abide by the Fourteenth Amendment, stop mandating a census question on immigration status, end its attack on the Affordable Care Act, focus on providing clean air and water, create a humane immigration policy, and end child detention—at the gate. We would return another day.

Learning when to refuse and/or redirect privilege-based attention, or step or roll back when the leaders of the action are centering voices and visibility from the impacted community, rather than use the privilege, is not always clear. I will not claim to get it right, or even to do it gracefully, but I have found if I start with the question "How can I best serve?"—not as an internal reflection, not as a prayer, but as a question to the leaders—I'm less likely to get it wrong.

AFTERWORD

OPENING BORDERS
STRETCHING HUMAN COMPASSION

Mary Elizabeth Moore

As we close *Deep Understanding for Divisive Times*, recall the introductory words of Axel Takacs. Inspired by bell hooks and the power of transgressing boundaries, he argues that "movements that unite transgress the boundaries that divide."[1] The chapters in this volume are themselves transgressions of divisive boundaries. They stand alongside the scream of cyberspace and media that announce closed and closing borders across the world. I use the term "border," which commonly connotes a political or structural boundary that is established by people of power. I recognize the need for boundaries in many contexts, but will speak here to the hardened borders—enforced by walls, fences, laws, social policies, and prejudices—that people create to prevent equitable and mutual interchange among peoples of different nations, religions, worldviews, ethnicities, abilities, and sexual and gender identities. Such borders create the conditions for abuses of power and the escalation of falsehoods, fear, and violence. The question here is whether opening borders of relationship—whether international, intergroup, or interpersonal—can stretch human compassion.

This book contains many personal and communal stories, as well as potent ideas and practices. The inclusion of narratives is not surprising because narratives play a critical role in human efforts to learn with and from others and to foster personal, social, and ecological transformation.[2] With that recognition, I share a narrative of my life, one that is seemingly small, even trivial, but was compassion-stretching for me.

REMEMBERING MOMENTS

Many years ago, I was part of an interreligious group that appealed to Houghton-Mifflin to revise some of the portrayals of religion in the social sciences series the company was piloting. I share this story because it took place during divisive times, and it was formative for me in developing a new sense of urgency for deep understanding of religion and the enormous range of religious sensitivities, particularly the power of interreligious collaborations in cultivating compassion. It also helps me recognize the many values that are at stake in the more recent contestations about what should and should not be included in school textbooks.

Rabbi Alfred Wolf led the group, bringing his long experience in the Wilshire Boulevard Temple, Los Angeles, and in interreligious leadership. By the end of the process, our efforts had effected some changes in the texts, though the changes were not as extensive as we had hoped. Thus, Rabbi Wolfe negotiated with Houghton-Mifflin for a team to write a teachers' guide for teaching about religion with the new textbook series, which we did as a collective effort, learning and teaching about the complexities and possibilities of such teaching.[3] I share two particular stories of discovery here to make a case for interreligious engagement that opens borders and stretches human compassion.

The first discovery took place in our first group meeting in Rabbi Wolfe's home, where we shared our common concern about misrepresentations of religion that reinforce stereotypes and fuel misunderstandings and antipathy regarding the religious diversity of the United States. Rabbi Wolfe shared an example that awakened me in a new way; the "Good Samaritan" story (Luke 10:25–37) had been used to introduce a chapter on Christianity. Wolfe pointed out that, of all the texts that could have been chosen, the editors had selected one that cast Jews and Judaism in a negative light. In the story, the Jewish scribe and Pharisee both pass by an injured man on the side of the road, and a Samaritan walks along the same road, sees the injured man, and tends him, even taking him to an inn and paying the innkeeper to continue the man's care. Throughout my life, I had loved this story and thought it represented the love and power of being a neighbor to all people; I had never once seen the anti-Jewish interpretation that runs through it. That was the beginning of new awareness in me—one that opened borders and stretched my compassion. I regularly see these problematic stories and issues now, though I am quite sure that my Christian eyes still see far less than I should. I also learned that ideology-infused interpretations of sacred texts can be broken open by compassion-infused readings. That is why I need continuing engagement with people of other faiths and with the multiplicity of religious traditions.

The second discovery came later when I was leading a workshop with a group of teachers to introduce the Handbook and its purpose, as well as its potential to guide teaching in the classroom. The teachers had many questions of me and themselves and more than a little resistance. One woman spoke most strongly when she expressed skepticism that any form of teaching about religion in the classroom would lapse into proselytism in many if not most classrooms. She told her own story of being a Jewish child in a public school in which one teacher advocated for Christianity and disparaged other religions, including her own Judaism. Now a teacher herself, this woman responded viscerally. She awakened me to the dangers of interreligious engagement in the public square (in this case the public schools) when unchecked by the claims of justice and compassion for all peoples. I could identify with her fear and resistance, yet I was and am convinced that less knowledge of diverse religions and less teaching about them have potential for far more danger.

How might people engage religion in public spaces to open borders and stretch human compassion? Power-constructed walls and other structural and relational barriers make space for prejudice, discrimination, and violence. In this moment of history, people across the world participate in ideologies and practices that perpetuate ignorance, denial, and violence. Many chapters in this book shine light on these concerns. Where is hope? The very question is a challenge, but the authors of *Deep Understanding* identify many religious, interreligious, and relational pathways. Bringing their work into conversation with my own,

I propose two approaches that can make space for hope: mutual questing for a better world and opening structural and existential borders.

MUTUAL QUESTING FOR A BETTER WORLD

Interreligious relationship-building has long been seen as vital for building human and earth relationships and thus contributing to movements of justice, reconciliation, peace-making, and ecological well-being. Religious leaders across traditions have sought to make that possible by sharing gifts from their own traditions with the larger public and by gathering and writing interreligiously in the shared work of what Jewish peoples call *tikkun olam*, or repair of the world. Many interreligious movements are established for these purposes. Note, for example, that Eboo Patel "founded Interfaith Youth Core on the idea that religion should be a bridge of cooperation rather than a barrier of division. He is inspired to build this bridge by his identity as an American Muslim navigating a religiously diverse social landscape."[4] This quote expresses both hope and challenge for religion's potential to be a force for cooperation rather than for division, while connecting with Patel's own personal search, grounded in his experience as an American Muslim.

Another exemplar of interreligious work toward goodness is the Yale Forum on Religion and Ecology, founded by Mary Evelyn Tucker and John Grim. The Forum's mission is "to inform and inspire people to preserve, protect, and restore the Earth community," recognizing that "[t]he religions of the world transmit ecological and justice perspectives in their scriptures, rituals, and contemplative practices as well as in their moral and ethical commitments."[5] Here, as above, the potential of religious and interreligious traditions and communities is focused on doing good, in this case doing good for the threatened and severely damaged ecology.

The quest for a better world is evident in many interreligious movements across the United States and world. In my home city of Boston, the Greater Boston Interreligious Organization (GBIO) describes its localized vision for goodness in this way: "Our mission is to build POWER by developing local LEADERS so we can ACT together on issues that matter to our communities" (emphasis theirs).[6] The focus here is local and regional; yet the issues addressed are wide-ranging and interconnected, including housing, healthcare, racial inequities and injustice, criminal justice, and schools. Similar organizations exist across the US and world—local communities focusing on local concerns in the quest for a better world.

Global justice and peacemaking movements exist for similar reasons and often on an international scale. Angeliki Ziaka, writing in the context of Christian engagement with Jewish and Muslim communities in Europe, describes the focus of interreligious dialogues as: "common themes found in all religions" focused on concern for humanity and creation, with the most common focus being on peace.[7] She recognizes the importance of weaving these interreligious emphases into the fabric of life through religious education in Europe: "A religious education which respects religious diversity and makes religion a subject for study, developing critical thinking and common responsibility, is perhaps the only bright path for the secular societies of Europe."[8] Conversations across Asia reveal a similar hope that the very practice of religion and interreligious dialogue and action will contribute to humanization, justice, and peace.[9]

At the same time, interreligious leaders are often quick to decry the destructive potential of religion and the casualties of history, especially when traditions are interpreted and practiced within enclosed borders that diminish opportunities for transformative relationships with others.[10] If people are to open borders for goodness to emerge, they (we) will have to be honest about the dangers, seeking pathways that protect the dignity and wellbeing of all.

OPENING STRUCTURAL AND EXISTENTIAL BORDERS

Opening borders is central to the quest for goodness because it creates long-term possibilities for people to diminish fears, cultivate genuine empathy, and work together in interreligious, intercultural relationships. The value of border-opening is well documented in the case studies and life narratives gathered by interreligious researchers and activists. The word "opening" is itself more complex than I can consider here, but borders can be opened literally, with walls and rules dismantled; they can be made more permeable with movement back and forth; and they can be transcended by establishing relationships that continue in spite of walls and fences. Different strategies are fitting or necessary in different contexts and moments of time, but border-opening is critical if people are to build just structures and relate in ways of compassion.

Structural and existential borders are enmeshed with one another. Structural borders instate and reinstate existential ones, and vice versa. Psychologically, studies of intergroup contact have been conducted since the 1950s, building on Gordon Allport's early work on prejudice. A number of studies were done in the 1960s to discern the correlation between contact and racial and ethnic prejudice in the US, and the focus on intergroup contacts has continued, with enlargement to include religion and other forms of difference. In a recent metanalysis of these studies, Thomas Pettigrew and Linda Tropp analyzed 515 studies with a total of 250,000 participants in 38 countries to discover the factors that best correlated with prejudice reduction.[11] They discovered that three factors play a role—increased knowledge, reduced anxiety, and increased empathy and perspective taking; the highest correlations were found with the anxiety-reduction and empathy-increase factors. In 94 percent of the studies, they found an inverse relationship between contact and multiple forms of prejudice.

Drawing from this metanalysis, one can conclude that structural border-opening and existential border-opening are intertwined and mutually influential. Thus, I will identify three interreligious practices that open borders in different ways, all with hope to expand compassion and effect transformation. I encourage others to enlarge on these practices in the future and to give further attention to social-structural and political border-opening. My purpose here is to identify practices that have proven to be vital in building interreligious understanding and partnerships and are well represented in the chapters of *Deep Understanding for Divisive Times*. I invite you to reflect on the practices of encountering, sharing, and seeking.

ENCOUNTERING THE OTHER

The personal stories with which I began this chapter are small stories of existential encounters with others. I shared them not because of their inherent importance to anyone other than myself, but to point to the power of encounters to awaken and turn a person in a new direction. I had many other experiences before and after these, and some were more dramatic. None was more important in planting seeds. Now, I can look back and realize what a rich and messy garden has grown from those seeds.

The idea of planting seeds is not limited to interpersonal exchanges. John Paul and Angela Jill Lederach have journeyed with communities traumatized by violence, and they have witnessed countless ways these communities plant seeds for social healing—through storytelling, music, poetry, and other arts and rituals.[12] Such practices open spaces so people can encounter one another and their horrific experiences in a new, more life-promising way, even as the memories and scars remain. The Lederach work is an important reminder that encounters may take many forms and are often grounded in the particular experiences and cultures of a people.

Encounters have power. I have just concluded nine interviews with interreligious leaders, with more to come. One striking theme is the power of interreligious encounters in the leaders' lives and practices. Globally, religious education has been one field rich with research on encountering difference and building transformative relationships. Many religious education studies focus on public spaces and state schools,[13] and some also on faith communities themselves. Sheryl A. Kujawa-Holbrook, for example, has made a very strong case for interreligious learning in religious spaces, recognizing the power of interreligious encounters in human thriving.[14]

Finally, encounters need to be real, building toward and engaging in hard conversations about issues of justice and peace among peoples and with the earth. Such conversations require relationship-building, careful planning for honest sharing and listening, and a commitment to continue conversations over time. Whereas political negotiations usually take place within a circumscribed group of leaders, the seeds that allow high-level negotiations to succeed are planted and watered across a land by communities who encounter one another with respect and courage.

SHARING TRADITIONS

A second practice by which people engage with one another interreligiously is in sharing riches from their own traditions, especially traditions that are, to some extent, "portable." Consider, for example, practices of mindfulness, compassion meditation, and walking meditation from

Buddhist traditions, and spiritual seeking and Sabbath in Jewish traditions. Thich Nhat Hanh has been very generous in sharing Buddhist practices with a large community of readers and fellow travelers.[15] Drawing from his Zen tradition, he shares the arts of meditation, living in peace, and mindfulness as guides to human life practices. Similarly, His Holiness the Dalai Lama, drawing upon the Tibetan Buddhist tradition, shares practices of mindfulness and meditation in multiple venues for the sake of guiding people to live meaningful and ethical lives.[16] He has also encouraged scientific studies of the potential healing effects of compassion meditation, and the studies have multiplied to form a major of body of data to support the healing potential of this meditation practice. Within Jewish traditions, spiritual leaders and theologians have shared the rich traditions and practices of Sabbath and of seeking God and the self and the world, writing for readers in their own and many traditions.[17]

In addition to the public sharing of one's tradition with others, some sharing takes place in interreligious relationships themselves. Consider the collaboration on the subject of joy by His Holiness the Dalai Lama and Archbishop Desmond Tutu. The two spiritual leaders came together for several days to reflect together on joy in relation to their different traditions and experiences. Their conversations and time together are recorded for posterity in *The Book of Joy*,[18] thus offering an important resource for others. In addition to such topical explorations, interreligious sharing can also draw upon practices of a particular tradition. For example, leaders in the Jewish community have often shared their ancient practice of studying in havruta pairs, stretching the practice into interreligious settings in which two partners learn with and from one another as they reflect on their respective texts and traditions.

I have shared some exemplars here to demonstrate the broad reach of tradition-sharing and the values that such practices contribute to the larger human family. The exemplars will be expanded in the future to include leaders from Hindu and Sikh traditions, which are quite generous in such sharing, as well as others. For some traditions, including many indigenous ones, sharing includes a strong caution against "stealing" or wanton borrowing from a sacred tradition, raising a concern that needs to be considered carefully in future work. As people share from their traditions what they judge to be most fitting to share, they open possibilities for mutual understanding and appreciation. Such sharing opens borders of spiritual knowledge, experience, and practice in an invitational way that honors the dignity and values of other religious communities. Such sharing inspires compassionate relationships to grow.

SEEKING RESONANCES ACROSS TRADITIONS

Interreligious discourses also have potential to unearth central themes that thread through diverse traditions, albeit in quite different ways. For example, the sacrality of human life is deeply influential in Judaism, Christianity, and Islam, potentially contributing to a respect for the dignity of every person and community in the human family.[19] Many religious people have sought to identify such resonances for the sake of fostering deeper and more life-supporting relationships. Consider the work of Thich Nhat Hanh and His Holiness the Dalai Lama, who have both sought resonances between Buddhist teachings and Jesus in Christian traditions.[20] Such works do not seek sameness, but the kind of resonances you find in music, in which one note brings out another and creates a harmony that is permeated with difference. Imagine the resonances that are sounded from the depths of different religious traditions. These add depth and fullness to the whole experience of interreligious engagement. The very search for resonances is an experience in mutual learning. Even the understanding and practice of compassion are enriched by the life stories and perspectives that arise in diverse traditions.[21]

LOOKING AHEAD

As I draw this book to a close, the potential is clear that, even in such divisive times as these, interreligious relationships carry extraordinary potential to open borders and stretch compassion. Compassion is a central value in building just and peaceful societies, and is a priority value in many, if not most, religious traditions. Not surprisingly, compassion is also a central theme in leadership and peacemaking literatures.[22] Opening borders creates spaces for compassion to emerge, and compassion heightens the potential of interreligious relationships to contribute to the flourishing of the human and earth family. During its second decade and beyond, may the opening of borders and the stretching of compassion be recurrent themes of the *Journal of Interreligious Studies*.

NOTES

1   See Axel Takacs, "Introduction," xi in the present volume; see also: bell hooks, *Teaching to Transgress: Education as the Practice of Freedom* (New York: Routledge, 1994).

2   From the Tannenbaum Center for Interreligious Understanding, see Joyce S. Dubensky, ed., *Peacemakers in Action* (Vol. II): *Profiles in Religious Peacebuilding* (New York: Cambridge University, 2016); Jennifer Howe Peace, Or Rose, and Gregory Mobley, eds., *My Neighbor's Faith: Stories of Interreligious Encounter, Growth, and Transformation* (Maryknoll, NY: Orbis, 2012); Marc Gopin, *Bridges Across an Impossible Divide: The Inner Lives of Arab and Jewish Peacemakers* (Oxford: Oxford University Press, 2012); Mary Elizabeth Moore, "Disrupting White Privilege: Diving beneath Shame and Guilt," *Religious Education*, 114, No. 3 (2019): 252–61; Mary Elizabeth Moore and Shin Myoung Kim, "Encountering Dignity: Building Human Community," *Religious Education*, 113, No. 3 (November 2018), 314–25.

3   Elliot N. Dorff, Robert Ellwood, Fathi Osman, and Mary Elizabeth Moore. *Teaching about World Religions: A Teacher's Supplement,* eds. Alfred Wolf and Robert Ellwood (Boston: Houghton Mifflin, 1991).

4   See: https://ifyc.org/eboo (accessed on 20 August 202).

5   See: https://fore.yale.edu/About-Us/Mission-and-Vision (accessed 16 August 2020).

6   See: https://www.gbio.org/ (accessed 16 August 2020).

7   Angelica Ziaka, "Interreligious Challenges and Engagements for Churches and Islam in Europe Interreligious Dialogue as mediator of nonviolence, understanding and reconciliation," in *Ortodoksia* 61 (2016): 86, and 86–116.

8   Ziaka, "Interreligious Challenges," 105.

9   Simone Sinn and Tong Wing-sze, eds. *Interactive Pluralism in Asia: Religious Life and Public Space* (Geneva: The Lutheran World Federation, 2016); Simone Sinn, ed., *Deepening Faith, Hope, and Love in Relations with Neighbors of Other Faiths* (Geneva: The Lutheran World Federation, 2008). These books focus largely, but not exclusively, on Christianity and other religions, but they give a glimpse into global hopes.

10 Marc Gopin, *Between Eden and Armageddon: The Future of World Religions, Violence, and Peacemaking* (Oxford: Oxford University, 2000).

11 Thomas F. Pettigrew and Linda R. Tropp, "How Does Intergroup Contact Reduce Prejudice? Meta-analytic Tests of Three Mediators," *European Journal of Social Psychology* 38 (2008), 922–934, esp. 922, 927–30.

12 John Paul Lederach and Angela Jill Lederach, *When Blood and Bones Cry Out: Journeys through the Soundscape of Healing and Reconciliation* (Oxford: Oxford University, 2010).

13 One collection highlights many of the major contributors to work on religious education as encounter: Siebren Miedema, ed., *Religious Education as Encounter: A Tribute to John M. Hull* (Religious Education and Diversity in Europe) (Münster: Waxmann Verlag GmbH, 2009).

14 Sheryl A. Kujawa-Holbrook, *God Beyond Borders: Interreligious Learning Among Faith Communities* (Eugene, OR: Pickwick, 2014).

15 Thich Nhat Hanh, *The Art of Living: Peace and Freedom in the Here and Now* (New York: Unified Buddhist Church, Inc., HarperCollins, 2017); Thich Nhat Hanh, *Being Peace* (Berkeley: Parallax, 2005, 1987).

16   His Holiness the Dalai Lama, transl. and ed. Jeffrey Hopkins, *How to Practice: The Way to a Meaningful Life* (New York: Simon & Schuster, 2003); *Beyond Religion: Ethics for a Whole World* (New York: Houghton Mifflin Harcourt, 2011); His Holiness the Dalai Lama, ed. Nicholas Vreeland, *An Open Heart: Practicing Compassion in Everyday Life* (New York: Time Warner Trade, 2001).

17   Abraham Joshua Heschel, *The Sabbath: Its Meaning for Modern Man* (New York: Farrar, Straus and Giroux, 2005); Arthur Green, *Seek My Face: A Jewish Mystical Theology* (Woodstock, VT: Jewish Lights, 2003).

18   Dalai Lama and Desmond Tutu, with author Douglas Carlton Abrams, *The Book of Joy: Lasting Happiness in a Changing World* (New York: Penguin Random House, 2016).

19   Mary Elizabeth Moore, "Sacred, Revolutionary Teaching: Encountering Sacred Difference and Honest Hope," *Religious Education* (April 2020), 1–13.

20   Thich Nhat Hanh, *Living Buddha, Living Christ* (New York: Riverhead Books, Penguin Putnam, 1995); His Holiness the Dalai Lama, *The Good Heart: A Buddhist Perspective on the Teachings of Jesus* (Somerville, MA: Wisdom Publications, 2016, 1996).

21   Mary Elizabeth Moore and Shin Myoung Kim, "Encountering Dignity: Building Human Community," *Religious Education*, 113, No. 3 (November 13, 2018), 314–25.

22   Mary Elizabeth Moore, "Building a Non-Violent Organization: Religious Leadership in a Violent World," *Religious Education*, 110:4 (July-Sept. 2015), 435–50.

ABOUT THE EDITORS

Lucinda Allen Mosher, ThD, senior editor of the *Journal of Interreligious Studies*, is faculty associate in interfaith studies at Hartford Seminary. As well, she is the rapporteur of the Building Bridges Seminar (an ongoing dialogue of Muslim and Christian scholar-practitioners under the stewardship of Georgetown University) and Fellow Emerita of Virginia Theological Seminary's Center for Anglican Communion Studies. The author of seven books—among them *Toward Our Mutual Flourishing: The Episcopal Church, Interreligious Relations*, and *Theologies of Religious Manyness* (2012)—plus numerous chapters and articles on multifaith concerns, she is the editor (seven volumes with David Marshall; now, solo) of the Building Bridges Seminar series from Georgetown University Press comparing Christian and Muslim perspectives on theological themes—including *Sin, Forgiveness, and Reconciliation: Christian and Muslim Perspectives* (2016), which was the recipient of a Catholic Press Association of the United States and Canada Book Award. With Vineet Chander, she is the editor of *Hindu Approaches to Spiritual Care: Chaplaincy in Theory and Practice* (2020), winner of *DĀNAM-Takshāshilā Book Award for Excellence in Indic Studies: the Rajinder and Jyoti Gandhi Book Award for Excellence in Theology/Philosophy and Critical Reflection*. As well, she has guest-edited thematic issues of *Teaching Theology and Religion, The Muslim World*, and *The Anglican Theological Review*. She holds a doctorate from the General Theological Seminary (NYC), where she focused on moral theology and Anglican-Muslim concerns.

Axel Marc Oaks Takacs, ThD, editor-in-chief of the *Journal of Interreligious Studies*, is an assistant professor in the Department of Religion at Seton Hall University. He completed his doctorate at Harvard Divinity School in comparative (interreligious) theology, Islamic Studies, and Catholic theology in 2019. As a constructive theologian, he aims through his scholarship to read pre-modern sources as resources to contemporary questions. His dissertation and current research focuses on poetry, poetics, the imagination, and social imaginary as ways to understand the Christian theology of the Incarnation and the Islamic theology of the imagination. His tangential academic interest attends to how the ideology of capitalism functions as a modern religion that effectively restricts our collective imagination of alternative ways to relate with each other.

Rabbi Or N. Rose is the founding Director of the Betty Ann Greenbaum Miller Center for Interreligious Learning & Leadership of Hebrew College. Before assuming this position in 2016, he worked in various administrative and teaching capacities at Hebrew College for over a decade, including serving as a founding faculty member and Associate Dean of the Rabbinical School. He is co-editor of *Words To Live By: Sacred*

Sources for Interreligious Engagement (Orbis, 2018) and *Rabbi Zalman Schachter-Shalomi: Essential Teachings* (Orbis, 2020). Rose is also the creator of the weekly scriptural commentary series *70 Faces of Torah*, curator of the web-based project *PsalmSeason*, and co-publisher of the *Journal of Interreligious Studies*.

MARY ELIZABETH MOORE, PhD, is Dean of the School of Theology and Professor of Theology and Education, Boston University. Her books include *Education for Continuity and Change, Teaching as a Sacramental Act, Ministering with the Earth, Covenant and Call, Teaching from the Heart,* and *The United Methodist Diaconate* (co-authored). In addition, she has published three edited volumes, *Children, Youth, and Spirituality in a Troubling World; Practical Theology and Hermeneutics*; and *A Living Tradition: Critical Recovery of the Wesleyan Heritage.* She has engaged in interreligious relationship-building in local, professional, and academic settings and is presently working on a project to develop interreligious approaches to practical theology. She is *publisher emerita* of the *Journal of Interreligious Studies.*

ABOUT THE CONTRIBUTORS

RUSSELL C. D. ARNOLD, PhD, is an Associate Professor of Religious Studies at Regis University in Denver, CO. He teaches courses in Interfaith Studies, Biblical Studies, and Jewish Studies. He came to the study of religion in college in an attempt to understand why and how Jews and Christians read the shared texts of the Hebrew Bible/Old Testament, but come to understand them very differently. He earned his doctorate from UCLA in Hebrew Language and Literature, focusing on the Hebrew Bible, Dead Sea Scrolls, and Early Judaism. His first book, *The Social Role of Liturgy in the Religion of the Qumran Community*, focused on the ritual and liturgical practice of the community associated with the Dead Sea Scrolls in the context of Second Temple Judaism and early Christianity. Since moving to Regis, he has been active in interfaith dialogue and building strong relationships between Regis and local Muslim and Jewish communities. His teaching focuses on building the skills and capacities needed to achieve religious and worldview pluralism on our campuses and in our communities. He serves on the leadership team for the recently launched Association for Interreligious/Interfaith Studies (AIIS).

THOMAS CATTOI, PhD, earned his doctorate in Systematic and Comparative Theology at Boston College. Currently, he is Associate Professor of Christology and Cultures at the Jesuit School of Theology at Santa Clara University in Berkeley, California. A scholar of Buddhist-Christian dialogue (with a special focus on Tibetan Buddhism) and of early Christian theology and spirituality, he has led a number of theological immersions to India and Nepal. He believes that comparative theology should be constructive, historically informed, and grounded in the broader Catholic tradition. Cattoi's publications include *Divine Contingency: Theologies of Divine Embodiment in Maximos the Confessor and Tsong kha pa* (2009), *Theodore the Studite: Writings on Iconoclasm* (2014), *Theologies of the Sacred Image in Theodore the Studite and Bokar Rinpoche* (forthcoming), as well as numerous articles. Since 2015, he has co-edited the journal *Buddhist-Christian Studies*. Cattoi is also a licensed psychotherapist in the state of California.

ABIGAIL CLAUHS, MDIV, BCC, is a chaplain, activist, and scholar whose work focuses on the intersections of spiritual care and social justice. An ordained Unitarian Universalist minister and Board Certified Chaplain, Rev. Clauhs holds a Master of Divinity in Interfaith Chaplaincy from Claremont School of Theology and a BA in Religion from Boston University. She has served as a Contributing Scholar for *State of Formation*, a program of the Betty Ann Greenbaum Miller Center for Interreligious Learning & Leadership at Hebrew College and Boston University School of Theology, and is the author of the *Protest Chaplain's Handbook: A Guide for Spiritual Care at Protests*. Currently, she serves professionally as a palliative care chaplain, and is a member of the Portland Interfaith Clergy Resistance, an interreligious collective of religious leaders providing presence and spiritual care "in the streets" at protests and within social justice movements in Portland, Oregon.

RABBI MICHAEL MARGARETTEN COHEN is a faculty member of the Arava Institute for Environmental Studies and Bennington College. He teaches courses on conflict resolution, the Bible, and the environment. Cohen, the rabbi emeritus of the Israel Congregation in Manchester Center, Vermont, is the author of *Einstein's Rabbi: A Tale of Science and the Soul* (2009), plus numerous articles that have appeared in the Middle East and the United States. He has a regular column in the *Jerusalem Post* called "Letter from America." Cohen co-founded of the Green Zionist Alliance. He serves on the Board of Trustees of the Burr & Burton Academy, the Mount Equinox Preservation Trust, the Green Sabbath Project, KaTO Architecture, Shomrei Breishit: Rabbis and Cantors for the Earth, and the Jerusalem Peacebuilders. He is a recipient of the Eliav Sartawi Award for Middle East Journalism from the Search for Common Ground.

PAULA GREEN, PHD, is the founder of Karuna Center for Peacebuilding and Professor *Emerita* at the School for International Training Graduate Institute. She has won many awards, including being honored by the Dalai Lama as an *"Unsung Hero of Compassion."*

RUBEN L. F. HABITO, PHD, is Professor of World Religions and Spirituality, and Director of Spiritual Formation at Perkins School of Theology of Southern Methodist University. He is also a Zen master in the Sanbo Kyodan lineage. His research interests include Japanese medieval Buddhism, comparative theology, spirituality, and socio-ecological engagement. He is the author of several books, including *Zen and the Spiritual Exercises: Paths of Awakening and Transformation* (Orbis, 2013).

RACHEL A. HEATH, MDIV, is a PhD student and a Theology and Practice Fellow at Vanderbilt University. Her research interests center on the intersections of multiple religious belonging, theologies of multiplicity, queer and feminist theories, and interfaith praxis in U.S. contexts. Prior to doctoral studies, she worked in multifaith chaplaincy at the University of Chicago and served on the executive committee for the National Association of College and University Chaplains (NACUC). She currently sits on the leadership council for the newly emerging Association for Interreligious/Interfaith Studies (AIIS) and on the Board of Advisors for the *Journal of Interreligious Studies*. She holds an MDiv from Yale Divinity School and a certificate in Religion and the Arts through the Yale Institute of Sacred Music. In May 2020, she ran her first ultramarathon through the rolling hills of rural Tennessee.

SOREN M. HESSLER, MDIV, is Director of Graduate Academic Services at Drew University and Instructor of Christian and Interreligious Studies at Hebrew College. He holds master's degrees in church administration, divinity, and higher education administration and is a PhD candidate in practical theology at Boston University. His dissertation, "Adjudicating Orthopraxies: A History and Practices of Accreditation in Theological Education in the United States, 1918–1968," examines the practices surrounding Christian leadership formation in the early twentieth century as a means of contributing to broader conversations in American higher education about the training of Muslim, Buddhist, and other non-Christian religious leaders in the twenty-first century. Hessler is co-editor of *Words to Live By: Sacred Sources for Interreligious Engagement* (Orbis, 2018), a member of the *Journal of Interreligious Studies* advisory board, and an ordained elder in the United Methodist Church.

WAKOH SHANNON HICKEY, MA, MDIV, PhD, is is a scholar and educator specializing in American religious history, Buddhism in Asia and the West, religion and medicine, and interreligious dialogue, with particular interests in issues related to race and gender. The author of *Mind Cure: How Meditation Became Medicine* (Oxford University Press, 2019), she is also a priest of Sōtō Zen Buddhism, a certified leader of InterPlay, and a professional chaplain, currently serving hospice patients and their families in Northern California.

JEANNINE HILL FLETCHER, ThD, is a constructive theologian whose research is at the intersection of Christian systematic theology and issues of diversity (including gender, race, and religious diversity). She is the author of three books that examine the intersectional realities of religious diversity: *The Sin of White Supremacy: Christianity, Racism and Religious Diversity in America* (Orbis, 2017); *Monopoly on Salvation? A Feminist Approach to Religious Pluralism* (2005); and *Motherhood as Metaphor: Engendering Interreligious Dialogue* (2013). She is Professor of Theology at Fordham University, Bronx NY, and board member of the grassroots social justice organization the Northwest Bronx Community and Clergy Coalition, an intergenerational, multiracial, multireligious group organizing to address social justice issues in New York City and beyond.

AMIR HUSSAIN, PhD, is is Chair and Professor of Theological Studies at Loyola Marymount University in Los Angeles, where he teaches courses on religion, with a focus on contemporary Muslim societies in North America. From 2011 to 2015, he was the editor of the *Journal of the American Academy of Religion*, the premier scholarly journal for the study of religion. He is on the Board of Directors of the American Academy of Religion. In both 2008 and 2009, Hussain was chosen by vote of LMU students as the Professor of the Year. He is the author of *Muslims and the Making of America* (Baylor University Press, 2016). He is the co-editor for the fourth edition of *A Concise Introduction to World Religions* (Oxford University Press, 2019). He is also the co-editor for the fifth editions of the pair of textbooks *World Religions: Western Traditions*, and *World Religions: Eastern Traditions* (OUP, 2018).

CELENE IBRAHIM, PhD, is a faculty member in the Department of Religious Studies and Philosophy at Groton School. She is the author of *Women and Gender in the Qur'an* (Oxford University Press, 2020) and the editor of *One Nation, Indivisible: Seeking Liberty and Justice from the Pulpit to the Streets* (Wipf & Stock, 2019). Her next book, *Monotheism in Theory and Praxis: An Islamic Perspective on the Potentials and Limits of Human Knowing*, is forthcoming from Cambridge University Press. Ibrahim holds a PhD from Brandeis University, a master's degree from Harvard University, and a bachelor's degree with highest honors from Princeton University. She is a frequent public speaker and consultant for educational and civic institutions and is the recipient of many awards and honors.

NANCY FUCHS KREIMER, PhD, is Associate Professor Emeritus of Religious Studies and founding director of the Department of Multifaith Studies and Initiatives at the Reconstructionist Rabbinical College. A 1982 graduate of RRC, she also holds a master's degree from Yale Divinity School and a doctorate in religion from Temple University. With support from the Henry Luce Foundation, Kreimer has pioneered innovative community-based learning opportunities for rabbinical students from across the denominations and their peers of other faiths—including Dialogue Retreats for Emerging Muslim and Jewish Leaders; Cultivating Character: A Conversation Across Communities; and Campus Chaplaincy for a Multifaith World. A past president of the Reconstructionist Rabbinical Association, Kreimer served on its Ethics Committee. She is a founding board member of the Interfaith Center of Greater Philadelphia, Shoulder-to-Shoulder (an Islamic Society of North America initiative), and the Sisterhood of Salaam Shalom. She co-edited *Chapters of the Heart: Jewish Women Sharing the Torah of Our Lives* (2013) and co-authored *Strangers, Neighbors, Friends: Muslim-Christian-Jewish Reflections on Compassion and Peace* (2018).

SHERYL A. KUJAWA-HOLBROOK, EdD, PhD, an Episcopal priest, is vice president for academic affairs and dean of the faculty, and professor of practical theology at Claremont School of Theology, and professor of Anglican Studies at Bloy House, the Episcopal Theological School at Los Angeles. Active as a professor, scholar, equity trainer, and theological educator for over thirty-five years, she is the author of twenty-four books, handbooks, and numerous articles and reviews. She serves on the board of the *Journal of Interreligious Studies*. Among her recent books is *God Beyond Borders: Interreligious Learning Among Congregations* (Pickwick, 2014). During 2010–2011 she was a fellow in the Christian Leadership Initiative of the American Jewish Committee and the Shalom Hartman Institute in Jerusalem, and is currently a distinguished fellow of the Interfaith New Testament Comparative Passage Project of the John A. Widtsoe Foundation.

JOEL LOHR, PhD, is the President of Hartford Seminary, where he also serves as Professor of Bible and Interreligious Dialogue. He is an award-winning author, scholar of religion, and passionate leader in interreligious relations and higher education. His teaching and research have focused on the Bible, specifically the Torah (or Pentateuch), as well as Jewish-Christian relations and dialogue. He has published ten books. His first monograph, *Chosen and Unchosen: Conceptions of Election in the Pentateuch and Jewish-Christian Interpretation*, was given the R. B. Y. Scott Award by the Canadian Society of Biblical Studies for "outstanding book in the areas of Hebrew Bible and/or the Ancient Near East." He has also published numerous articles in popular media and in respected dictionaries and peer-reviewed journals such as the *Journal of Biblical Literature, Zeitschrift für die Alttestamentliche Wissenschaft, Catholic Biblical Quarterly, Horizons in Biblical Theology,* and *Journal of Interreligious Studies.*

Jeffery Long, PhD, is Professor of Religion and Asian Studies at Elizabethtown College, where he has taught since receiving his doctoral degree from the University of Chicago Divinity School in the year 2000. He is the author of *A Vision for Hinduism, Jainism: An Introduction, the Historical Dictionary of Hinduism* (first and second editions), and *Hinduism in America: A Convergence of Worlds,* as well as the editor of *Perspectives on Reincarnation: Hindu, Christian, and Scientific* and the co-editor of the Buddhism and Jainism volumes of the *Springer Encyclopedia of Indian Religions.* In 2018, Long received the Hindu American Foundation's Dharma Seva Award for his work to promote accurate and sensitive portrayals of Hindu traditions in the American education system and media. He has presented in venues around the world, including three presentations at the United Nations in New York. Long is an avid fan and aspiring author of science fiction.

Luis Menéndez-Antuña, PhD, is Assistant Professor of New Testament at Boston University School of Theology. He is interested in liberation theologies, cultural studies, and critical theory. Previously, he was Assistant Professor at Pacific Lutheran Theological Seminary and served as Core Doctoral Faculty at the Graduate Theological Union (Berkeley, CA). He has published his research in journals such as *Estudios Eclesiásticos, Ilu. Revista de Ciencias de las Religiones, Biblical Interpretation, Journal of Religious Ethics, Early Christianity, Critical Research on Religion,* and *Journal of Biblical Literature.* His first monograph on Revelation, *Thinking Sex with the Great Whore: Deviant Sexualities and Empire in the Book of Revelation* (Routledge, 2018) offers an emancipatory reading of Revelation 17–18 using postcolonial and queer historiographies to explore emancipatory paths for identity formation in biblical texts. He is currently working on his second monograph, which focuses on theoretical and hermeneutical developments in New Testament Studies.

Rabbi Rachel S. Mikva, PhD, serves as the Herman E. Schaalman Chair in Jewish Studies and Senior Faculty Fellow of the InterReligious Institute at Chicago Theological Seminary. The Institute and the Seminary work at the cutting edge of theological education, training religious leaders who can build bridges across cultural and religious difference for the critical work of social transformation. With a passion for justice and academic expertise in the history of scriptural interpretation, Rabbi Mikva teaches courses and writes publications that address a range of Jewish and comparative studies, with a special interest in the intersections of sacred texts, culture and ethics. Her most recent book is *Dangerous Religious Ideas: The Deep Roots of Self-Critical Faith in Judaism, Christianity, and Islam* (Beacon, 2020).

Thomas Mitchell, a native of Knoxville TN, earned his BA in Political Science and Educational Studies from Rhodes College. Currently, he is a Master of Divinity Candidate at Harvard Divinity School. His studies focus on the intersections and relationships between religion, society, and public policy. In exploring those relationships, Mitchell is particularly interested in how a greater understanding of religious language and dialogue could create a healthier environment in which difficult political and societal conversations could take place.

SHELTON OAKLEY HERSEY has sought out, participated and facilitated spaces for reconciliation over the past decade. Her Bachelor degrees are from Rhodes College (Memphis TN) in Religious Studies and Sociology. From Los Angeles and Fuller Theological Seminary, where she obtained a Master's in Intercultural Urban Development, to Mexico and South Africa, she has worked cross-culturally as pastor, spiritual director and community development specialist. She has served on several boards and other nonprofit and church-related councils. All of this has provided skills and experiences in cultural and bridge-building competence and youth leadership development. Under Shelton's direction of the Interfaith Youth Initiative for four years, the program expanded to create more spaces designed for young leaders in greater Boston to recognize their significant role in unlearning and relearning that which divides and unites us. She has now transitioned to Hebrew College to lead the Dignity Project, a program of the Miller Center for Interreligious Learning & Leadership for high school students and graduate theological students.

JUDITH OLESON, MSW, MA, DMIN, is the Director of the Tom Porter Program on Religion and Conflict Transformation Program at the Boston University School of Theology, preparing religious leaders to become a resource for peace in a multicultural, multi-faith world. Dr. Oleson coordinates a clinic/internship program, intercultural and interfaith partnerships, interdisciplinary learning events, and research initiatives. As a lecturer in the School of Theology, she teaches courses in Conflict Transformation, Transitional Justice, and Reconciliation with both graduate and doctoral students. Dr. Oleson held a tenured position in in the Sociology/Social Work Dept. in an undergraduate liberal arts college for ten years where she developed and directed a minor in Peace and Conflict Studies. She also teaches in Croatia with the European Center for the Study of War and Peace in Zagreb, Croatia. Previous to joining academia, she was a social worker for over twenty years, facilitating collaborative partnerships for social change and collective healing in organizations and community systems.

EBOO PATEL, PhD, is the Founder and President of Interfaith Youth Core (IFYC), a nonprofit organization working to make interfaith cooperation a social norm in America. A key figure on issues of religious diversity and democracy, he has spoken on over 175 college campuses, served on President Obama's Inaugural Faith Council, was profiled in *Time Magazine* as one of the People Bridging Divides Across America (March 26, 2020) and as one of America's Best Leaders by *U.S. News & World Report* (2009). The author of many books, including *Interfaith Leadership: A Primer* (2016) and *Out of Many Faiths: Religious Diversity and the American Promise* (2018), he also publishes the blog "Conversations on Diversity" for

Inside Higher Ed. Patel holds a doctorate in sociology of religion from Oxford University, where he studied on a Rhodes scholarship. He has been awarded the Louisville Grawemeyer Prize in Religion, the Guru Nanak Interfaith Prize, the El Hibri Peace Education Prize, the Council of Independent Colleges Academic Leadership Award, and many honorary college degrees

JENNIFER HOWE PEACE, PhD, has been an interfaith organizer and scholar since the 1990s. Dr. Peace was the first associate professor of Interfaith Studies at Andover Newton Theological School, where she cofounded and co-directed the Center for Interreligious and Communal Leadership Education (CIRCLE). Founding co-chair of the Interreligious/Interfaith Studies program unit at the American Academy of Religion (AAR), in 2017 she launched the AAR-affiliated Association for Interreligious/Interfaith Studies. She has authored numerous articles, essays, and chapters on interfaith cooperation; her publications include co-edited volumes, *Interreligious/Interfaith Studies: Defining a New Field* (Beacon: 2018), and *My Neighbor's Faith: Stories of Interreligious Encounter, Growth, and Transformation* (Orbis: 2012). From 2019–2020 Dr. Peace was the Tufts University Chaplain, *ad interim*. She currently serves on the advisory board for the Pluralism Project at Harvard University.

ANANTANAND RAMBACHAN, PhD, is Professor of Religion, Philosophy and Asian Studies at Saint Olaf College. Rambachan has been involved in the field of interreligious relations and dialogue for thirty years, as a Hindu participant and analyst. Among Rambachan's many publications, his major books include *Accomplishing the Accomplished: The Vedas as Source of Valid Knowledge in Śaṅkara, The Limits of Scripture: Vivekananda's Reinterpretation of the Vedas, The Advaita Worldview: God, World and Humanity, A Hindu Theology of Liberation: Not-Two is Not-One,* and *Essays in Hindu Theology.* He has contributed chapters to numerous scholarly works, and his writings also appear in various journals, including *Philosophy East and West, Religious Studies, Religion, Journal of Ecumenical Studies, Journal of Hindu Christian Studies, Journal of Hindu Studies, Journal of the American Academy of Religion* and *Current Dialogue.* The British Broadcasting Corporation (BBC) also transmitted a series of 25 lectures on Hinduism by Rambachan to audiences around the world.

DAVID RHODES, MA, is an education consultant developing programs and curricula related to dialogue, pluralism, and climate change leadership. He holds a Master's degree in Education Policy and Management from the Harvard Graduate School of Education. Rhodes taught middle school social studies and Spanish for seven years, working with students to explore how to engage across differences, analyze systems, and learn from the past. He also worked with a health clinic for migrant farmworkers and co-founded an organization to help welcome people coming as refugees to the Finger Lakes region of Upstate New York. Currently, he lives in Newton, Massachusetts, with his wife and three children.

JUDITH SIMMER-BROWN, PhD, is Distinguished Professor of Contemplative and Religious Studies at Naropa University and Acharya in the Shambhala lineage of Chogyam Trungpa. She serves on the Board of the Society of Buddhist-Christian Studies and has been active in interreligious dialogue internationally since the 1980s. She directed the Naropa dialogues (1981–1988), was a member of the Cobb-Abe Theological Encounter (1984–2004), and the Gethsemani Encounters (1996 & 2002). Currently she co-chairs the American Academy of Religion's Contemplative Studies Unit and lectures and writes on Tibetan Buddhism, American Buddhism, women and Buddhism, and interreligious dialogue. She is the author of *Dakini's Warm Breath: The Feminine Principle in Tibetan Buddhism* (Shambhala, 2002), co-author of *Meditation and the Classroom: Contemplative Pedagogy in the Religious Studies Classroom* (SUNY, 2011), and contributor to *Benedict's Dharma: Buddhists Reflect on the Rule of St. Benedict* (Riverhead, 2002).

ROBERT J. STAINS JR, MEd, is Principal of Bob Stains and Associates Conflict Transformation, Senior Associate at Essential Partners, and Visiting Researcher at the Tom Porter Program on Religion and Conflict Transformation at the Boston University School of Theology, where he is also adjunct faculty teaching about dialogue. For the past twenty-six years, Bob has been designing and facilitating inter-religious dialogue and training religious leaders from across the US, Europe, Asia, Africa, and South America in dialogic thinking and practice. He currently works with individual congregations, clergy associations, seminaries and regional, national, and international governing bodies to respond dialogically to disruptions in community life related to differences in belief, race, gender, social class, politics and age.

RABBI JOSHUA STANTON is Rabbi of East End Temple in Manhattan and a Senior Fellow at CLAL—The National Jewish Center for Learning and Leadership. Previously, he served as Associate Rabbi at Congregation B'nai Jeshurun in Short Hills, New Jersey; and, before that, as Associate Director of the Center for Global Judaism at Hebrew College and Director of Communications for the Coexist Foundation. Currently, he serves on the Board of Governors of the International Jewish Committee for Interreligious Consultations, which liaises on behalf of Jewish communities worldwide with the Vatican and other international religious bodies. Stanton was in the 2015–2016 cohort of Germanacos Fellows, a member of the inaugural group of Sinai and Synapses Fellows (2013–2015), and one of just six finalists worldwide for the $100,000 Coexist Prize. Stanton is a Founding Co-Editor Emeritus of the *Journal of Interreligious Studies.*

STEPHANIE VARNON-HUGHES, PhD, is the Director of the Claremont Core and Teaching & Learning Specialist at Claremont Lincoln University, and an award winning teacher and interfaith leader. She is the host of the religion & culture podcast "In Times Like These" and author of *Interfaith Grit: How Uncertainty Will Save Us* (2018). Varnon-Hughes was a co-founder and editor-in-chief of the *Journal of Interreligious Studies* and its sister publication, *State of Formation,* an online forum for emerging religious and ethical leaders. She holds a PhD from Claremont Lincoln University, an MA and STM from Union Theological Seminary, and undergraduate degrees in English and Education from Webster University.

REV. WENDY VON COURTER, DMin, graduated with her Master's of Divinity from Boston University School of Theology (BUSTH), and was ordained in 2005 (Unitarian Universalist). She received her Doctor of Ministry in Transformational Leadership from BUSTH in 2017 and was named Distinguished Alum in 2016. A fifth-generation UU, she served for 14 years as parish minister in Marblehead MA and held national roles in her denomination: Accessibilities Committee, Journey Toward Wholeness Transformation Committee (chair), Council on Cross Cultural Engagement, Allies for Racial Equity (President), Right Relationship Team. She was co-chair of the Essex County Community Organization, and convenor of the Marblehead Ministerial Association. Her current role is as the Mentor to the UU Community of Learning at BUSTH and adjunct faculty. A long-time activist, she has a lengthy record of civil disobedience in support of immigrant justice, racial justice, and LGBTQIA rights. She and her wife, Gini, live in Buckley, MI.

MICHELLE VOSS ROBERTS, PhD, is Principal and Professor of Theology at Emmanuel College of Victoria University in the University of Toronto. She is the author three book-length works in comparative theology: *Dualities: A Theology of Difference* (Westminster John Knox, 2010); *Tastes of the Divine: Hindu and Christian Theologies of Emotion* (Fordham University Press, 2014), which received the Award for Excellence from the American Academy of Religion; and *Body Parts: A Theological Anthropology* (Fortress Press, 2017). She is the editor of *Comparative Theology: Insights for Systematic Theological Reflection* (Fordham University Press, 2016)—a volume that brings interreligious comparison to the introductory study of theology. Her most recent project is the *Routledge Handbook of Hindu-Christian Relations*, which she is co-editing with Chad Bauman. Dr. Voss Roberts has served as President of the Society for Hindu-Christian Studies and co-chair of the Comparative Theology Group of the AAR.

ABOUT THE *JOURNAL OF INTERRELIGIOUS STUDIES*

The *Journal of Interreligious Studies (JIRS)*—a peer-reviewed publication of the Boston University School of Theology, Hebrew College, and Hartford Seminary—is a forum for academic, social, and timely issues affecting religious communities around the world. It was founded in 2008 as the *Journal of Inter-Religious Dialogue* by a pioneering group of young scholars, with its first issue released in February 2009. In Winter 2014, it became the *Journal of Interreligious Studies*, a name better reflecting its primary purview, well-defined by scholar Kate McCarthy as:

> a subdiscipline of religious studies that engages in the scholarly and religiously neutral description, multidisciplinary analysis, and theoretical framing of the interactions of religiously different people and groups, including the intersections of religion and secularity. It examines these interactions in historical and contemporary contexts, and in relation to other social systems and forces. Like other disciplines with applied dimensions, it serves the public good by bringing its analysis to bear on practical approaches to issues in religiously diverse societies.[1]

Over the years since, it has developed into a significant medium for the exploration of interreligious engagement in theory and practice.

As a premier online publication, *JIRS* is poised to impact interreligious dialogue and work substantially to increase both the quality and frequency of interchanges among religious groups, their leaders, and confessional or non-confessional academic scholars. With the understanding that clergy and lay leaders greatly affect the dynamics within their congregations and religious movements, the *JIRS* offers a novel way to establish long-term dialogue and collaboration among religious communities and the academy. By fostering conversation, the *JIRS* hopes to increase religious and interreligious literacy, contribute to the field of interreligious hermeneutics, and address the issues surrounding interreligious relations, dialogue, theology, and communication.

To this end, *JIRS* solicits articles of an interdisciplinary nature as it aims to produce resources for interreligious education, pedagogy, and cooperation. It also encourages submissions from the related fields of interreligious, intercultural, and comparative theology. Finally, it seeks articles that feature careful and critical engagement with how race, gender, class, sexuality, nationality, and dis/ability intersect with religious identities and communities in the public sphere or secular domain. More specifically, *JIRS* seeks to:

- Feature articles on cutting-edge research and scholarship taking place at theological seminaries and universities concerning the field of interreligious studies, comparative religion, comparative theology, and interreligious/ intercultural theology.

- Promote innovative ideas, methodologies, pedagogies, and hermeneutics for interreligious work to ensure that best practices are shared and replicated.

- Express challenges facing religious communities and openly discuss interreligious disputes and their possible solutions.

- Provide a means for religious leaders to engage in interreligious work and learn about traditions other than their own.

- Utilize the increasingly "global" nature of religious communities to promote religious literacy and appreciation both within and beyond the United States.

- Attend to the intersectional nature of interreligious studies, dialogue, and community engagement that illuminates how race, gender, class, sexuality, dis/ability, nationality, and more impact the relationship among religious communities and the secular domain.

Now in its second decade of publication, *JIRS* continues to build an interreligious community of scholars in which people of different traditions learn from one another and work together for the common and public good.

NOTES

1   Kate McCarthy, "(Inter)Religious Studies: Making a Home in the Secular Academy," in *Interreligious/Interfaith Studies: Defining a New Field*, ed. Eboo Patel, Jennifer Howe Peace, and Noah J. Silverman (Boston: Beacon, 2018), 12.

GRATITUDES

The publication of this volume and the continued presence of the *Journal of Interreligious Studies* remain a communal undertaking of love. The editor-in-chief and senior editor wish to thank Mary Elizabeth Moore and Or Rose for their many years of service to the *Journal of Interreligious Studies* and for their contributions to this book. In addition, we are grateful to Joel Lohr, president of Hartford Seminary, for joining the team publishing the *JIRS* and contributing to this volume. Without the partnership among Hebrew College, Boston University School of Theology, and Hartford Seminary, neither this volume nor the *JIRS* would exist. The same must be said of our funders over the years. The generosity of the Henry Luce Foundation, the Russell Berrie Foundation, the John Paul II Center for Interreligious Dialogue, and various friends of *JIRS* is deeply appreciated.

The editors are sincerely thankful for the logistical and administrative support provided with good humor and pastoral care by Soren Hessler, Director of Graduate Academic Services at Drew University, and Tom Reid, Associate Director of the Miller Center for Interreligious Learning & Leadership at Hebrew College. Finally, the volume's contents would remain merely plain text in digital documents without the expert layout design provided by Barrie Mosher of NeighborFaith Consultancy, LLC, plus wonderful production assistance from Paraclete Press (Brewster, MA)—particularly, Sister Brigid Minor and Sister Anna-Hope Mitchell. Gratitude abounds.